Burma's Pop Music Industry

Eastman/Rochester Studies in Ethnomusicology

Ellen Koskoff, Series Editor
Eastman School of Music

(ISSN: 2161–0290)

Burma's Pop Music Industry:
Creators, Distributors, Censors
Heather MacLachlan

Burma's Pop Music Industry

Creators, Distributors, Censors

Heather MacLachlan

UNIVERSITY OF ROCHESTER PRESS

First published 2011
Transferred to digital printing and reprinted in paperback 2013

University of Rochester Press
668 Mt. Hope Avenue, Rochester, NY 14620, USA
www.urpress.com
and Boydell & Brewer Limited
PO Box 9, Woodbridge, Suffolk IP12 3DF, UK
www.boydellandbrewer.com

ISSN: 2161-0290

hardcover ISBN-13: 978-1-58046-386-7
paperback ISBN-13: 978-1-58046-471-0

Library of Congress Cataloging-in-Publication Data

MacLachlan, Heather.
 Burma's pop music industry : creators, distributors, censors / Heather
MacLachlan.
  p. cm. — (Eastman/Rochester studies ethnomusicology, ISSN 2161-0290 ; v. 1)
 Includes bibliographical references and index.
 ISBN 978-1-58046-386-7 (hardcover : alk. paper) 1. Popular music—Burma—
History and criticism. 2. Popular music—Social aspects—Burma. 3. Music trade—
Burma. 4. Popular music—Censorship—Burma. I. Title.
 ML3502.B86M33 2011
 781.6309591—dc23

                                                        2011021934

A catalogue record for this title is available from the British Library.

This publication is printed on acid-free paper.
Printed in the United States of America

This book is dedicated to the many Yangon dwellers
who graciously granted me interviews, invited me
into their homes, and shared their lives with me.

They lived out one of the highest ideals of their society:
They warmly welcomed me, the visitor.

Contents

Illustrations

Acknowledgments

I completed this book, as the saying goes, "by the grace of God and the goodness of the neighbors." I thank all of the following people for their encouragement and guidance:

My academic mentors, for graciously taking the time to advise me—Martin Hatch, Steven Pond, Magnus Fiskesjo, Ward Keeler, San San Hnin Htun, Eric Tagliacozzo, Rhoda Linton, Gavin Douglas, Sean Turnell, Carol Babiracki, and Ian Holliday.

My writing group partners, for sharing the journey with me—Clifford Crawford, Alexa Yesukevich, Matthew Hoffberg, and Baran Han at Cornell University; and Mari Rapela-Heidt, Laura Grimes, and Samuel Dorf at the University of Dayton.

The dedicated staff at the University of Rochester Press, for helping me to craft a better book—Carrie Crompton, Ryan Peterson, Suzanne Guiod, Ellen Koskoff, and two anonymous reviewers.

The GCF early morning prayer group, for repeatedly lifting me up in prayer—Heidi Park, Andrew Yeo, Thea Sircar, and David and Rita Hjelle.

My prayer partners, for being shining examples of faith and calm—Heather Edvenson and Minnita Daniel-Cox.

My translator in Yangon, for her gift of time and expertise—Daw Pa Pa.

Other friends in Yangon, for their interest, support, and friendship—Rachel Tha Hla, Rova and Mawite, Pastor Stanley, Pastor Ler Wah, and the congregation of the Ahlone Sanchaung Karen Baptist Church.

My Karen friends in Ithaca, for answering so many questions and for adopting me as their "pi"—Paw Pha, Moo Lerh, and Blu Paw.

And my precious husband and son—Christopher St. Amand and Riel St. Amand—for everything.

Introduction

In 1755 King Alaungpaya, the founder of the last great Burmese monarchical dynasty, arrived at the small fishing village of Dagon. At the end of a long campaign to conquer and unify much of what we now know as Burma, he decided to found his new capital. He renamed the location Yan-gon, meaning "the end of strife." Standing in modern-day Yangon (also known as Rangoon), it is easy to imagine what Alaungpaya must have seen. Undoubtedly he raised his eyes to the glorious sight of the Shwedagon Pagoda, where devout Buddhists have venerated a shrine containing eight hairs from the head of Gautama Buddha for more than a millennium. He must have seen small family homes made of bamboo, and women carrying their produce to market in baskets balanced on their heads. He would have given alms to saffron-robed monks who wandered the streets at dawn, begging bowls in hand.

It is easy to picture the scene as it looked 250 years ago because, in many ways, the city still resembles the village where Alaungpaya rested. Nowadays, of course, the bamboo huts are interspersed with concrete and steel; there seems to be a new construction project on every major thoroughfare. Cars race past the open-air markets, and monks wear eyeglasses and ride public buses. But glimpses of the older Yangon are everywhere in the contemporary city.

We can still see some of what Alaungpaya saw, and we can still hear some of what he heard. The musical tradition that flourished in the courts of kings like Alaungpaya, known as the *Maha Gita*, continues to develop today as a vibrant and important part of Burmese life in the twenty-first century. The *Maha Gita* is a body of song texts written down some centuries ago; the melodies that accompany these texts have been passed down orally. The songs are accompanied by a variety of distinctively Burmese musical instruments, such as the *saung gauk* (harp) and the *pattala* (xylophone). The king's mighty instrumental ensemble, known as the *hsaing waing*, includes a set of pitched drums called the *pat waing*; tuned gongs; and the *hnay*, an aerophone with a particularly piercing sound.[1] Now, as then, singers and instrumentalists trained in the *Maha Gita* perform for Buddhist rituals and at weddings, and play an important part in public festivals. *Maha Gita* performers appear frequently in government-sponsored television shows, and young people study the tunes and techniques of the *thachin kyi* (great songs) at Yangon's University of Culture.[2]

Figure I.1. Workers' house next to a mansion they are building, Dhamma Zedi
Lan, Yangon

From our historical vantage point, we can also hear Burmese musical sounds
that Alaungpaya could not have imagined. His dynasty ended, slowly and pain-
fully, as the British colonized Burma in waves of invasion during the nineteenth
century. English cultural products, including musical instruments, came to
Burma with the colonists, and the resourceful Burmese adopted them for
their own use. Through the twentieth century, Burmese musicians developed
uniquely Burmese ways of playing the piano, the violin, and the guitar.[3] The
nomenclature evolved to reflect the change. Today, when Burmese musicians
use a piano to play European classical music, they call it a piano, but when they
use it to perform *thachin kyi*, they call it *sandaya* (just as, in the English-speaking
world, a violin is called a fiddle when it is used to play bluegrass repertoire).
In addition, they combined their own melodies and singing style with Western
instruments (in the 1920s, the slide guitar, and later, electronic keyboards and
guitars) to create a new style.[4] This fusion genre is known as *kalabaw* or *mono*,
after the single-track recording devices on which it was first recorded in mid-
century. The moniker *mono* also serves to distinguish the fusion of traditional
music with Western instrumentation from the third important genre of Burmese music, called *stereo*, which is the focus of this study.[5]

Stereo (pronounced "sah-TEE-ree-oh") musicians are unabashed admirers of
Anglo-American pop music, and *stereo* aims to fit squarely within the Western
pop and rock tradition. The term *stereo*, however, has become rather dated, and
most Burmese people no longer use it. Because of this, and in deference to my

Figure I.2. *Hsaing waing* ensemble performing at a wedding in Yangon, January 2009

English-language readers, in this book I usually refer to *stereo* as "Burmese pop music," which is indeed widely popular in Burma. (The term "popular music" embraces many musical genres created during the twentieth century, including pop and rock and other genres such as rhythm and blues, disco, country, and soul.)[6] Burmese pop music—like pop music around the globe—consists of short songs, recorded in a studio and performed live by (usually) solo singers accompanied by the rock instrumentarium: electronically amplified guitars, a drum kit, and a keyboard. These songs are always constructed using tonal harmonies and organized in verse-and-chorus form.

It is important to note that the entire Burmese pop music industry is located in Yangon: virtually all recordings are made in studios in Yangon, and everyone who wishes to make a career in pop music must live in Yangon.[7] Because the recordings eventually make their way to other large urban areas and even to small villages across the country, the music is understood to be "Burmese" pop rather than a solely Yangon-based genre; but the fact remains that Yangon is the cradle of this music.[8]

Stereo music is now the dominant music on the airwaves in Yangon, and concerts given by the best-known artists attract thousands of ticket-holders. Photos of the beautiful young singers who perform in these shows appear weekly in tabloid-style journals. Hundreds of people make their livings working in the

Yangon-based industry. It is clear that the Burmese pop music scene is increasingly important in Burmese life generally. (Hip-hop, which has exploded in Burma during the past five years, is becoming important as well, but it is unfortunately outside the purview of this book.[9] Hip-hop artists do have some links to the *stereo* music world in Yangon, but industries are independent of each other.) In this book I will discuss many of the salient aspects of the Burmese pop music scene. For now, it will suffice to make one important point: Burmese pop music cannot be dismissed as just another instance of cultural imperialism.

Cultural imperialism has been a favorite theory of scholars seeking to explain the ubiquity of Anglo-American pop music around the globe.[10] National leaders, too, have deployed the term when expressing their hostility to Western pop music: Indonesia's Soekarno, for example, condemned the presence of rock music in his country as "cultural imperialism,"[11] and spokesmen for the government of the People's Republic of China railed against Mandopop as "spiritual pollution" from the West.[12] Despite its widespread use, the term "cultural imperialism" is notoriously difficult to define. In his book of the same title, John Tomlinson spends nine pages explaining why he cannot provide a short and coherent definition of it.[13]

Pop music scholar Keith Negus argues that whatever else we might say about it, cultural imperialism must be understood as the dominance of certain ownership structures, media technologies, and cultural products in a given market.[14] Following Negus's definition, I argue that the Burmese case cannot be dismissed as a straightforward imposition of American cultural values and products on a vulnerable foreign population. Quite the opposite, in fact: Burmese musicians, until very recently, have gone to great lengths to acquire Western-made recordings, instruments, and recording equipment. These products were not (legally) available in the early days of *stereo*, and even now must be smuggled into the country in defiance of international sanctions. None of the Big Four oligarchic recording companies—Sony Music Entertainment, Warner Music Group, Universal Music Group and the EMI Group—has ever had a corporate presence in Burma.

Why, then, the deep attraction to Anglo-American cultural products and to English pop songs in particular? During the colonial era, which lasted until 1947, British overlords promoted all things English to their subject population. They managed to convince at least some Burmese people that the English education system, the English language, and the British way of life were markedly superior to their Burmese analogs. Even today, it is possible to meet self-confident Burmese people (I met some of them during my research) who believe that their own society is somehow lacking in comparison to the West. So we must acknowledge that Burmese people are living with the legacy of an explicit cultural and military imperialism that predisposes some of them to valorize, among other things, Anglo-American pop music.

This aspect of the Burmese pop music scene has led Western journalists to describe the music, and its creators, as little more than the dregs of the American rock and roll movement. Phil Zabriskie, for example, articulated this view in his 2002 *Time* magazine piece, as did Scott Carrier in a longer piece called "Rock the Junta."[15] In the view of these journalists, who usually stay in Yangon for only a few days and who do not speak Burmese, musicians are sad, uncreative figures who do nothing but imitate the great music of the West. Zabriskie describes Zaw Win Htut as a rocker who performs "watered-down Burmese covers of rock relics by the Eagles, Rod Stewart and the Beatles" and who "cannot afford to be . . . idealistic." And Carrier dismisses the whole city of Yangon with a sniff: "While there was a lot of rock and pop music being played all over town, most of it was just awful." Perhaps it seems like tilting at windmills to take issue with these short articles. But this type of literature is virtually all that English-speaking international audiences ever read about Burmese pop musicians; therefore, it is important to scrutinize their accuracy.

In this book I argue that the assessment of Zabriskie and Carrier is too simplistic. Yes, Burmese musicians do work hard to learn and reproduce the Western rock and pop traditions, but they do not do so because their airwaves, retail shops, and concert stages are being overtaken by Hollywood-based multinationals. And while they do prize English-language pop songs, they do not do so simply because their grandparents were the colonial subjects of Britain. Rather, these musicians exercise agency and considerable ingenuity in their pursuit of "international music" (as they frequently call it). In many cases, they have done so in defiance of their own government.

In 1962, after a short-lived era of independence and parliamentary democracy in Burma, a group of generals overthrew the elected government and installed their leader, General Ne Win, as the supreme ruler of the country. Ne Win established the Burma Socialist Programme Party (BSPP) as the only legal political party and launched the Burmese Way to Socialism, the ideology that shaped the country for most of the next three decades.[16] One of the most important features of this policy was the extreme isolation it imposed on Burma. In the interests of creating a self-sufficient socialist economy, the new military government severely restricted trade with other countries and access to foreign goods. Within months, almost all foreigners were expelled from the country, and tourist visits were limited to seven days.[17] At the same time, the junta promoted its own narrow vision of "Burmese culture," modeled on Ne Win's understanding of the former kings of Burma. The BSPP rejected most forms of Western culture as "decadent," and Ne Win reserved a special hatred for American rock and pop music.[18]

It was during the early part of the BSPP era that young Burmese grew their hair long, built their own electric guitars, and listened to clandestinely obtained recordings of the Beatles and the Rolling Stones. Since pop music was not allowed on government radio—only *thachin kyi* and *mono* were acceptable—they had to circulate their music via friends and family. They relied on the few of their peers who were allowed to travel abroad (mostly to Eastern European socialist countries) to obtain recordings and musical instruction books. They cultivated friendships with the few Western diplomats they met in order to obtain precious foreign-made instruments and recording equipment. And their music-making moved into the open in 1973 when the BSPP co-opted their new *stereo* style in order to promote a government referendum.[19] Since that time, the Burmese regime has tolerated pop music and even exploited it for its own purposes.

The BSPP was succeeded in 1988 by a government first known as the SLORC (State Law and Order Restoration Council) and later as the SPDC (State Peace and Development Council). This government, like the BSPP, was a military dictatorship that repeatedly showed its utter disregard for its citizens' wishes and needs. For example, in 1989 the SLORC changed the name of the country to the Union of Myanmar. This move was vigorously protested by the National League for Democracy, the political party that received the lion's share of the popular vote in elections in 1990—but which was never allowed to assume power. (Note that in this book I refer to the country as Burma, out of respect for the NLD's position, except when I refer to government ministries or publications that use the word Myanmar.) All of the events discussed in this book took place during the SPDC era, which ended on March 30, 2011, when the SPDC was formally dissolved. The fraudulent election of 2010 brought a supposedly new and democratic government to power. However, the new government is dominated by the Union Solidarity and Development Party, a group that is almost indistinguishable from the former SPDC. As this book went to press, Burma was still, in effect, controlled by a corrupt and unjust military junta.

Burma's successive military governments have distinguished themselves by their willingness to murder citizens who speak in opposition to them. Notoriously, the BSPP massacred university students demonstrating for democratic rights in 1962 and 1974, and citizens at large who marched for democracy in 1988. The SPDC, for its part, jailed thousands of opposition leaders, including the elected head of state, Aung San Suu Kyi. This regime sponsored a mob which murdered prodemocracy supporters (at the Depayin Massacre of 2003) and sent soldiers to abduct and kill Buddhist monks during the short-lived Saffron Revolution of September 2007. Although the SPDC was not as isolationist as was the BSPP, and in fact worked hard to increase tourism in Burma, it remained suspicious of any force which might draw the loyalty of its citizens—for example, rock stars on stage in front of thousands of screaming fans. It continued to censor pop music rigorously, and it made no bones about banning or even jailing entertainers who might promote any kind of change (say, free and fair elections) that would threaten their dominance.

In this book I contest the notion that Burmese pop music is nothing more than the outworking of either Western cultural imperialism or local military totalitarianism. While both of these historical forces have deeply affected the development of Burmese pop, neither can claim to be its *raison d'être*. As the history of the genre shows, reality is more complex, and more interesting.

A Brief History of Pop Music in Burma

In 1903, the Gramophone Company made the first recordings of Burmese music, and by 1910 more than five hundred recordings had been released.[20] These early recordings captured the classical music of the *Maha Gita* tradition. The engines of the industry, however, were located outside the country: for the first few decades, Burmese recording companies pressed their 78 LPs in Calcutta. The first recording studio inside Burma was built in 1952, and pressing plants appeared in the 1960s. Before the 1962 military coup, at least eighty different recording companies specialized in recording various genres of Burmese music.[21] The A-1 recording company, for example, made its mark by specializing in recordings of *kalabaw* (or *mono*) songs. *Kalabaw*, as we have seen, represents a fusion of local and Western traditions. During the early twentieth century, prosperous Burmese in Yangon also enjoyed music that was imported intact from outside. American big band jazz was particularly popular; some of the greats performed in Burma in the 1930s and in the wake of their shows, jazz nightclubs sprang up to serve audiences who wanted to continue to enjoy jazz. The last of these nightclubs closed in the 1970s. By that time "fusion between Western styles and Burmese modern traditional music slowed significantly."[22] The balance tipped in favor of foreign music that was closely imitated, rather than transformed, by Burmese musicians.

Burmese pop music got started in the early 1960s, when young Burmese people became enamored of electrified or amplified music. In fact, several of the older musicians interviewed for this book remembered the 1960s as a turning point, because "electronic music" became available then. The most compelling manifestation of this new kind of music was American rock and roll, always performed by ensembles centered on the electric guitar. The style was particularly popular on the campus of Rangoon (now Yangon) University, where young men strummed their guitars and sang outside women's dorms in the evenings. The first few Yangon-based rock bands were cover bands dedicated to reproducing Anglo-American hits. They were composed of entrepreneurial young men whose families had enough resources to purchase instruments—and the patience to listen to hours of practicing.

During this era, aspiring teenagers were supported in their quest to master American rock by the Burma Broadcasting Service. The BBS, which had been established by the British colonial regime, was maintained after independence in largely the same format. Importantly, it required that all programming be in English. Young rock bands were given the chance to play for a national audience—and even earn an honorarium—during the BBS's amateur talent hour. Their repertoire fit the bill because it consisted entirely of "English songs" (cover songs). A member of one of the most successful bands of this era, the Playboys, recalled performing Elvis, Cliff Richard, and Beatles songs for the BBS as a teenager: "We could play five songs in forty-five minutes, and we got forty-five *kyat* to cover our transportation costs." He pointed out that the BBS was extremely helpful to young pop musicians because it had close ties to the Voice of America. Because of this connection, his band and others like them had access to the American-produced records they wanted to cover. He estimated that his band got about 90 percent of their records from the BBS.

As Burmese musicians mastered the performance techniques and the repertoire of Western pop music, they began writing Burmese lyrics for the American and British melodies they liked so much. This kind of composition, called *copy thachin*, remains important in Burma today. In 1967, university student U Htun Naung wrote what is now identified as Burma's first *own tune* (original) pop song, "Mommy I Want a Girlfriend." The melody, rhythm, and harmony, as well as the lyrics, were all of his own creation. He recorded this song on equipment he kept in his dorm room at Rangoon University.[23] By 1969, copies of this song were delighting fans all over Burma. And in 1971, when entrepreneur U Ba Thein opened the country's first *stereo* recording studio, *stereo* music (named after the dual-track tape recorder featured in the studio) took off.[24] Local pop musicians were then able to create professional-quality recordings and sell them to fans.

In 1973, Sai Htee Saing and his band The Wild Ones made history as the first to commit to performing nothing but *own tunes*. In 1976, the Yin Mar Music Store opened in downtown Yangon. This was the first store devoted entirely to stocking foreign-made recordings, and it served (and still serves) as a mecca for young Burmese who want to learn how to play and sing pop music. Inspired by recordings acquired at Yin Mar, Sai Htee Saing's increasingly large number of peers created, performed, and recorded *copy thachin* and *own tunes* through the 1980s and 1990s. In the 1980s, a handful of bands (including Iron Cross, The Wild Ones, and Emperor) recorded between thirty and fifty albums per year, usually serving as backup ensembles for a rotating cast of singers. (This pattern persists today, as I discuss at length in this book.) During this era, the Burmese pop scene even produced a handful of all-female bands. Together, these pop music bands became the entertainment of choice for many parties, weddings, and professional functions. And Burmese pop musicians continued to work in tourist venues, impressing foreigners with their note-perfect renditions of English hit songs.

By the close of the 1990s, live performances for large Burmese audiences had grown rare, in part because of the government's reluctance to allow large crowds to congregate. On January 27, 2001, Zaw Win Htut and a handful of other famous Burmese singers performed at the first "big show" of the new millennium. At this show, the Emperor band accompanied a handful of different singers, each of whom contributed a few songs. This concert serves as a convenient marker for the beginning of the contemporary era of Burmese pop music history. Importantly, it fits the marketing model for Burmese pop that developed in the 1980s. Now virtually all live shows feature one band backing multiple soloists, and so-called group albums (which include a variety of songs performed by a variety of artists) are the best-selling kind of recordings in the country.

Burma's first call-in radio station, Yangon City FM, began broadcasting on January 1, 2002.[25] This station plays mostly pop music and has been important in the dissemination of Burmese pop to a wider audience in recent years. In addition, consumers are now able to purchase VCD (video compact disc) recordings of their favorite songs. VCDs—the most popular version of modern pop recordings—include audio, video of the performers, and lyrics scrolling across the screen. For this reason they are also known as "karaoke" CDs (one of my friends laughingly calls them "three-in-one"[26]). In 2007, Myawaddy TV, a government-run television station, premiered a song contest modeled on *American Idol.* The show, called *Melody World,* was an immediate success and went on to a second season. And in March of 2008, Mandalay FM (another call-in radio station modeled on Yangon City FM) started broadcasting in both Mandalay and Yangon.

As these examples show, the current era is one of dramatic expansion. However, it is also marked by deep uncertainty. Many of the full-time professionals who work in the Burmese pop music scene worry that their industry is in grave danger. Piracy is rampant, and it is driving profits down so far that some careers have already been lost. Other industry insiders are struggling financially and are pessimistic about the future. Nevertheless, Burmese pop musicians persist in their efforts to create meaningful and commercially successful music.

They say that their music, or more precisely their musical activities, come "from the heart." When they use this expression, in English or in Burmese, they mean the same that English-speakers do when they use it: their decisions are based on their emotions, and their musical efforts are the logical outcome of their own feelings. Singers say that their singing comes from their hearts; audio engineers say that their editing decisions come from their hearts; and even producers say that music producing is a reflection of what is in their hearts.[27] Interestingly, composers say that emotion is so important to the process of composing that it makes a significant difference in the amount of time it takes to compose a song. If Burmese pop music composers feel very deeply, they say that they can compose a song in a matter of hours—otherwise, it may take weeks or months.[28]

Albin Zak writes that American pop musicians make exactly the same claim.[29] When asked, they aver that "there are no rules," because all of their artistic decisions are based on intuition or emotion. Yet the fact remains that their industry has developed conventional practices that guide musicians, whether they are aware of this or not. The same is true in Burma: the work and lives of pop musicians there are marked by norms and patterns. My goal in this book is to delineate these norms and patterns without implying that the real people involved in them are ever entirely predictable. I aim here to reveal the heart of the Burmese pop music industry, as I learned about it through observation, participation, and conversation.

Conducting Research in Burma

The particular social context of Burmese pop music has not, until now, been explored in depth, either by scholars of popular music or by contributors to Burma studies. By writing this book, I hope in some small way to contribute to both of those disciplines. The newspaper articles by Carrier and Zabriskie, mentioned above, represent two of only a handful of scholarly and journalistic treatments of pop music in Burma. No extended study, based on the statements and behaviors of Burmese pop musicians themselves, has previously been conducted.

In colonial times, English-language anthropological study of Burma focused on the amazing ethnic diversity in the country. In fact, one of the field's most enduringly influential books is Edmund Leach's *Political Systems of Highland Burma: A Study of Kachin Social Stuctures.*[30] Today, the government claims that there are 135 different "national races" in the country, including the majority Burmans (also known as the Myanmar people). Although no accurate census has been conducted since the 1930s, the consensus is that ethnic minority groups, like the Kachin, Chin, Karen, Shan, and others comprise about 30 percent of the total population of about 50 million. Members of these groups play a disproportionately important role in the pop music industry, as I explain in detail later. Out of respect for my informants' preferences, I usually refer to ethnic minority groups, or national races, as *tain-yin-tha.*

Much of the more recent research on Burma has focused on political histories.[31] Recent important contributions to the field continue this focus, with scholars examining the pressing question of Burma's political future in light of its past.[32] Two books which treat this theme, and which are based on interviews conducted with Burmese people, have been published recently.[33] However, most of the outstanding work in Burma studies does not privilege the voices of Burmese people themselves.[34]

This book does privilege Burmese voices. From 2007 to 2009, I spent nearly six months living in Yangon, interacting with people in the center and on the fringes of the pop music industry on a nearly daily basis. I attended concerts and rehearsals, music classes, recording sessions, and religious services. I purchased music, and I even contributed in a small way to the production of music (by playing the keyboards for one track on one recording, as I describe in chapter 3). But my main research method was the interview. I conducted seventy-seven interviews, most of them lasting approximately two hours, with people from across the industry. I interviewed some of the highest-paid, most recognizable performers in the country, as well as young people struggling to break into the music business. In addition, I interviewed composers, producers, audio engineers, concert promoters, radio station management personnel, and others, such as music teachers, whose work is more tangential to the industry. Many of the assertions I make in this book are based on these interviews.

And I include my interviewees' first-person statements at every juncture. I do so because I believe, along with Robert Walser, that "ultimately, musical analysis can be considered credible only if it helps explain the significance of musical activities in particular social contexts."[35]

One aspect of the Burmese pop music industry is not explored in detail in this book: the perspectives and contributions of fans. There are a couple of reasons for this. First, making any kind of broad claims about consumer reception of Burmese pop music would require a significant data sample. In Burma there are no fan clubs or similar organizations, so there is no obvious way to collect data about preferences and trends. Even sales numbers are hard to verify, as I explain in chapter 4. Of course, during my time in Yangon, I met many people who could be described as fans of pop music, and I did learn about the music industry from them. However, formal interviews in Burma are difficult, since people can easily fall under suspicion if it becomes known that they are having significant conversations with foreigners. Therefore, I limited my formal (quotable) interviews to industry insiders, all of whom gave their oral or written consent to be interviewed, and most of whom were promised confidentiality. Only a handful of interviewees are identified by their real names in this book; all of the others have been given pseudonyms. The pseudonyms are a mix of Burmese names and English names (usually a first name only), as is typical in any cross-section of the population in Yangon.

I have been asked by many people how I managed to conduct research for this book. The truth is that it was rather straightforward. I first became interested in Burma in the late 1990s, while living in my native Canada, where I met some Burmese refugees. In late 2001, I traveled to the Thai-Burma border to do humanitarian work in refugee camps there. Subsequently, while a PhD student at Cornell University, I published an article about Karen young people dancing in the Mae Khong Kha refugee camp.[36] Later, I conducted fieldwork among the Chin population of Indianapolis, Indiana, which resulted in another article about music among Burmese people outside of Burma.[37] In June 2007, I got on a plane and flew to Yangon, ready to research music-making inside the country. Within two weeks I had met a number of amateur musicians and had been invited to teach at a church-sponsored music camp. When I returned to Yangon in December of that year, my contacts quickly led to interviews with significant public figures in the pop music industry.

Of course, I understand why I have been asked so often about my research methods. It is logical to wonder how any foreigner could conduct extensive interviews—that is, engage in illegal activity—in one of the world's most notoriously repressive states. In fact, this very question has spawned a small but significant literature of the "I-bravely-went-to-Burma-and-talked-to-regular-people-and-heroically-emerged-to-tell-the-tale" variety. Books and articles in this genre paint the country as a hellish police state, and then glorify the author for having the nerve to spend time there.

One example is particularly germane, because the author, Manny Brand, writes about his attempt to research music education. The title of his chapter gives a fair indication of his perspective: "Hopelessness and Despair in Yangon, Myanmar."[38] Brand spent a week in Yangon attempting to "find a music teacher, one who could tell me about teaching in such an isolated, regimented and discouraging place."[39] Brand recounts a cloak-and-dagger tale: he was questioned by threatening government officials, received a surreptitiously passed note directing him to a secret music school, and finally interviewed a music teacher who told him, "Living here means: no job, no personal development, no integrity, no truth, no pride, no momentum, no goals, no happiness and certainly no freedom. It means waking up every morning with fear—fear of repression, fear of arrest, fear of torture and fear of prison. . . . Now, I teach music lessons, but I am afraid to perform anymore. All my musician friends are afraid."[40]

My own experience was, in many ways, the polar opposite of Brand's. For example, I interviewed a teacher at the State High School for Fine Arts that Brand tried to visit. Unlike him, I was not interrogated by menacing officials as a result. I also visited three other privately run music schools, none of which was an underground operation hiding from military intelligence. And although the teachers and students at those schools were honest about the challenges they face as citizens of Burma, they did not express existential hopelessness and despair. Certainly I neither heard nor perceived that all Burmese musicians are constantly afraid. Rather, I came away from this project profoundly impressed by, and grateful for, the consistent hospitality at the heart of Burmese society. I was able to write this book because dozens of Burmese people—Buddhists, Christians, and Muslims—invited me into their homes, offices, and recording studios. They listened patiently to my efforts to express myself in Burmese, gave me copies of their recordings for analysis, and generously answered my many questions. In fact, my sojourn in Burma stands out in my memory as a time when I was surrounded by welcoming, friendly people. This book represents my best effort to do justice to their ideas and experiences.

In chapter 1, I describe some of the creators of Burmese pop music and outline the career path that musicians typically follow. I examine the degree of autonomy that musicians enjoy in relation to their colleagues, their fans, and the Burmese regime.

In chapter 2, I describe the music that these musicians create. This chapter looks at the issues of innovation and of imitating the Western model. I analyze three examples of fusion music created by Burmese pop musicians, but I also investigate why it is that so many of them spend so much time focusing on imitation rather than innovation.

In chapter 3, I describe the learning and rehearsal culture created by these musicians. I discuss their ideas about talent, showing that these beliefs affect their perceptions about rehearsing, for example. Furthermore, I argue that these beliefs intersect with their religious beliefs, so the current learning and rehearsal culture will likely resist significant change.

In chapter 4, I turn from the creators of music to the distribution side of the industry. Using sociologist Richard A. Peterson's production perspective, I examine six facets of the distribution of pop music in Yangon. I argue that a close look at Burma's pop music industry forces us to reconsider Peterson's own theories about cultural production.

In chapter 5, I take on the exercise of state power in Burma, as manifest in the censorship system. I look at controllers of music (censors) and delineate the relationship that exists between them and their putative subjects, the musicians.

Chapter One

The Creators of Burmese Pop Music

Gita Studio is located in a nine-story building on one of Yangon's major thoroughfares. The building is only a few years old and boasts an elevator that works virtually every day, thanks to the enormous, noisy generator that squats in front of the entrance. The owner of the building, who built it as an investment, now lives in Singapore. The rumor is that he is laundering money for the military junta, and that the building is a respectable front for his seamier activities.[1] The building is located in the heart of one of the city's Karen Christian neighborhoods, and it serves as a focal point for professional Karen musicians living in the area. They gather in the ground-floor café to eat and talk; they record their *series* (albums) in the Gita Studio upstairs; and they even have their music videos edited by the movie editing business located on the eighth floor.

The building also contains apartments, some of which are occupied by members of this musical community. Aung Shwe, who works full-time in Gita Studio as an engineer, keyboardist, and arranger, lives there, as does one the country's most famous "pretty boys" (handsome young models and actors), who recently launched a singing career. Pretty boy Taylor's star is on the rise, but he continues to live with his parents in a modest apartment near the top of the building. Like most young adults in Burma, he respects the idea of a family home and expresses no desire to reside by himself, though he could well afford to do so. His apartment, like so many others that I visited while living in Yangon, is a small space where multiple generations live together, seemingly in harmony.

The recording studio itself, which occupies an entire floor of the building, is an active but not frenzied space. Though the heavy doors to the various rooms are clearly marked with "Do not open while recording is in session" signs, people merrily disregard the instruction, wandering in and out frequently. Clearly, they know each other well. Morale seems high; people greet each other happily and settle into their work quickly. The industrious atmosphere I sense may have something to do with how people working in this studio (and in other studios across Yangon) conceive of a working day: one day of recording time, about ten hours worth, is called *duty*. One *duty* typically costs 20,000 to 30,000 *kyat* ($20–$30) at well-equipped studios like Gita Studio, although customers frequently pay a flat fee of around 600,000 *kyat* ($600) to record an entire *series*.[2] (Another studio owner quoted prices to me in typical Yangon style: one *duty* costs 30,000 *kyat*, and 5,000 more if the customers ask the owners to fire up the generator.)[3] Artists who come here to record their work, or to have their work recorded or mixed, are paying large amounts, by local standards, for the use of the studio. After repeatedly attending recording sessions here and elsewhere, I decided that customers are getting good value for their money. The musicians work efficiently; that is, they do their *duty* diligently. In addition, the studio contains world-class digital recording equipment, and the air-conditioning runs constantly in order to protect that equipment.

Recording sessions follow an unvarying pattern. To begin, a producer who wants to record an album composes, or pays someone else to compose, a *demo* (pronounced "DEE-moh"). Full-time producers are rare now in Yangon, for reasons that I explain in chapter 4, so the producer is frequently a singer or instrumentalist who has raised money privately in order to fund a recording project. The *demo* cassette usually consists of sung melodies with harmonic accompaniments played on guitar or keyboard. The producer or singer supplies this *demo* to the arranger (the person who makes a plan for how the song will be recorded). The arranger then supplies this arrangement to the players who will record the *series*. In the studio, the recording engineer records first the "body," that is, the drum part, by itself. Second, he records the "multiple," or the guitar and keyboard parts. Third, he records the vocals; at this point, the singer records the melody over the full accompaniment created during the first two steps. Finally, the vocal harmonies are recorded. The finished tracks are sent across the hall to the audio engineer, who employs the very latest computer technology to mix the tracks and create a polished, finished product.

This bare-bones description of the recording process was given to me by a well-known professional musician. To put flesh on it, I decided to spend a day observing him and his colleagues at work in Gita Studio. On February 12, 2008, I arrived early, greeted a few acquaintances who were breakfasting in the café, and headed up to the studio. A number of musicians were gathered to record a song that had been requested—or more accurately, demanded—by the government. The ceremonial opening of new bridge was to be broadcast on Myanmar TV, and the powers that be wanted a song to accompany the video. In this case, the producer—the person or entity funding the recording—was the federal government.

Soe Htun, the musician who first explained the recording process to me, is a Karen Christian and a well-known professional guitarist.[4] Soe Htun arrived early that morning, *demo* tape in hand. He listened to the tape and wrote down the chord progressions almost simultaneously. His notated score, with neatly printed eight-measure lines of chords, was complete after he had played the cassette through twice. (As per the conventions of Burma's C Rule notation—

more about this in chapter 2—he wrote the chord progressions in C major, although the song was actually in A major.) "It's easy," he said; the song contained only three chords (the tonic, the subdominant, and the dominant) organized in predictable tonal progressions. He pointed out that this is the usual way of things: the government likes simple songs. Government songs can be challenging to record, though, because the bureaucrat in charge will often demand that the song include "cultural sounds." This was the case that day, and so Soe Htun's notation arrangement included a pause (or rest) where the sound of a *bohn*, a traditional Burmese drum, would later be inserted. After writing out his arrangement, Soe Htun proceeded to record a rhythm guitar part, simply strumming the chords on the beat, four per measure, for the length of the song.

Just before 11:00 a.m., the drummer arrived. Hlaing Kyi is also a Karen Christian, and happens to be the son of one of Burma's most influential *stereo* musicians.[5] With Soe Htun, who was functioning as both guitarist and arranger for this recording, he ran through the various sections of the song. Although the two were seated in different rooms, they were able to speak to each other through the sound system, and I could hear what I came to think of Burmese "rock talk": all of the technical vocabulary pertaining to the music is in English, and the English words are embedded in Burmese sentences. An English-only speaker would likely be able to discern what was going on as the two men talked to each other about the "verse," the "chorus," the "fade-out," and so on.

After Hlaing Kyi and Soe Htun played through the entire song once, they spent ten minutes experimenting with the sound of the drums; the guitarist wanted to be sure that the sound was *hla deh* (pretty). Just as the men got set to record, the electricity went out. Although the studio was dark for only a few seconds, when the power returned, the recording engineer had to plug and unplug numerous wires, delaying the whole procedure. Everyone remained good-humored, though; this is a daily occurrence, and they have all learned to cope with it. Finally, Hlaing Kyi recorded his drum part, playing along with the guitar track. He played the same pattern throughout the song, with no tempo changes and few fills. As soon as he completed the task—that is, as soon as he had played the piece once—he was off. He had to play at a wedding. Like many studio musicians in Yangon, he performs live at private functions as well as in the recording studio. Conveniently for him, most weddings in Yangon happen during business hours.

Soe Htun did not bother to listen to the recorded tracks, but proceeded immediately to the bass guitar part. Like a number of other professional guitarists I met in Yangon, he is equally adept on bass guitar and electric guitar. His approach was straightforward: he played the root of the chord on the first beat of each measure, and then another chordal note (the root, third or fifth), creating this rhythm for each set of four beats:

At the chorus he varied this slightly; the rhythm became:

At a few points, Soe Htun encountered difficulty—unsurprisingly, since he had not rehearsed this part—and therefore had to stop and restart. It was fascinating to see that he and the recording engineer worked very closely together. The engineer seemed to be able to anticipate Soe Htun's need to restart, stopping the recording one second (or less) after Soe Htun stopped playing. They spoke to each other seldom, and then only in short phrases. Very little time was lost: they seemed almost to read each others' minds. The bass guitar part was not recorded in one take, exactly, but it was completed quickly, with a minimum of discussion.

Without listening to the finished product, Soe Htun proceeded to the next task at hand: recording another rhythm guitar part, this one an octave higher than the first. Again, without taking time to listen to the sound of the tracks he had just recorded, he moved on to the lead (electric) guitar part. Here he played little more imaginatively, creating short melodic motives to fill in two- or three-beat sections where the singer would pause for breath. In two hours, Soe Htun supervised or recorded five tracks.

The composer arrived around 1:00 p.m. and recorded the sung melody over the drum and guitar tracks. His purpose in doing so was simply to provide a vocal guide; the featured singer would record the melody the following day. A modest man, the composer seemed happy to hear how his song was developing so far. He offered no criticisms or suggestions to Soe Htun, who was clearly in charge here. As arranger-guitarist, Soe Htun made all of the artistic decisions—or so it seemed until the keyboard player arrived.

The keyboardist worked in the same way that Soe Htun did; that is, he recorded his part without rehearsing it first, performing from the C Rule notation at sight. He, too, had a formulaic approach to the work, playing solid triads in the same rhythm in most measures:

He added a few complementary rhythms, and employed some passing tones and neighbor tones to vary the pitches. He also requested, a few times, that the recording be stopped so that he could rerecord something he was not happy with. I noticed that he never played a wrong note (in the sense that he never played a note that did not belong in the chord progression). His requests to rerecord stemmed from his own judgment about his playing. If it was not adequately *hla deh*, he simply replayed it. Generally, his changes resulted in a more complex keyboard part; he crafted the sound as he went along. Like Soe Htun (who was now working the recording console, the engineer having disappeared), the keyboardist listened while he played and made corrections as he went, feeling no need to listen to the track once it was complete. And although Soe Htun was present throughout, he gave no verbal directions to the keyboardist—despite holding the title of arranger for the project.

When the work wrapped up for the day, the body and the multiple were complete. The next day the singers would record the vocal and the harmony— and play the *bohn* for a few beats to satisfy the government's requirement for cultural authenticity.

Soe Htun, Hlaing Kyi, and the other musicians who worked at Gita Studio on February 12, 2008, embodied the realities of the Burmese pop scene in a number of ways. Specifically, this small group demonstrated the tendencies of the larger community with regard to gender, religion, and career path. The largely egalitarian social structure in this particular studio is also typical of the Burmese pop industry at large. However, this description of one recording studio on one day is only a snapshot. As we shall see, viewing the situation with the widest possible lens, these musicians live and operate in a uniquely Burmese context of religious, commercial, and gender traditions which color the relationships they have with their colleagues, their fans, and their government. The nature of these relationships accounts for the sharp distinction between the Burmese pop music industry and the Anglo-American industry.

Gender and Religious Norms

Generally, the Yangon pop music scene is male-dominated, and a sharp gender divide exists. Women are quite visible in Burmese pop music, to be sure, because they principally work as singers, and thus are inevitably front and center during live shows and on album covers. Less frequently, they work as composers and as producers, but usually only when they compose for themselves or when they self-produce their *series*. They never work as arrangers or recording engineers, and they virtually never play instruments. Throughout the course of my research, I met only two women instrumentalists.

When Zeya Win was a child, her parents paid for lessons in classical Burmese dance and singing ("*Maha Gita myo*" or *Maha Gita* type). At age nineteen, she developed an interest in rock guitar, and her father paid for her to have lessons with a professional (male) guitarist. She says that both she and her father were "unusual": she because she wanted to play guitar and he because he supported her in this goal. Her teacher eventually helped her earn a spot in one of Yangon's successful all-female bands, and with this band she spent a few years performing for weddings, *Thingyan* festivals, and the like.

One year, Zeya Win recalls with a smile, her band was named "Best Band of the Year" by the Burma Broadcasting Service's Local Talent program. She says that she never thought of herself and her peers as "professionals" because their income was so small compared to that of their male counterparts. Of course, the all-girl band was restricted in the amount of money it could earn because it was "not culturally acceptable" for the women to travel by themselves to other cities to perform. In order to travel, they needed to be accompanied by male performers who would be appearing on the same concert program. Eventually, Zeya Win says, her band broke up when the members decided to pursue more financially viable careers.

The only other woman instrumentalist I met was Ma Khin Sein. She is currently working full-time in the Yangon pop music industry as a percussionist. She is a remarkably self-confident person. "If I can get an instrument, I can play it!" she says happily, explaining how she has come to be a proficient performer on a variety of drums from around the world.[6] This self-confidence no doubt accounts for her professional success. During our interview Ma Khin Sein emphasized also that she has received tremendous support from two men: her former employer, who first encouraged her to purchase and play a drum; and her husband, who is himself a professional musician, and with whom she performs nightly at one of Yangon's most expensive tourist hotels. And she is becoming known to the larger public due to her work on recordings with some of Burma's most popular bands.

Zeya Win and Ma Khin Sein are singular figures in their industry. The Yangon pop music scene is hardly unique in this respect; women are largely underrepresented in rock music the world over, and they play instruments much less frequently than men do.[7] When I asked Burmese industry members about the gender divide among them, they had no quick answers. They assured me that there is no rule barring women from playing instruments, working a recording console, or anything else. (And when I looked doubtful at this response, male informants sometimes invited me to play with them, proving that they were not rigid sexists.) The general feeling was that somehow it just happens that women choose to limit their involvement to singing.

No doubt this is true on some level; expectations regarding appropriate gender roles are powerful in every human society, all the more so when they are not questioned. In the Burmese case, musicians model themselves on British and American superstar pop groups—which are themselves male-dominated, and in which women are usually only visible as lead singers (if they are present at all). And I think there is another, more locally grounded reason for this phenomenon.

In Burma there are a number of long and living traditions of groups of musical instruments playing together. The most famous and most common is the *hsaing waing*, a classical orchestra of membranophones (principally the drum circle), idiophones (gongs) and an aerophone (the oboe-like *hnay*). The *hsaing waing* developed in the courts of Burmese kings. Today it performs for traditional puppet theatre, Buddhist rituals, and cultural shows. Although both men and women sing the lyrical melodies of Burmese classical music, generally it is only men who play the accompanying instruments. There are major exceptions to this rule, of course. Women do sometimes play certain instruments, particularly the *saung gauk*, or Burmese harp, and less often the *pattala* (wooden xylophone) and the *sandaya* (Burmese piano). They also frequently play the *si neh wa* pattern, which establishes the meter in Burmese classical music, on a wooden clapper and a pair of finger cymbals. But they generally play these instruments only indoors, in small chamber ensembles, to accompany their own singing. Women do not play in the large *hsaing waing* ensemble, which most often performs outdoors and accompanies other performers.

In *tain-yin-tha* communities (ethnic minority groups, or "the national races," as the government usually translates it), the same is true. Men and women sing and dance, but only men play musical instruments. In fact, in some communities there are explicit rules forbidding women from playing instruments. One Karen Buddhist woman, a member of a traditional dance troupe, told me that women are not allowed to play instruments because "the *nats* (spirits) would not like this, and it would bring suffering [on the group]."[8] Other Karen Christians, both men and women, affirmed the same kind of prohibition against women playing, or even touching, certain traditional musical instruments. One female seminary professor showed me a number of instruments in the school's library collection, but would not play the drum (*tabluh*) nor the bronze drum (*glo*), not even to demonstrate the sound for me, out of respect for this age-old rule.[9] The Karen Christians' faith includes a continuing belief that some traditional instruments are living creatures and that the instruments themselves are gendered. They therefore continue to restrict the playing of most instruments, especially the *glo* and the *gweh* (buffalo horn), to men, even as they include these instruments in Christian services.

I suggest therefore that women are underrepresented in Burmese pop music for a multiplicity of reasons. They are participating in an art form that is dominated by men wherever it appears, and therefore they have few role models other than women-as-singers. They are, like women in most societies, generally less economically powerful than men, and therefore may not have the financial resources to purchase expensive digital equipment and set up recording studios. And they are the inheritors of a custom that has, for some centuries now, exercised a taboo on women participating in instrument playing.

This custom, though, is changing. In recent years, the University of Culture has trained many female students to play the whole range of Burmese instruments, with the result that the annual national *Sokayeti* Competition has recently featured classes for all-female *hsaing waing* groups.[10] And a recent documentary movie about Karen refugees on the Thai-Burma border features a scene in which a group of women play instruments to accompany their sisters who are performing a *don* dance.[11] It is therefore entirely possible that the Yangon pop scene, too, will soon see a loosening of the current seemingly rigid boundaries surrounding women performers.

Gender norms are determined in part by religious beliefs. And in Burma, religion often implies ethnicity, because religion tends to map fairly neatly onto ethnicity. Most Chin, Kachin and Sgaw Karen people are Christians; most Indian people are Muslims; and most Shan, Pwo, Karen, and Burman people are Buddhists. In the case of the people working at Gita Studio, Soe Htun (the guitarist), Hlaing Kyi (the drummer), and the keyboardist were all Sgaw Karen Baptists, while the composer and the recording engineer were Burman Buddhists. As I noted earlier, this particular studio is located in a Sgaw Karen neighborhood, and therefore it is to be expected that members of that community would appear there. However, this microcosm of the Yangon pop music scene is actually a fairly accurate reflection of the larger community.

Exact population statistics are impossible to come by, but we can say with certainty—and many of my informants did say this—that Christian *tain-yin-tha* musicians are largely over-represented among creators of music in Yangon. One of my Burman Buddhist friends, Ko Htet Aung, summed it up rather rue-fully: "Everyone thinks I'm Christian because I sing," he said.[12] This was not always the case. When Burmese pop got started in the early 1960s, most of the participants, especially those who were stage performers, and therefore known to the public, were Burman Buddhists.

Today, a significant number, perhaps half, of the best-known singers in the country are *tain-yin-tha* Christians, mostly from the Karen, Chin, and Kachin ethnic groups. (Examples include Phyu Phyu Kyaw Thein, currently the high-est-paid performer in Burma; Rebecca Win, Song Thin Par; Lay Lay Wah; Mee Mee Kay; Kabya Bwe Mhu; and Hackett.) In addition, a large number of others work as composers and instrumentalists; some of the best-known include Chit San Maung (the lead guitarist in the Iron Cross band) and Saw Kuh Hser, a noted composer. Ma Khin Sein is an Anglo-Burmese Christian, and Joyce Win, who has recorded best-selling albums since the 1970s, is a Burman Christian. In light of the fact that Christians constitute only four or five percent of the total population of Burma, this overrepresentation of Christians in the pop music industry is startling.[13] Musicians themselves—Christians and Buddhists alike—account for this phenomenon by pointing to the informal but persis-tent musical training that young Christians receive in Burmese churches. Ther-avada Buddhist ceremonies held at pagodas, by contrast, include no singing.

Career Development

Although the Buddhist, Christian, and Muslim musicians working in the Bur-mese pop music industry come from different religious and ethnic backgrounds,

their working lives generally conform to a pattern. These musicians tend follow the same path, and during interviews they highlighted the same kinds of
events as important to their development as professional musicians. Typically,
they had supportive parents. Many of my informants talked about the emotional support their parents gave them, in the form of verbal encouragement
and prayer for their future musical success. In addition, parents who could
afford it paid for instruments (usually piano or guitar) and formal lessons.
Furthermore, some parents modeled musical success for their children, giving
them living examples of possible musical careers. Aye Kyi, one of Burma's most
famous singers, vividly recalls her mother and two aunts forming a singing trio
and performing at venues around Yangon.[14] And Ohnmar Tun, who has had
a long career as a singer, is now encouraging her son and daughter in their
careers as a punk rocker and a pop singer, respectively.

Of course, these experiences were not universal. Some musicians
recounted that they had serious conflict with their parents over the issue of
pop music. For example, Maung Maung Zin, now a successful performer and
teacher, remembers that when he said that he wanted to study Western music
in Singapore, his father told him,"You're stupid."[15] Moe Lwin, a highly successful composer and performer, recalls that his father was so enraged at the
sound of his young son's guitar playing that he smashed the guitar.[16] Guitarist Htay Cho says that this kind of tension persisted even after he left home.[17]
When he was a university student he lied to his parents about the amount
of time he was spending practicing his guitar and hanging out in recording studios, letting them think that he was devoted to his studies in zool-
ogy. Later, he financed the purchase of a new electric guitar by selling a gold
necklace his grandmother had given him—and he lied about that, too. It was
years before he was able to be completely open with his parents, because they
disapproved so strongly of his desire to pursue a career in the Yangon pop
music industry. However, all of these men said that their parents' "scolding"
stopped after they became financially successful, and that their parents are
now proud of them.

The Yangon-area pop musicians that I interviewed for this book were all
largely self-taught. Their self-teaching seems to go hand in hand with their high
degree of self-motivation. For example, several musicians recounted going to
great lengths just to acquire an instrument, either borrowing one or building
one of their own. Typically they develop a deep desire to become musicians
early in their teen years. They then take steps to educate themselves, working
independently to master the craft. For example, a composer named Michael
shared that when he was a teenager he practiced the piano eight hours per day,
with no guidance from a teacher, out of sheer love for the music and a desire to
improve.[18] Performer Myine Myat shared that he learned how to play rhythm
guitar, beginning at age thirteen, on his own at home.[19] After high school, he
went to Thailand to pursue a musical career, initially playing folk songs in cof-

fee shops. Later, he learned picking technique from a Yamaha Music school book that he purchased.

Virtually all of the now-successful recording artists in the Burmese pop scene got their start performing Top 40 hits, in English, for business and diplomatic travelers. For example, James Thiri, a veteran of the industry, explained that he began his career playing in a band with his cousins; they earned money and a good reputation playing at many foreign embassies. And Aye Kyi, one of the most successful recording artists in Burma, shared that she got her start singing at the Dolphin Restaurant, an upscale eatery owned by a family friend. Currently, the most consistent work for up-and-coming Burmese pop musicians is found in hotels and restaurants that cater to foreigners. Many interviewees mentioned that they had regular gigs at downtown hotels prior to making their first recordings.

In fact, playing at such venues is often the culmination of a professional career in pop music in Yangon. Quite a number of people who make a full-time living as singers and instrumentalists work five or six nights a week at hotels and focus their energies on this kind of live performance, rather than trying to break into the recording industry. For example, Myine Myat has spent the past eight years performing nightly at a long-stay condominium complex in central Yangon. He likes the work and is grateful to be able to earn enough to support his wife and daughter while working far fewer hours than the average Yangon resident.

Virtually all of the performers active in the Yangon pop scene, even those at the pinnacle of popularity, combine time spent performing live with time spent in the studio. Many of the live shows occur in hotels, which provide the best indoor performance venues in the city. Others are at private parties—weddings, reunions, birthdays, and other celebrations. In fact, it is these small functions, not the "big shows" or stage concerts for which the public buys tickets, that pay the rent. Most musicians receive an average of 50,000 *kyat* per night when playing at a small function.[20] Because Yangon's upper middle class is growing, partly due to Chinese immigration, and because members of this class often hire bands rather than DJs to provide music for their family functions, professional musicians can be assured of a steady income from live performance opportunities.

Celebrity, Burmese Style

A number of scholars have concerned themselves with musicians' status in the larger society they inhabit. Alan Merriam argued that this question is part of one of the six critical areas of enquiry for ethnomusicologists.[21] After surveying the field research that had been completed up to that point, he asserted that musicians across cultures usually constitute a separate and socially marginal group.[22] According to Merriam, they often occupy a low social rank, while simultaneously retaining a high importance in society and permission to indulge in deviant behavior.[23]

"Big name" Burmese pop musicians, however, are hardly marginal; they are, rather, privileged members of Yangon society—and they know it. They make more money than do most of their fellow citizens, and they do so in congenial circumstances. They spend many hours in air-conditioned studios (experiencing physical comfort that can be hard to find in hot and humid Yangon), and they exercise a large degree of autonomy. Moreover, they are "famous."

People who work full-time as professional pop musicians in Yangon are usually called, by themselves and others, "famous musicians." Of course, there are many musicians in Yangon who are hoping to break into the industry, or who have achieved only marginal success as yet, and cannot be considered famous. But most of the musicians I interviewed are commonly considered to be famous, and their stories reveal what it does, and does not, mean to be a famous pop musician in Yangon.

Burmese people who speak English use the word "famous" to mean "well-known by many people," as American English speakers do. In Burmese, the equivalent word is *nammeh gyi deh*, or "big name." In Yangon, the category of big-name pop industry professionals includes many people who are not stage performers. Notice, for example, how the word is used in this 2001 posting on an English-language news website where you can find out "What's happening around good ol' Yangon." Evidently pop singers can be famous, but so, too, can beauticians:

> Silver Oak is a trendy bar opened by two hairstylists/beauticians Ko Ko and Nyi Nyi. It is located on Bo Aung Gyaw Street (lower block). Their beauty salon is next to the bar. Ko Ko and Nyi Nyi, who circulate in the entertainment industry, have their close singer friends and new music groups entertain at their bar. On June 22nd, they had Graham and audiences went gaga over his performance. Graham sings for many television commercials and is also a famous singer. One famous beautician hired a photographer to take pictures of this night with Graham.[24]

The pop music industry contributes to this phenomenon in the way it advertises new *series*. The names of the musicians are prominently listed on the covers of most CDs, along with the instruments they play or their roles as composers or singers. The name of the studio is also listed, and often, the names of the audio engineer and the photographer who created the cover art. These CD covers are then used for billboard advertising, blown up to thousands of times their original size and displayed at major intersections. It is therefore literally true that, in Yangon, one can become a big-name video editor, for example.

Figure 1.1. Billboard advertising a new *series*, showing names of all involved, including the recording engineer

One man whose name appears frequently on such billboards is Pee Paw, or White-Hair Pee Paw, as he is often known. Pee Paw is an impresario, the go-to guy for anyone who wants to organize a live show inside (and increasingly, outside) of Yangon. He is "the most famous stage show organizer in Burma"; he was described to me this way by a number of people. Like other famous music industry members that I met, he claims this status for himself without braggadocio. "Everyone knows me as 'the best'" he told me calmly.[25]

As our interview continued, it became clear that Pee Paw has worked hard to achieve that staus, and continues to work very hard to maintain it. The son of a movie-making family, he was the personal manager of Zaw Win Htut, one of Burma's best-selling rock stars, for six years before launching into the live show business. Live shows (that is, concerts on stage in front of audiences) had almost disappeared from the Burmese music scene when Pee Paw decided to organize one. Realizing that many fans of Zaw Win Htut had never actually seen him perform, Pee Paw put together a live show in 2001. Since that time, he has organized 135 live shows. His company now employs twenty-two people. He claims, with justification, that his work resurrecting the live show tradition has fundamentally changed the nature of the pop music industry in Yangon in the twenty-first century. He is therefore comfortable asserting that he is famous; he can claim this status for himself with good reason.

From the musicians' perspective, fame is much to be desired. A number of already-successful members of the industry identified this as one of their goals. "I want to be the most famous audio engineer in Burma," said Aung

Shwe, reminding me that fame is not limited to stage performers. Interestingly, most members of the pop music community talk about fame as something to be used strategically, rather than as an end in itself. Pee Paw, for example, says that his big name is a kind of quality assurance for fans: "People know, if it's a Pee Paw show, it's a good show," he points out. And a guitarist called Johnson, who like a number of his fellow evangelical Christians works as a professional musician in Yangon, says that his fame helps him to spread the gospel.[26] Speaking about the crusade-style shows at which he often performs, the man asserts "I'm famous, that's what makes people come [to hear the preaching]."

Other Karen Christian musicians talked about using their fame to uplift the Karen people, to be shining examples of Karen-ness and thereby improve the reputation of Karen people among the Burman majority and ultimately, in the world. Taylor, a Karen singer who has already achieved some recognition with his first *series*, says, "I want my name to be known all over the country." He points out that by becoming famous he will be in a position to help his fellow Karen and other *tain-yin-tha* groups who are materially impoverished and suffer from a sense of inferiority. Soe Htun articulated the same kind of goal, saying that he wants to take advantage of his fame in order to promote a nationalist agenda, that is, to convey the strength and beauty of the Karen people. He referred to other musicians who have accomplished this for their own ethnic groups, including the *luk thung* singers from Isan who have rehabilitated that province's reputation in Thailand, and African American blues musicians who garnered unprecedented respect for their community and its art forms in the United States and the United Kingdom.[27]

Being famous means being well-known to the general public in Burma. Industry insiders also emphasized the importance of being known within the industry, saying that being widely-known inside the Yangon music scene is crucial to their work. Ma Khin Sein, for example, says that she is always working to achieve more recognition from her fellow musicians so that she can build her career. "It is important that people know me; after they get to know me they will call me [to perform]" she says. U Hla Myint Swe, the director of City FM radio station, says that being known by musicians is central to his and his radio station's success.[28] He argues that City FM has prospered because many popular musicians support it by appearing on its programs. And they appear on these programs because he invites them to do so: "Everybody knows me," he says, arguing that he is able to gain the cooperation of artists because he is known by them.

For all that fame can be a useful tool, it can also be a liability. In Burma, having a big name means that one's name is known to all, including the government. Famous people are therefore more likely to be scrutinized by the regime, a possibility that is an ever-present concern to musicians. Author Phil Zabriskie, who profiled Zaw Win Htut for *Time* magazine in 2002, focused on this negative aspect of fame for Burmese musicians. After describing how the singer had to submit to interrogations about his lyrics, Zabriskie concluded, "For Burmese artists and performers, fame is less about feast and more about frustration." Composer Ko Chit Min confirmed this, saying that the best approach is to cultivate a big name only within the music industry.[29] He says that being well-known to the general public can be more trouble than it is worth. "If you're famous with the public, then you get more pressure from the government," he claims.

In addition, people who are under government surveillance are less likely to be granted permission to leave the country, so their freedom is restricted in a very tangible way. Two well-known singers and a composer whom I interviewed identified surveillance by the government as one of their biggest concerns. Many other interviewees requested that I not write down other complaints that they voiced, fearing that a government representative might someday read this book. For the same reason, some performers requested that I not mention their song titles, since identifying song titles is tantamount to identifying performers, at least when the performers are famous. Fame in Burma, then, can be a double-edged sword.

The most significant difference between the Western and Burmese notions of fame is that in Burma, fame is not linked with wealth. Americans talk about celebrities who are "rich and famous." But in Burma, no such assumption is made. It is quite possible to be famous without being rich. In fact, most of the famous musicians that I met while conducting this research were not particularly rich. They tended to live in rather larger apartments than my nonfamous friends, and they tended to own cars and employ house servants, but they did not occupy the top rung of the income ladder. They were able to travel outside the country (rarely), and they were able to educate their children. They did not, however, live in the upscale suburban neighborhoods around Yangon where mansions sell for $70,000–$80,000, and they often experienced a lack of money as a constraint on their careers, saying that they would be able to do more if only they had more money.

In fact, being a pop musician has not historically been viewed as a road to financial success in Burma. James Thiri stated flatly, "By doing music you can never be a rich man." He is now, arguably, a rich man, but he assures me that he did not earn his wealth principally from his music career. He was lucky enough to be born into a rich family, and then emigrated to Australia during the 1980s. Currently, he owns a business that is part of a joint venture with the Myanmar Government Ministry Number One. The business is profiting handsomely by selling multivitamin injections to the millions of diaspora Burmese who cherish local medicines.

Some of James Thiri's peers say that while they have earned significant income over the course of their careers in music, they always held other jobs (as dentists or English teachers, for instance) to supplement their musical earnings.[30] Younger musicians at the beginning of their careers tend to focus exclusively on their music-making as a way of earning money. However, a number of them are married to spouses who work in other fields that provide regular paychecks. Soe Htun, for example, is married to a fashion designer. Myo Myo Thant, a singer who has had some success, is married to woman who works for the United Nations; he emphasized during our interview that she is the main breadwinner for their family.[31] Nu Nu Win, a young female singer, is married to another famous singer, and together they earn enough for the Jeep which she drove to our interview.[32]

In comparison with the large numbers of Yangon residents who live on the equivalent of one US dollar per day, professional musicians are doing extremely well. And they are generally doing better than government workers, who earn such paltry salaries that they are often accused of demanding bribes to supplement their income. Public school teachers, for example, have raised the art of augmenting their earnings to new heights. Many of them work after school hours as private tutors. Some, in order to guarantee themselves a pool of students who need tutoring, refuse to teach the entire curriculum during the school day. The phenomenon of teachers working as tutors has become an industry in Yangon, and it even has a name: *tuition.* All parents who can afford it send their children to *tuition* after school, mostly to ensure that their children will be able to pass the rigorous national exams for which they are supposed to be prepared during regular classes.

The professional musicians I met in Yangon were, by and large, able to send their children to *tuition.* (When I met a musician with children, I asked about this as a way of gauging family income. Burmese people, like Americans, tend to be uncomfortable with a direct question like, "How much money do you make?") These musicians, then, are more economically secure than teachers. Rather than having to supplement their incomes, they are able to purchase the services of those who are earning a second income. Furthermore, they usually do their work in air-conditioned studios and hotels, meaning that their working lives are less physically demanding than those of most Burmese workers.

Of all the musicians I interviewed in Yangon, the one who seemed to have the most luxurious lifestyle would probably be described as "upper middle class" in North American terms. Moe Lwin drives a late-model minivan with all the extras, rents a penthouse apartment in a premium building, and sends his three children to school in Singapore. However he, like virtually all of the others that I met, insisted that he does not "have a big [music] business" and that he was only able to purchase equipment for his new recording studio because he spent nearly a decade working in the IT industry in California. Like many of his peers, Moe Lwin does not view himself as rich, although millions of Burmese people would beg to differ.

As an outsider, I found it somewhat difficult to assess industry members' repeated claims that they are not rich. Of course, their incomes vary quite widely, and so it is probably impossible to make any kind of blanket statement about their economic status. Nonetheless, virtually all of the famous musicians (and audio engineers, and managers, and composers, etc.) that I met own cell phones. Ownership of hand phones (as they are called in Burma) marks this particular group of people as earning more, even much more, than the norm. According to United Nations statistics, in 2004 there were 92,007 mobile telephone subscribers in Burma. At that point, hand phone users constituted a tiny elite (less than 0.25 percent of the population). By 2010, Myanmar Post and Telecommunications estimated that 4 percent of the population used hand phones; ownership of such a phone is a daunting proposition in a country where a phone costs approximately $1,500 and a phone card even more.[33] Today, a cell phone owner in Burma is still one of a privileged few.

Another significant difference between Burmese pop musicians and their American peers is that Burmese performers are not antiestablishment figures, either in their public profiles or in their private lives. During one of my trips to Burma, I amused myself in my guesthouse at night by reading back issues of *Rolling Stone* magazine, which reminded me how important a rebellious attitude is in Western conceptions of rock and pop music. In the "Special Troublemaker Foldout," which contained a "Rebel Hall of Fame" to recognize the "Badasses and Bombthrowers" of American rock music, *Rolling Stone* wrote:

> What makes a rock & roll rebel? It's about sound. It's about style. It's about attitude and arrogance and ignoring all the codes of the day. It means keeping control over your own music, rather than tailoring it to please everybody else. It's about challenging the rules, politically and sexually and creatively. There's more to rock rebellion than just being an asshole, although sometimes that's part of the job. . . . We salute the musical visionaries who have stuck to their guns creatively, refusing to kiss ass. . . . We salute the ill-mannered, the obnoxious, the unmanageable, the absurd. We raise a toast to the rock heathens who keep teaching us new ways to destroy our lives and poison our minds.[34]

The article goes on to celebrate musicians who defied the rules of the industry (such as Eddie Vedder, who testified against Ticketmaster's monopoly before Congress) equally with those who behaved rudely, or even illegally, in public (like Avril Lavigne, who spat on a paparazzo, and Pete Doherty, who struggled with a career-destroying drug addiction and once burglarized a bandmate's apartment). After reading this faintly repellent article, I realized that such a thing could never be written about Burmese rock stars. And this is not just because of the extreme censorship of print media in Burma. Rather, it is because Burmese pop musicians value their public respectability, and generally do not participate in these kinds of behaviors. To wit, here is an internet posting by "K.K." on YangonNow.com. K.K. writes about another famous entertainer in Yangon, Yaza Ne Win, and directly links his career success to his adherence to conventional respectability:

> He appears in films, ads and VCDs. His father was a famous actor. His sister is a famous singer. He suddenly becomes famous just after 40. He has a good name without any scandal with girls. Is it because of good teaching of his mother. Media says nothing ill about him. They said his goods, interesting action, has become the same. Everyone wants to use him in their movies . . . He becomes an important actor. His recent CD was sold well. (K.K.)[35]

Indeed, Burmese pop musicians have gone some distance to emphasize this point with their audiences. For example, the Myanmar Musicians Association began sponsoring a soccer team in 2006. The team, which includes a number of famous pop singers, plays exhibition matches around the country. Myo Myo Thant, one of the founding members of the team, says that one of the main goals of the team is to demonstrate to the public at large that the singers are physically healthy people, "not a bunch of drug addicts." Johnson, the evangelical guitarist, who usually exhibits the reserved demeanor common to many Burmese people, became visibly emotional when I questioned him on this point. He insists that most musicians in the Yangon pop industry—and he knows many of them—do not take drugs. Furthermore, he says, most of them are just people trying to make an honest living.

Other musicians agreed with this assessment. Although it is impossible to know for sure what their colleagues do in private, musicians say confidently that they do not show up for recording sessions or concerts visibly drunk or high. Furthermore, like most Burmese people, famous musicians are adherents of Buddhism, Christianity, or Islam, and so they are reluctant to violate the precepts of their faith. In addition, they usually live with their extended families, and so do not want to participate in behavior that might bring trouble or shame to their loved ones. I did meet one musician (a Christian) who admitted to being a drug user; he said that he is "ninety percent clean now" and that he began to kick his habit when he got married three years ago.[36]

Another pronounced contrast between famous Burmese pop musicians and their Western counterparts is that the Burmese are not celebrities, at least not in the Hollywood sense. They are not stalked by paparazzi. They do not employ security teams or have entourages. Indeed, it proved easy to contact them, even for a foreign researcher who began her study with no acquaintances inside the country. Furthermore, they do not employ agents or publicists. While their photos often appear in the glossy privately owned newspapers sold on Yangon street corners, they do not seem to be the creatures of the media that American pop stars so often are. Although a handful of Burmese singers have recently appeared in billboard advertisements for products including laptop computers and iced tea, no famous musicians have turned themselves into a brand in order to sell sneakers or perfume.

Figure 1.2. Advertisement featuring one of Burma's most famous singers, Lay Phyu

Figure 1.3. Lay Phyu selling Yum Yum noodles

I interviewed a singer named Thuza who was, in early 2009, one of the most highly paid performers in Burma. He earns approximately $1,500 for one evening's performance. Thuza exemplifies all of the trends I outline above. For example, although he is earning a good living in pop music right now, he says he is actively looking into other business opportunities because he cannot count on his music income to sustain him and his family long-term.[37] A devout Buddhist, he says that he does not want to participate in the sexual profligacy and "selfishness" associated with rock stardom in the West. Rather, he says, he hopes his fans will think he is "decent." He does not have an entourage, although his wife does act as his manager, helping him to coordinate his many activities. He does not have any paid bodyguards either, although he spends a lot of time with his brother and a small group of male friends who usually accompany him when he goes out in public. And when he does go out in public, he is never fearful, because autograph seekers and photojournalists are "always very respectful. They ask permission to take my picture."

Other industry members share Thuza's perception that fans are usually respectful, even adoring. A manager at Yangon's City FM radio station says that the reason the station has become so successful so quickly is that it is the first and only one in the country which provides listeners the opportunity to phone in and chat with famous singers.[38] He claims that during the bimonthly Star Online show, when Yangon residents call the station and ask questions of the invited musical guest, callers are sometimes so overcome by emotion that they cannot speak.

I saw this kind of reaction myself, in less extreme form. A friend of mine named Rebekah, a well-educated woman who owns her own business and is widely respected in her community, agreed to help me contact one of Yangon's famous singers by phoning her on my behalf. She had obtained the singer's phone number from the singer's uncle, who was a good friend of hers. Still, the singer seemed to her to be a special person, inhabiting another plane. "I hardly dare to phone her and ask!" Rebekah said to me, before nervously dialing.[39] On another occasion, when a different friend arranged for me to meet with another famous guitarist, she and some family members tagged along, thrilled to have the opportunity to meet the man. (Although he was a colleague of their cousin's, somehow, they had never met him before and they jumped at the chance.) As we pulled up to the meeting point, they spotted a Lexus. "That must be his car!" they exclaimed—and photographed it.

It is important to note that even the most famous Burmese pop musicians are, at this time, famous only among Burmese people. Those musicians at the very height of popularity, such as Phyu Phyu Kyaw Thein, R Zani, members of the Iron Cross band, and others, have performed concerts outside of Burma in recent years in countries including Malaysia, Singapore, Thailand, England, and the United States. However, in each of those cases, they performed for predominantly Burmese audiences, and the concerts were organized by Burmese diaspora organizations. Therefore, at this point in history, famous Burmese singers are not reaching foreign audiences in the way that their English-language models in the West have done.

Some musicians I interviewed identified this as a goal—but they spoke about it wistfully, rather than in the context of a concrete plan. Nu Nu Win, for example, said that she dreams of writing songs "for the whole world," but immediately added that she thinks this is currently impossible, due to the political situation in Burma. And Ko Htwe, a Karen composer and performer, said that he would like to write English words for his Burmese- and Karen-language compositions, so that they could be understood by international audiences.[40] But he intends to do this, he says, at some undefined time in the future. Both of these musicians are reaching around the planet via YouTube. However, they know that, like all of their colleagues in Yangon, they are still very much Burmese singers, famous with Burmese people and literally unknown to anyone else.

Burmese Musicians as Autonomous Social Actors

Burmese pop musicians are sometimes specialists, in the sense that they play only one role in the larger scene, but more often they are generalists. (For this reason, I often refer to them as "creators of music.") An individual may be, and often is, a composer and a singer, or an instrument player and a producer, and so on. For most Burmese pop musicians, divisions between various roles are not rigid. Soe Htun, for example, works as an arranger and also plays electric guitar and bass guitar. He also owns his own recording studio, and is therefore comfortable operating a recording console. The audio engineer at Gita Studio began his musical career at the age of sixteen when he started playing keyboard for one of Burma's best-known early rock bands. He continues to work as a keyboardist, performing semiregularly around the country. These two men are typical of people working full-time in the Yangon pop scene. They demonstrate multiple skills that reinforce each other.

Burmese instrumentalists also demonstrate versatility within the realm of music performance. That is, they do not usually specialize in playing one particular style of music (rock, country, pop, and the like). Rather, they make themselves available to accompany singers, who do tend to specialize in one style or another. For Soe Htun, this is a point of professional pride. He says that he regularly watches Asian MTV to discover which new musical styles are becoming prominent internationally, in preparation for learning them himself. Singers confirm that the instrumentalists they work with are well-versed in a variety of popular styles. Ohnmar Tun assures me that instrumentalists are very skilled and "know all the styles." She says that before she sings a song, she simply informs the players of the tempo, the style ("like foxtrot, country rock, R and B . . ."), and the key of the song. "And they can do it right away!" she says brightly.

The kind of confidence that Ohnmar Tun has in her colleagues pervades the pop music industry in Yangon. Creators of music are largely confident in one another's abilities to do the job well, and this confidence reveals itself not so much in what they say about each other, but in what they do not say to each other. Take, for example, the kinds of interactions that occurred (or did not occur) at Gita Studio: although the participants created a collegial atmosphere, by way of their friendly greetings and gentle joking with each other, it is hard to argue that they worked as a team. The guitarist, drummer, and keyboardist arrived one after another, and each recorded his part with a minimum of input from the others. Each of them relied on the notation developed by the guitarist—but that notation was a skeletal C Rule score (to be discussed in chapter 3), with only chord progressions, structural markings and some basic metric information. The score contained no melodic pitches or indications regarding rhythm, dynamics, or style.

Each instrumentalist recorded his parts as he saw fit, telling the recording engineer when to stop and restart the sound. The audio engineer, who worked in a room across the hall, had a profound impact on the nature of the final sound product—and he, too, worked utterly independently. He used the most up-to-date computer software to isolate and manipulate the sounds of various instrumental tracks. He worked without reference to any opinion but his own. In short, all of these creators of music were largely autonomous, at least insofar as their own responsibilities extended. They created their own music and were not subject to any criticism or even much direction from anyone else.

When I pointed this out to the audio engineer, he smiled. He and the others were amused by my repeated questions ("Did you rehearse that before today?" "How did you decide what to play?"). He assured me that what I observed that day was representative; Burmese pop instrumentalists generally create their parts as they record them, and they do so independently. This way of operating is common to recording studios across Yangon. All of the professional musicians I observed worked this way, evincing a great deal of trust in each other's musical choices. Instrumentalists in particular functioned with a great deal of autonomy, using minimal notation and improvising their parts. In Burmese pop music, there is no analog for the producer in a Western music studio. (The word "producer," as it is used by Burmese pop musicians, means a person or institution that funds a recording project.) There is no person who listens to others, telling them to play it again, to make certain changes, to try this or that riff. There is no authority figure who makes "key decisions about how specific material should be recorded in a studio and [who supervises] the sessions."[41] We might point to the arranger as a kind of leader, but the reality is that, as I saw at Gita Studio, the arranger arranges very little. He does create basic notation, as a guide to help the musicians, and he does have some say in who will be hired to play which instrument, but beyond that he does not dictate what should be played, nor how.

Htay Cho, a professional guitarist who is passionate about music and full of ideas about shaping sound, says that his dream is to one day become a Western-style music producer. He acknowledges that this will be a challenge. Right now there are no other music directors working in the Yangon industry, so there are no models for him to follow. In addition, he says, Burmese musicians do not see the need for this. He imagines that he will have to spend a long time proving the worth of his services and earning the trust of his peers. At this time Htay Cho is concentrating on saving enough money so that he can work as a producer for free, volunteering his services to wary musicians who are used to working autonomously.

Interestingly, even the almighty junta exercises very little control over the creation of the music, as became evident on the day I visited Gita Studio. Although the musicians were recording a government song, there was no government representative present to comment on the proceedings. The composer had to create his lyrics according to the government's expressed wish for a song that would be appropriate for a bridge opening, but he was not required to include any particular words or phrases. The arranger did submit to the requirement that the song contain "Burmese sounds"—but barely. He allowed just one four-beat rest for a token solo on the *bohn.*

Creators of Burmese pop music enjoy the benefits of being famous and of exercising a good deal of control in their everyday working lives. They are privileged people. During interviews, however, they most frequently emphasized another privilege they enjoy: the opportunity to make a career out of creating and performing music. They conceive of their work as a fortuitous connection between something they enjoy and something that pays well. In response to the question, "Why do you pursue a career in music?" almost all of my interviewees used the same expression: *wah-tha-nah ba-deh.* The dictionary translation of this expression is "It's my hobby." Indeed, some fluent speakers of English among my respondents said exactly those words when answering this question. However, as I talked with each of them more about what this means to them, I came to the conclusion that in this context, a more appropriate translation would be, "It's my passion."

In one typical interview, Myo Myo Thant explicitly contrasted this notion of a "hobby" with the idea of making money. He said that he works as a musician because this is his hobby and that his goal in doing so is not to make a large amount of money. On another occasion, Hlaing Kyi said, "Music is in my blood. I love it so much that I always listen to music when I come home at the end of the day, no matter how much I've already played that day." Composer Shway Nyunt elucidated this notion more poetically: "I was born with music and I will die with music. It's my hobby, not my profession. I love music so much, all kinds of music!"

Musicians' Relationships with Their
Colleagues, Fans, and Government

Burmese pop musicians value the generally good working relationships that exist between musicians in their industry. Soe Htun, who has the chance to observe and participate in many interactions in his work as a performer and arranger, says his peers usually respect each other: "They listen to each other and do not fight." Composer and arranger Theingi Zaw, who has been working in the industry for more than two decades, says that in his experience, industry workers usually get along well. "Mostly people aren't jealous of each other, and they respect each other," he claims.[42] He links these good relations directly to musicians' job satisfaction: Burmese musicians are usually *jay-nah deh* (satisfied) with their work, and therefore they are relaxed and kind when dealing with each other.

Of course, this perception is not universal. Ko Chit Min is a Myanmar Musicians Association member who sits on the organization's dispute-resolution committee, and therefore sees frequent conflict between industry members. He believes that many of them do not respect each other. He claims that composers, for example, do not seem to appreciate all the work that producers do, and so on. "They get along fine until money is involved," Ko Chit Min says. "Then, they don't seem to follow the Buddha, or Jesus, or Mohammed, or whoever they say they're following." Producer Chit Nyein says that many famous singers behave like divas, demanding that recording schedules be arranged to suit their own convenience. He claims that the Burmese public would be shocked to know how some of their favorite singers behave toward their colleagues in the industry. Kenneth, a manager at Yangon City FM, concurs, saying that some of the famous musicians are "difficult to cooperate."[43]

Burmese pop music industry members may not be unanimous in their reports on how they relate to each other. However, they seem to be in agreement about the relationships they have with their audiences. As I noted earlier, most musicians perform live rather frequently. A number of them talked about how much they enjoy their audiences' responses, as evidenced in their behavior at concerts. Aye Kyi talked about receiving e-mails and phone calls from her fans encouraging her to record another *series*; she had stopped recording and performing when she had a baby because she became embarrassed by her weight gain. She says that fans addressed this directly in letters, saying things like, "I still love you whether you're fat or not." Htay Cho said that when others listen to him making music, he feels an "incomparable happiness."

As positive as the relationship between performers and fans generally is, most of my interviewees emphasized that they did not take fans' appreciation for granted. They spoke about the responsibility a performer has to gauge an audience's mood and respond to it. Hpone Thant, a young composer, says "Without music, people would be deaf and dumb."[44] He believes his job is to create music that affects listeners' emotions and "gives them energy." Moe Lwin, who has considerably more experience, agrees: he says that his goal, when onstage, is to "give the audience more pleasure. But not just pleasure, more feeling . . . more intense feeling matching the mood of the song."

Taylor outlined how this belief—that the role of the performer is to respond to and intensify an audience's mood—plays out in practice. A professional singer will arrive at a concert with the notation for five songs in hand, intending to sing only three. He will select these three on stage, basing his choice on his assessment of the audience. "For example, if they [the fans] are energetic and standing up, then you should sing a hard rock song," Taylor says. For him, and for a number of others in his industry, this is the essence of communicating with audiences: reflecting their feelings back to them. This belief, and the accompanying behavior, can only operate in the Burmese pop scene because of the kinds of skills and expectations around playing that we saw up close in Gita Studio. It is only because professional instrumentalists can perform from notation at sight that singers can walk on stage and decide on their song choices there and then.

Burmese pop performers seem confident that they are not only able to directly communicate with their audiences, but that this communication effects some change in the fans themselves. They believe that their music "reaches" their audiences. One young singer known as Julia said that her goal is to make her audiences "happy."[45] She believes she accomplishes this, partly because she can observe fans clapping and singing along with the music, and partly because she knows that she herself feels happy when she listens to music. Therefore she assumes that fans are happy too, when they listen to her. Myo Myo Thant says that he is convinced that his fans hear the messages in his songs. He describes his songs as "spiritual" rather than "political," and says that the proof of his success is that listeners, having heard his music and absorbed its message of love and freedom, interact with their family and friends accordingly. Aye Kyi, who records both secular and gospel songs, says that she heard that a man converted to Christianity after listening to one of her gospel *series*.

As these examples show, Burmese pop musicians maintain this belief—that their music directly affects their listeners—with little evidence to support it. Their comments are more like statements of faith than of verifiable fact. Scholar Jason Toynbee is deeply skeptical of the notion that musicians can communicate with audiences and that audiences can understand the message being communicated.[46] Nevertheless, he acknowledges that the idea plays an important role in performers' approaches to their audiences. He outlines three predominant strategies, or modes, that pop musicians use when communicating with audiences. First, the expressionist mode, in which the musician attempts to express his or her inner being; second, the transformative mode, in which the musician performs "music which maintains a vision of a better world" in an attempt to transform that world; and third, the reflexive mode, in which a strongly self-aware musician displays his or her skills and presents the music to an audience.[47]

As Toynbee points out, most performances use more than one of these strategies, and this is, of course, true in Burma. However, my research suggests that Burmese pop performers most often use the transformative mode; that is, they aim to transform their audiences, and thereby, their world. Interestingly, Toynbee argues that musicians who most often use this mode of communication usually perform music that is "a variation of that which has already been played and sung," rather than original music (as expressionist musicians would do).[48] Again, the Burmese pop scene seems to support his analysis. Its repertoire has historically been dominated by *copy thachin*, or songs that are variations of Anglo-American hits (more about this in chapter 2).

Burmese pop musicians make a number of different claims about their relationships with their fellow musicians and with their audiences. However, they all make identical claims about their relationship to the government: to a man, and to a woman, they say that they are independent of the SPDC. They insist that they do not actively support the government, and that they do not work for it. This is a point of pride for many of them. Kyaw Naing Oo, for example, is a Myanmar Musicians Association committee member who pointed out to me that he was elected to his position by the membership (rather than being appointed by the government, as other committee members were). "The government doesn't like me much," he said happily.[49] James Thiri, who is one of the leaders of the newly reconstituted MMA, took pains to explain to me that this organization is not a creature of the government, nor a professional association or labor union for musicians. Rather, he says, the MMA is a "bridge" that lies "in between" the two camps. And Thet Htaw Mya, the manager of one of Burma's busiest rock bands, eagerly pointed out to me that he never deals directly with government functionaries when organizing concerts: "That's the contractor's job," he emphasized.[50]

Industry members insisted on their independence from the military government even when this claim seemed tenuous at best. For example, U Ye Zaw Tun, who has made a good living importing, selling, and installing recording equipment in government-run radio and television studios, began his interview with me by saying, "I have *never* worked for the government" (his emphasis). Leading figures at both Yangon City FM and Mandalay FM emphasized to me that their radio stations are "private" and "not like the government radio stations," even though their broadcasts, like all media, must be sanctioned by the SPDC, and their stations are under the direct control of government ministries.[51] Theingi Zaw made caustic comments about "some other composers" who are disliked by all the rest because they "write songs for the government and get favors in exchange." In the next breath he admitted that he had recently performed for, and been paid for, a government-organized sports event. "You cannot say no. If you do, they will take action. Like, they will make sure that you do not get a pass [from the Press Security Board, which censors all commercial recordings] for your next album," he explained.

In truth, it seems that most, if not all, of the people working full-time in the Burmese pop industry are obligated to cooperate with government at one point or another. (And some of them said as much to me.) The SPDC is constantly asking musicians to create and perform music for government-sponsored events and TV shows. When a "request" is made, musicians are under tremendous pressure to cooperate, and they usually do. In order to square this behavior with their antigovernment stance, musicians must parse their words. For example, they distinguish between more and less acceptable types of "government songs." Policy songs, understood to be propaganda, are the most morally objectionable subgenre of government songs. These songs generally promote government policy; one recent example was a song that told listeners to vote "yes" in the national referendum of 2008. Other kinds of government songs are more like public service announcements. These songs announce upcoming public health campaigns, for example, or give information about how disease is transmitted.

Generally, composers and performers acknowledge that they sometimes participate in government songs, but claim that they never write or sing policy songs. They then go on to define policy songs as those songs which they personally refuse to create (or have, fortunately, not been asked to create). For example, Ko Chit Min says that he has written some PSA-type songs at the government's behest, but that he never writes policy songs, and that when he is asked to do so, he refuses. For him, all songs requested by the government that treat topics other than public safety are unacceptable policy songs. Prominent composer Htin Thu acknowledged that he has written a song to promote a vaccination campaign, and other songs for bridge openings and the like, but that none of these are policy songs.[52] In his view, a song that celebrates the opening of a bridge (that is, which touts one of the SPDC's accomplishments) is not a policy song—although some of his peers would disagree. Moe Lwin (the composer who created the referendum song mentioned above) admitted that he does sometimes write "political" songs for the government. But he added instantly that when he does so, he tries to redeem the work by making it worthwhile for the audience. He adds "interesting parts, and funny jokes." He says that his goal is to write a "fair" song, one that takes a stand somewhere between the government and the prodemocracy forces. So even he is unwilling, at least in his own mind, to write a song that does nothing but serve the government's agenda.

The Wider Context: Civil Society in Burma Today

One important way in which Burmese pop musicians assert their independence from the SPDC is by contributing to Burma's growing civil society. As many commentators on politics, freedom, and Burma understand, the simple equation of social progress with democratic elections is naïve. This has become particularly evident in some of the G8 countries in recent years, where liberal democratic governments have enacted laws and pursued policies which infringe on the historic rights of their citizens, in the name of fighting the war on terror.[53] Therefore, much of the scholarly discourse surrounding Burma now focuses on the health of the country's civil society. Civil society consists of voluntary organizations of people (other than political parties) who work together for the common good, such as NGOs, community clubs, religiously motivated groups who care for the marginalized, and so on. Such organizations require trust, cooperation, and disinterest (that is, the opposite of self-interest) from their members if they are to succeed. They are thus the building blocks of a democratic society, and the relatively democratic nature of a community or country can be assessed, in large part, by gauging the strength, autonomy, and accountability of civil society organizations.

Burma's civil society is almost always portrayed in the international media as being extinct, or nearly so. A number of Burma scholars concur with this assessment. David Steinberg, for example, asserts that the military regime has effectively destroyed the country's formerly robust civil society.[54] Monique Skidmore points out that the regime's policy of forced relocation of populations (both in rural and urban areas) disrupts the local social networks that develop over many years and which are necessary for the formation of civil society.[55] Zunetta Liddell cites a list of government infringements on freedom of association and freedom of speech in Burma and argues that civil society has "no room to move."[56]

There are some dissenting voices. Calvin Khin Zaw, who now works for one of Burma's most respected NGOs, and who spent more than a decade as a political prisoner, asserts that civil society does exist in Burma.[57] Furthermore, he argues that international focus on individual leaders such as Aung San Suu Kyi does a real disservice to institutions, including those that constitute the civil society, which will be crucially important to any democratic transition in Burma. Brian Heidel, author of the first comprehensive survey of NGOs and CBOs (community-based organizations) in Burma is categorical: "Civil society is alive in Myanmar today."[58] And a recent article in the *Irrawaddy* online magazine points out that in the aftermath of Cyclone Nargis (which killed and displaced hundreds of thousands of people in Burma in May, 2008), the country's civil society organizations rose up to help the victims. The result was that in the wake of the government's restriction of international humanitarian aid, the most-feared outcomes did not come to pass. Epidemic disease, for example, was thwarted. The hundreds of examples of small and large groups of Burmese people who worked hard to help their fellow-citizens proved the existence and effectiveness of the country's civil society.[59]

My experience of living in Yangon tended to support the idea that civil society exists in Burma, and that it operates in all kinds of everyday contexts. Living in Yangon for an extended period, spending time in the homes and workplaces of many citizens, conversing with them in their native language and observing their patterns of behavior and belief, led me to this conclusion. For example, I rode Yangon's public buses daily and was impressed by my fellow-riders' commitment to helping each other during what can be long and uncomfortable commutes. On these buses, those lucky enough to get a seat always offer to hold the bags and packages of those who are forced to stand. They make these offers—which are always accepted, since no one expects the holder of the goods to abscond with them—to strangers and acquaintances alike. Twice, I even observed seated passengers holding the small children of standing parents.

To give another example: as I mentioned above, very few people in Yangon have telephones. In low- and middle-income neighborhoods, those lucky enough to have a phone in their home will almost always share that phone with their neighbors, so that individual phone numbers are, in effect, party lines. The owners of the phones do not ask their neighbors to help pay for the service. In fact, they seem to view this way of helping their fellow-citizens as a kind of civic responsibility, one that is welcomed rather than resented.[60]

These are small things, perhaps. But they are near-universal behaviors, and they reveal the willingness of Burmese people to participate in and sustain their interdependent society. They are a testament to the continual willingness of the average Burmese person to subsume his or her individual interest to the common good, and they are therefore indications that civil society has fertile ground in which to grow.

Moreover, the research I conducted in Yangon revealed that at least one identifiable and influential group of citizens—creators of pop music—make frequent tangible contributions to civil society in Burma. These musicians do not usually talk of "civil society" or "democracy"—but they are practicing the essence of democracy, by working together for the good of society at large. Earlier in this chapter, I referred briefly to musicians' goals, showing that some of them desire to become famous in order to be able to further some social purpose, such as, for example, uplifting the reputation or morale of the minority population into which they were born. In addition, many Christian and Buddhist musicians work for low pay, or even donate their services, in order to help younger musicians or organizations in their faith communities who are creating recordings on low budgets. They also regularly donate their time and talents by performing for free at religious festivals.[61]

And musicians of both faiths are committed to helping to raise funds and awareness for causes that benefit Burmese citizens generally. For example, in January 2008, many of the most famous musicians in Yangon banded together for a concert held at Aung San Stadium. The concert, which lasted three hours and featured approximately twenty-five different acts, was performed specifically to raise money and public sympathy for AIDS patients. This event attracted a standing-room-only audience of about four thousand people and raised 78 *lakhs* (78 million *kyat*, or approximately $7,800).[62] All of this money was given to a Yangon hospital that treats AIDS patients.

The concert performers appeared for free; indeed, when I asked Taylor whether he had collected a fee for his performance, he seemed offended that I had even posed the question. "I would not have taken any money even if it had been offered," he assured me. As I spent more time with Yangon pop musicians, I came to understand why this singer had found my question inappropriate: he and his colleagues so frequently work for free, on projects benefiting others less fortunate than themselves, that it is almost inconceivable that any of them would attempt to profit from an opportunity to raise money for AIDS patients.

The AIDS fundraising concert was combined with an exhibition soccer game. After the concert, the Myanmar Musicians Association soccer team (composed of male members of the MMA, and other soccer players hired for the occasion) played a match against the country's national team. The game seemed to be as much of a draw as the concert itself; no one left after the singing concluded. Indeed, the audience seemed excited to watch the game, cheering equally loudly for both teams.

This match was one of a dozen or so that the MMA team plays in a normal year. The MMA founded this team at the behest of one of their members who is a former member of a professional team, and now it travels around the country, performing concerts and playing friendly soccer matches with local teams. Funding for uniforms and other costs is provided by another member of the MMA who is privately wealthy.[63] None of the musicians are paid for the trips, and they do not use the concerts or matches as opportunities to sell their *series*. Myo Myo Thant told me that the team's objectives are first, to show that they are not drug addicts, and thereby to present a good example to rural youth; and second, to "build relationships" and "create a network" between musicians and their fans.

During an interview, I asked Taylor, who also belongs to the MMA soccer team, about the team's second objective, which he labeled as "having fellowship" with villagers. When I asked him to define "fellowship," he responded: "That means talking together and listening to each other . . . like you and I are doing right now." Myo Myo Thant concurred, explaining that conversations become possible when people play sports together, and that the soccer team was created, in large part, to provoke conversations and create friendly ties between famous Yangon performers and their rural fans. By funding and participating in the MMA soccer team, Burmese pop musicians are providing opportunities for strangers across the country to work cooperatively and have dialogue. In other words, they are fostering the basis of democratic institutions.

Popular music scholar Reebee Garofalo argues that this kind of behavior has received short shrift in academic writing. He points out that intellectuals such as Karl Marx and Theodor Adorno had little patience with popular culture. Marx saw it as nothing more than a reflection of the ideology of the ruling class, and Adorno viewed it as a tool used by elites to turn the masses' attention away from the injustices of capitalism.[64] Later scholars of popular music, contesting the ideas of Marx and Adorno, emphasized that popular culture does have "progressive potential," because large numbers of people are able to "appropriate" it and craft their own meanings for it.[65] But Garofalo contends that scholars need to evaluate the political potential of "mass culture" (as he calls it) by examining the intentions and actions of artists and industry members, rather than just by analyzing the content of their artistic products (pop songs, in this case). He focuses on "mega-events"—pop music concerts that are organized to serve four purposes: fundraising, consciousness raising, allowing artists to be involved in the "cause," and mobilizing the general public, usually through mass media, in service of the cause. Garofalo argues that, insofar as mega-events succeed in achieving these goals, they succeed on a large scale. Therefore, they should be acknowledged as important factors that contribute to the political potential of popular music.

When Burmese pop musicians participated in the AIDS fundraising mega-event described above (and at other similar events), they advanced at least three of Garofalo's four purposes. First, they raised a significant amount of money for medical patients in need. Second, they lent their prestige to HIV/AIDS sufferers, who have not, until recently, been acknowledged by the Myanmar government as being worthy of help. Third, they reinforced their own (and, they hope, their fans') understanding of themselves as entertainers who are allied with their audience, not with their totalitarian government. By making a tangible, public contribution to a "good cause" that has not been adequately supported by the SPDC, these musicians were making a statement about their commitment to Burma's developing civil society.

By choosing to impact their society in this way, pop musicians in Burma are pursuing a line of action akin to what Gautama Buddha called "the Middle Way." The Buddha taught that the Middle Way—the path that lies between two extremes—is the best way to live. The Middle Way strikes me as an appropriate descriptor for the path pursued by Burmese pop musicians as they work toward societal change. These musicians usually do not confront the military government directly by penning lyrics critical of the regime. In other words, they do not choose a path of resistance, as Western scholars would understand it. Nor do they thoughtlessly accede to the government's demands. Rather, they leverage their fame to serve another purpose, giving their energy and skills to projects that are important to local communities.

At least one other scholar has argued for a similar conception of possible political change in Burma. Ardeth Maung Thawnghmung says that a growing number of Burmese people, disappointed with both the military's human rights abuses and the National League for Democracy's inability to effect change, are embracing a "new ideology in Myanmar" which is an "alternative, middle-way approach" to political progress.[66] Unfortunately, Thawnghmung does not say much about this middle way (or "third force," as she also calls it). However, she does contrast it with the cycle of repression and confrontation that has characterized the relationship between the SPDC and the NLD. In addition, she points out that this new approach is valued by people of diverse backgrounds who have come to the realization that they can work together because they have common goals (for peace and economic stability, for example). In other words, this middle way is the fruit of dialogue and cooperation between various parties.

All of this is not to say that Burmese pop musicians view themselves as social workers or political activists. (Indeed, had the AIDS fundraising concert been seen as "political" in the local context, the SPDC would never have allowed it to take place). As we have seen, these musicians say over and over that they decided to pursue their careers because they enjoy music making so much: it is their "hobby." However, when they perform for "good causes" without receiving much or any pay, something they all do fairly regularly, they deploy their ability to attract an audience for the common good. When they consciously set aside the opportunity to earn money for themselves and instead perform for the betterment of their fellow citizens, they underline one very important facet of their identities as famous Burmese musicians. They demonstrate to others and to themselves the depth of their stated commitment to care for their audiences.

Yangon-based pop musicians are, on the whole, happy and productive people. Their own statements and analyses of their situation account for this. They tend to exercise a great deal of autonomy in their work, while at the same time surrounding themselves with friendly colleagues in a collegial atmosphere. They earn enough to be able to access items such as cell phones that are out of the reach of most of their fellow citizens. Furthermore, they enjoy the work, since for most of them music making is a hobby, or passion, that they began to pursue long before they could expect to earn any money from it. They are largely respected for what they do by their fans. They are not expected to violate the social norms of their society, and most of them do not. Moreover, they experience their work as purposeful. Those who have an explicitly religious framework for understanding their lives see their careers as the unfolding of "God's will." Those who do not nevertheless believe that they are able to communicate with their fans and affect those fans for the better. And they make tangible contributions to those fans' lives by participating in the development of the country's civil society.

These creators of music are not naïve Pollyannas; in fact, they clearly articulated their struggles and challenges during interviews with me. Their most oft-repeated complaint is that they do not have enough money to pursue the recording projects that they wish to create. They are deeply worried about rampant piracy of recordings and are often frustrated by their government's irrational attempts to control musicians through surveillance, censorship, and other means. As people who rely on electronic instruments to make their living, they are regularly impeded by the unreliable electricity grid in Yangon. They know that their hopes to go abroad, either to perform or to pursue education, are unlikely to be fulfilled. Nevertheless, they are, for the most part, happy to be creators of music in Yangon and have no intentions of doing anything else. Although they walk a fine line in the work they do for the government, Burmese pop musicians are not mere puppets of a repressive junta. Rather, they are complex human beings who are seeking, and often finding, meaningful and fulfilling lives in the midst of a deeply challenging situation. As such, they merit serious attention from all who care about music and musicians.

Chapter Two

The Sound of Burmese Pop Songs

On February 16, 2008, I was among thousands of excited people attending an Iron Cross concert at Kandawgyi Park in Yangon. For the uninitiated (and this would exclude virtually every citizen of Burma), Iron Cross—or IC, as they are usually called—is the most famous and successful of contemporary Burmese rock bands. The group has sold many thousands of albums. The quickest way to mark IC's success is to point out that the band has toured outside of Burma. In 2004, for example, they played dates in Japan and the United States.[1] However, like the handful of other Burmese acts who have performed abroad, IC remains virtually unknown to the outside world. Its only audience is Burmese, at home and in the diaspora. That night, the excitement was palpable: the members of Iron Cross are veritable stars, almost heroic figures to their fans. Scalpers on the street hawked tickets for 5,000 *kyat* (or $5), a markup of 500 *kyat* from the official price.

My two companions and I abandoned our taxi at the gate, realizing that the crush of people would prevent us from advancing by car. As concert-goers surged past me, I noted that most seemed to be under thirty years of age; that men outnumbered women by about five to one; and that virtually no one was wearing a *longyi* (the traditional Burmese unisex skirt). Blue jeans were the uniform of the evening. And the slogans on t-shirts affirmed the wearers' affinity for international youth culture: I saw numerous shirts celebrating David Beckham, Che Guevara, the FBI, and the US Army, and a few young men sported defiant slogans such as "F**K the Revolution" and "God Made Grass." But I was most interested to see many people wearing the logos and names of pop bands. All of the groups represented were American and British bands; the misspelled Likin [Linkin] Park t-shirt was the most popular. There were no t-shirts representing any Burmese bands—even Iron Cross.

Arriving at the natural amphitheater where the stage was set up, we were enveloped by the crowd. There were no seats (as there had been for another concert I attended in the same venue a month earlier), and everyone was forced to stand. The luckiest were high up on the hills or very close to the stage. The dense crush of bodies in the darkness gave rise to the feeling of being in some different, out-of-the-norm place and time. And this was reinforced by the behavior of my friends, a man and a woman who were hugging—hugging!—each other in public. (I was amused to realize how shocked I was by this; clearly, after only a few weeks in Yangon, I had begun to absorb the mores of Burmese society.) Although we were packed in like sardines, there was a feeling of expansiveness and possibility. I experienced it because I was next to invisible in the crowd, and so was relieved of the constant polite attention I usually received as a foreigner. For the Burmese fans, this feeling of expansiveness came from participating in something normally forbidden—that is, a public meeting of more than five people after dark.

At 6:30 p.m., the official start time, the loudspeakers began blaring a recording of Mariah Carey. We listened to the album until, around 7:00 p.m., the concert began. When it did, I was intrigued to see that the band members simply walked onto the stage, took their places, and began performing. At every other Burmese pop music concert I have attended, the show begins with a long-winded introductory speech during which an announcer reads the biographies of the performers. This is such an integral part of public performances that recordings of live shows usually include the speech. (I always feel vaguely sorry for these announcers, because they are the subject of some heckling, although, since their speeches are rather boring, my sympathy is limited). But at the IC concert, the show began with the show.

And what a show it was! The first act was an extended instrumental improvisation in which each of the musicians (a drummer, a keyboardist, a bass guitarist, and a lead guitarist) performed a long, virtuosic solo. Chit San Maung, the lead guitarist, is a true showman: he played his guitar while holding it over his head, then behind his back, and finally like a keyboard, balancing the instrument on a roadie's willing back. That night, Maung's fingers performed seemingly impossibly fast runs, up and down the range of the guitar, the notes sizzling in the evening air.

After this, we were treated to a standard pop concert. Iron Cross served as an accompanying ensemble for much of the time, playing for a parade of guest singers who came forward one by one to perform two or three songs each. The singers included two women, one of whom opened with a copy of Avril Lavigne's "Sk8terboy," and four men. Each of these singers has achieved some success in their own right (Zaw Paing, for example, is a huge star whose face adorns billboards), but there was no escaping the fact that this concert with IC represented the pinnacle of achievement for each of the singers.

And their presence did not conceal the gaping absence of IC's own lead singer Lay Phyu, who had not performed with the group for years.[2] Rumors abounded as to why this was. One of my friends told me her version: Lay Phyu was forbidden to perform in public by the government because (1) he had refused to perform live on City FM, the Yangon pop radio station, saying that his songs were intended for the whole country and not just Yangon, and (2) he had sung something the government did not like. Whatever the case, the crowd clearly remembered him and missed him: they shouted his name before the concert began, during the lulls between songs, and at any other convenient moment.

The fans generously showered the other performers with their attention, too. They sang along very loudly (perhaps it would be better to say that they shouted along) to almost every song; they took off their shirts to wave them above the crowd; they lifted their hands into the air, clapped, hollered, and even danced where there was room. They did not, however, toss many items toward the stage, as crowds usually do at concerts in Yangon. At the gate, security personnel had confiscated all of the caps from our plastic water bottles, and no one was selling flowers or trinkets, so there was not much to throw. Some enthusiastic fans did manage to toss their water bottles, though.

Undoubtedly, if the staging permitted access to the stage, some members of this crowd would have mounted the stage and presented the performers with flowers or balloons, draping them over their necks. This lovely gesture, and the trust between performers and fans that makes it possible, is one of my favorite aspects of Burmese pop concerts. I was disappointed to realize that it would not happen at the IC concert, because the ramp leading to the stage was blocked. Normally, this ramp is wide open (indeed, I suspect it was built to make it easier for fans to access the stage), and fans use it with enthusiasm. The little ritual always reminds me of Buddhist blessings, during which devotees drape ropes of flowers over statues of the Buddha. It seems to be a direct descendent of audience behavior at traditional Burmese *bwe* (festivals), during which worshippers (usually women) approach the *nat kadaw* (spirit mediums) and lay flowers around their necks or pin money to their clothes.[3]

The barrier between the audience and the band that night was unusual, but many more of the features of their performance were standard practice. For example, family members and technicians were clearly visible at the side of the stage, where they hovered during the songs. Sometimes, the workers even moved equipment around the stage while a song was being sung. Because of this kind of behavior, there is a marked lack of staged formality to many Burmese pop concerts. The performers seem to be there to do a job, which they do competently and without fanfare. Singers will sometimes move about the stage, dance, and play air guitar, but the moment they finish singing their lyrics, they thank the crowd and walk offstage. (Or, they thank the crowd three or four times before walking off: Burmese pop singers are nothing if not polite.) They do this even if the band is still playing the final notes of the song. Bands do not usually play encores. The attitude seems to be, "When it's over, it's over."

Burmese pop music performers are limited by their technology: there are no rotating stages or strobe lights or multistory screens in Burma. The backdrop used at a stage show (a large piece of cloth hung across the back of the stage) presents a couple of logos representing the sponsor or the band, and the name of the event and the date in Burmese and, frequently, in English. The backdrop is never changed during a show, and performers never change their costumes (invariably casual Western wear, for both men and women). Bands do frequently use dry ice for effect—but without making it an integral part of the show. Normally, as at this IC concert, puffs of dry ice vapor appear at regular intervals, coordinated neither with the songs nor with the action on stage.

This concert, like most Burmese pop concerts, was rather longer than the typical American show: the musicians performed from 7:00 p.m. to 10:30 p.m. with no intermission. After the entire group of six singers had performed one by one, they repeated the lineup. All the songs they performed were Burmese pop songs, and quite a few were *copy thachin*, that is, Anglo-American hit melodies with Burmese lyrics. Although Iron Cross is sometimes described as a "heavy metal" band,[4] the format of Burmese pop concerts does not allow for pigeonholing bands into one musical style. Instrumentalists have to be prepared to play for singers performing a variety of styles. That night, the aesthetic was overwhelmingly middle-of-the-road rock. The entire band played for each number, with the drums and guitars filling in rhythms and chords in a relatively uniform fashion on each song. The singers generally used a clear head tone when singing, rather than shouting into the microphone. And their voices were paramount in the texture; although the band evinced great musicianship, clearly, they were accompanying the voices. There was none of the headbanging or smashing of guitars that I associate with heavy metal; rather, utmost decorum reigned on stage throughout the night.

In general, the crowd seemed interested and happy, although when a fight broke out during a lull around 9:00 p.m., I wondered if it weren't partly the result of boredom. Certainly the fight seemed to alarm onlookers, who tried to move away from it in the cramped space. But it was nothing serious. At least, this seemed to be the opinion of the security personnel, who watched with disdain from the sidelines and made no attempt to intervene. Dagon Beer Company was the sponsor for the concert, so beer was on sale and was imbibed in large amounts. I did not notice any open selling of drugs. My very half-hearted attempt to research this point (I asked two people if I could buy drugs at the concert) led nowhere: I was simply informed that there were no drugs available. Perhaps the most noticeable feature of this concert was the fact that the electric current ran steadily through the evening. There were none of the sudden silences or darkenings of the stage that I had come to expect at shows like this.

The show concluded with a copy of Collective Soul's "December," the bass guitarist drawing out the characteristic B♭–B♮–G riff in haunting fashion. This piece is one of IC's signature tunes—it was included on their fifteenth anniversary DVD—and I was struck by how representative this was of the larger Burmese pop scene: the most respected group in the country played a *copy thachin*, performing it with almost eerie exactness, and the crowd embraced the music as an artifact of international modernity that nevertheless expressed Burmese ideas using Burmese lyrics.

Categorizing Songs: Insiders' Perspectives on Terminology

Most of the Burmese pop songs I have listened to while researching this book can be grouped into one broad category: the ballad. Ballads are relatively short songs, organized into verse-chorus form, that imply some kind of real-life circumstance or evoke some narrative (often a love story); they are usually performed at a fairly slow tempo. The ballad has played an important part in Western European music for centuries, and in the twentieth century it became an important form of popular music.[5] Because ballads aim to tell a story, the words must be clearly understood by listeners. Therefore, the texture of a ballad always prioritizes the singer's voice. Even when ballads are performed by rock bands (as they often are now), the electric instruments deploy their powerful sound capabilities to accompany the voice of the singer, and on recordings, the mix will favor the singer.

Why ballads? One good reason is that this is the form of Western popular music that most Burmese people have been exposed to, until very recently. After 1962, Burmese government policy (and later, international sanctions) prevented foreign-made recordings from flowing freely into Burma. Any Burmese person who wanted to listen to English-language pop, for example, would have to be content with whatever recordings could be smuggled into the country.

I interviewed Khine Ta Htun, a man who worked as a "supplier" for one of Burma's best-known recording distribution companies from 2002 to 2005. During those years he traveled monthly to Bangkok in order to acquire original recordings for his employers to duplicate and sell. I asked him what kinds of recordings he chose to purchase, and he outlined three basic criteria. First, if the music was "melodic" he would purchase the recording. Second, if the album included a song that was currently playing in heavy rotation on Asian MTV (that is, if the video was already popular with other Asian audiences), he would purchase it. And third, if the recording was a new album from a big-name group ("like Metallica") he would purchase it. But Khine Ta Htun emphasized that the first of these criteria—the "melodic" nature of the music—was the most important. In fact, he said, he regularly purchased albums by unknown or indie artists if they sounded "melodic," because he knew they would be popular with Burmese audiences.

Pressed for a definition of "melodic," Khine Ta Htun said that the music could be in any style, from country to heavy metal, as long as the songs had strong melodies that fans could easily hear. This is a fair description of "December," IC's signature song, and for that matter, many of Metallica's greatest hits. And it is an important component of ballads. Like many of his peers in previous decades, Khine Ta Htun focused on importing "melodic" recordings, to the exclusion of other kinds of popular music, into Burma. His story helps to explain why Burmese pop music, which is self-consciously modeled on Anglo-American pop, so consistently focuses on the ballad.

Before continuing, I must acknowledge that virtually none of the Burmese pop music industry members I interviewed for this book would agree with my assessment. They would reject the idea that all of their songs belong to one genre, because this implies that all of their songs are somewhat the same. Interestingly, as I discovered in talking with them, they do not believe that another, more common, categorization is particularly relevant, either.

Commentators on Burmese pop music tend to describe the songs as falling into two categories: *copy thachin* and original pieces, called *own tune* by the Burmese.[6] While members of the Yangon pop scene do use the terms *copy thachin* and *own tune*, they almost never class their songs this way. Rather, they group the songs according to the themes in the lyrics. For example, Christian musicians tend to speak of "love songs" and "gospel songs."[7] Michael, a Christian composer, explained it this way: A love song is always in Burmese, with lyrics that speak about romantic heterosexual love. It has three verses and a chorus. A gospel song, on the other hand, can be in Burmese or in one of the many minority (*tain-yin-tha*) languages. The words may be about God, but also possibly about nature, family, Christmas, a wedding, or some other important event.

Both love songs and gospel songs can be composed in various styles, such as country or rock or blues. Michael notes that he usually earns more money writing love songs than gospel songs: he makes an average of $140 for a love song that is used on a CD or VCD, and $200 if it is used in a movie. Therefore, he sometimes writes love songs on spec, in the hopes that he will be able to sell them to well-known singers. When I asked him about the percentage of *copy thachin* versus *own tunes* in his oeuvre, Michael told me that all of his songs are *own tune* songs; but like other musicians I interviewed about this topic, he did not focus on the *copy thachin/own tune* distinction until I brought it up.

Soe Htun divided song types into three; he spoke of love songs, gospel songs, and *ah-kyoh-pyu-tay* ("beneficial songs" or "encouragement songs"). Encouragement songs can be recorded in both Burmese and in *tain-yin-tha* languages. They are songs that have lyrics of inspiration and encouragement, in which the basic message is: Be proud of your people, be proud of yourself, be strong, and pursue your goals. Again, these songs may be *copy thachin* or *own tune*; their distinguishing characteristic is not the origin of the melody and chords but rather the intent of the lyrics.[8]

Musicians, like all human beings, tend to classify concepts according to their own experiences. In the course of my interviews with Burmese pop musicians I found two in particular who clearly demonstrated this truism. Their very different experiences in the pop industry were reflected in the way they understood songs to be organized. The first was Esther, a "Karen singer" who identifies herself this way because she records only in the Sgaw Karen language, and never submits any of her recordings to the censors.[9] She believes that the most important distinction between pop songs in Burma is that between songs with Burmese words and songs with words in other languages. Esther's songs are all Karen songs, but they subdivide into three categories: love songs, gospel songs, and "national songs." National songs, she says, are "songs of loving your people." She sings them to remind her listeners to remember their ethnic heritage, to love it, and to live according the traditional values that she understands to be associated with that heritage.

U Maung Zaw is one of the most prolific composers in Burma. He is a Burman Buddhist who writes only in Burmese.[10] He has written many songs for the government over the course of his career. He divides songs into the two categories that most closely reflect his own experience: songs he has written "for himself" (that is, to sell to singers) and "government songs." Within the category of government songs, U Maung Zaw identifies five subcategories: songs about health; songs explaining traffic rules; songs announcing the opening of a construction project, such as a railroad or government building; songs about education; and finally, songs announcing government policy. Two well-known examples of government songs, he says, are the "Visit Myanmar Year" theme song and the "National Convention song."[11]

For all such songs, the composer works from a blueprint of sorts provided by the government—a thematic idea or a first line. Government songs stand in sharp contrast to all of U Maung Zaw's other songs, for which he creates all of the lyrics himself. In his own songs, he usually addresses one of three topics: peace in the world, Buddhist philosophy or thought, and love. Again, he acknowledges that he writes both *copy thachin* and *own tune* songs. But these two categories are not particularly meaningful for him, since he writes both *copy thachin* and *own tune* songs for himself and for the government.

Another reason that the *copy thachin/own tune* divide is not useful to community members is that the line between the two is not distinct. Some *copy thachin* are clearly copied from a foreign model: the rhythm, melody, and harmonization are lifted from an American or British pop tune with almost no variation. Others are not so clearly copied from another source, but they depend on that source to some extent. Some composers identified certain of their songs as *own tune* pieces, but acknowledged immediately that the songs relied to some degree on specific source tunes. For example, singer-songwriter Ko Htwe pointed out that one of his songs was based on a Japanese pop tune, but it was not an exact copy of that tune, although he had taken ideas from it. Aung Shwe, who has many years of experience arranging *own tunes*, said that "We never copy exactly." He explained that he listens closely to foreign recordings, takes ideas from them and inserts these ideas into an *own tune* composition as appropriate, but never adds Burmese lyrics to an intact foreign tune.

A comparison between Stevie Wonder's "I Just Called to Say I Love You" and a Burmese pop song called "The Last Time" exemplifies this principle.[12] The lyrics are utterly different; Wonder's song is a joyous expression of unconditional love, whereas the Burmese song is about breaking up. However, the verse sections of both songs have some important commonalities. In both cases, the verse is divided into two sections; the second section begins at the eighth measure. The first section opens with a I–I^{maj7} chord progression. In the original song, the harmony continues to alternate between these two chords through the rest of the A section, while in the Burmese song, the harmony moves to the dominant.

The similarity between the two songs becomes more evident at the start of the fifth bar (the B section): At this point, both songs use II–II^{maj7} chordal movement, and both melodies emphasize this by alternating between the supertonic and the note one semitone below. Furthermore, the characteristic upward-thrusting opening motive of "I Just Called" occurs in the Burmese melody, too. Importantly, it occurs at exactly the same pitch level, ending on the tonic, in both cases. In "The Last Time" (see fig. 2.1) this motive is preceded and followed by notes (instead of rests as in the original), but these notes simply reiterate the motive's destination pitch, so they do not draw attention away from the generating motive.

Like "The Last Time," many Burmese pop tunes cannot fit easily into either the *copy thachin* or *own tune* categories, since they use elements from, but do not exactly copy, source songs. Small wonder then that Burmese musicians do not usually reference this distinction when categorizing songs. Ultimately though, the reason that Burmese pop musicians do not usually distinguish between *copy thachin* and *own tune* songs is that they view all of their output as, literally, their own tunes. To a man, and to a woman, Burmese composers and performers insisted to me that their songs, whatever their origin, were expressions of their own ideas and their own artistic voices. U Maung Zaw, who has written hundreds of *copy thachin*, grinned wryly as he explained: when he listens to an original recording, he says, he frequently does not understand the English (or Japanese or Chinese) words. He does get a sense of the mood of the song, though, whether it be happy or sad, and

Figure 2.1. Melody and chords of first verse, "The Last Time," composer unknown

then creates his own lyrics according to his own feelings, or his own interpretation of the sounds.

U Maung Zaw's colleagues echoed his words, almost precisely; for example, Taylor told me that he composes both *copy thachin* and *own tune* songs—and immediately added that in both cases, his compositions represent an expression of his own mood. Michael said that although he always writes within the frame of a foreign (that is, non-Burmese) musical style, he uses these "beats" to showcase his own ideas, expressed in the lyrics. In fact, he invoked the deity when I inquired about his songs: "God gives me my *own* idea" he said emphatically.

Johnson, a guitarist and hotel bandleader, explained to me that this normal disconnect between the English and Burmese lyrics of a *copy thachin* has led to some disconcerting changes of category, at least for Western listeners. For example, he said, the English-language love song "Sometimes When We Touch" is, in Burma, a well-known gospel song called "Free of Charge."[13] (A few weeks later, I heard the song performed during a church service, and had to remind myself that, for the Burmese congregants, the song was entirely appropriate in the context.)[14] And some American Christmas songs, including "Jingle Bells," "Feliz Navidad," and "I Saw Mommy Kissing Santa Claus," have been reworked into Burmese love songs. For Burmese Buddhists, these *copy thachin*, with their Burmese lyrics, have no connection to a Christian holiday.[15]

For most Burmese pop musicians, the most important distinguishing characteristic of a song is the theme expressed in the lyrics. Therefore, the fact that a *copy thachin* has original lyrics makes all the difference in the world. A Burmese *copy thachin* may, and probably does, suggest to its listeners rather different ideas than does the English original (religious worship rather than romantic emotion, for example). It may in fact belong to an entirely different category of song. And because its most important identifying feature, the lyrics, is an original creation of a Burmese composer, the song is understood to be a form of Burmese, rather than foreign, artistic expression.

This brings us to another small but significant point about Burmese vocabulary: for Burmese pop musicians, the word "composer" (in English or in Burmese) means "a person who writes lyrics." A composer can, and often does, write rhythms, harmonies, and so on, but the salient point is that she or he writes the words for songs. Indeed, some of the most respected pop music composers in Burma virtually never write anything but words, since they compose only *copy thachin*. This idea was made most clear to me by Theingi Zaw, who frequently works as an arranger. In this capacity, he makes many decisions about instrumentation, form, and other musical elements in songs. In addition, he often writes out melodies for instrumental soloists to play during the break, which is common to most Burmese pop songs). However, he insisted that he is not a composer because, as he said, "I don't ever write words."

Comparing *Copy Thachin* to Original Recordings

As Johnson once suggested, the term "copy song" should perhaps be rethought, since it implies an intent that is opposed to that of Burmese *copy thachin* composers. Nonetheless, there is a good case to be made for this term. Comparing well-known Burmese *copy thachin* to the original (American) recordings makes it abundantly clear that the *copy thachin* sounds are usually very closely modeled on the sounds of the originals. The melodies and harmonies of the *copy thachin* are usually identical to those of the original. In general, the *copy thachin* are performed at the same tempo and in the same key (or within a whole tone) of the original recordings. In addition, *copy thachin* feature the same timbral effects as do the originals.

Compare, for example, Shakira's recording of "Wherever, Whenever" (which she herself subsequently sang in Spanish and recorded as "Suerte") to Phyu Phyu Kyaw Thein's copy version of the song. The Burmese version is in C♯ minor, just like the original, and it features the distinctive sound of pan-pipes, which are especially audible at the very end of the song. The Burmese singer's voice is a flexible alto, just like Shakira's. One small difference between the two is that Phyu Phyu Kyaw Thein tends to slide a bit between pitches, which Shakira never does. Although Phyu Phyu Kyaw Thein has to perform the melody slightly differently, because she sometimes has more syllables to sing, the two vocals are clearly intended to sound the same; even the vocables ("lay lo") are pronounced the same way. The attempt to make the vocal tracks match is most evident in the second phrase of the chorus. In the English version, the words are "I'll be there and you'll be near," and Shakira's voice is digitally processed to produce a robotic effect on the words "there" and "near." In the *copy thachin*, the same phrase is processed to produce roughly the same effect, although we do not hear the same emphasis on single syllables that is present in the original.

The biggest, most obvious difference between the two songs is not aural, but visual: Shakira's video features only the singer, dancing provocatively before a succession of images representing the wildness of the natural world. Phyu Phyu Kyaw Thein, on the other hand, is dressed modestly and is surrounded by a group of young people who dance energetically with (but hardly touch) one another. They perform in front of monochrome background screens, allowing the lyrics, rather than background visuals, to suggest images in the listener's mind. And, of course, the lyrics are far less sexually explicit than those of the original; the overall effect is innocently fun rather than sexually intense.

Another pair of examples shows the same tendencies. Two female Burmese singers, May Sweet (now living in the United States) and Lay Lay War (now retired in Yangon) recorded a copy of Madonna's "Like a Virgin."[16] The Burmese song is called "A pyo sin," which means "a single woman" (and, in Burma, this would imply that the woman is a virgin). The Burmese performers sing their copy song in D minor (the original is in E minor) and create the same texture that marks the original version. The instrumental accompaniment is marked by staccato chords on a synthesizer, and the two women are careful to sing separately or in unison so that their vocalization approximates Madonna's monophonic presentation as closely as possible.[17] The only obvious difference occurs at the chorus, where, in the original, Madonna sings an E above treble C. When May Sweet performs this note (in her case it is a D), the sound is more breathy and less sustained, and the pitch falls quickly. On the third iteration, this note is almost spoken. This is the highest note in the melody, and the fact that the Burmese singer performs it with a less piercing tone (and with seemingly less breath support) is a reminder that, in Burma, high notes are often considered especially foreign, and therefore difficult.

Again, the biggest difference between the two songs is found in the visual presentation. Madonna's original video, and her subsequent live presentations, could hardly be less stereotypically virginal. On the other hand, May Sweet and Lay Lay War are very modestly dressed in the kind of clothing that wealthy Burmese women wear to formal functions, with long sleeves and skirts and high-necked jackets. And again, their clothing matches the relatively more modest intent of the Burmese lyrics. Although these lyrics do speak of "a single woman who has never loved," this expression in Burmese does not carry the same weight of sexual connotation that it does in English. And of course the character in the Burmese *copy thachin* is a virgin, rather than someone who claims to feel like one.

Examples abound.[18] The similarities and differences are consistent: *Copy thachin* tend to sound like original recordings, but the visual presentations of the songs look different. The sound of the Burmese *copy thachin* aims to match the sound of the American recording, and usually succeeds. Musicians told me that their efforts to match the original extend past melody and harmony to elements like tempo. U Ye Zaw Tun, who sometimes works as an audio engineer, says that he regularly listens to original recordings with a metronome ("Dr. Beat") in hand so that he can set the click track for the *copy thachin* recording at exactly the same tempo. And composer Htin Thu says that when he writes *copy thachin* he often tries to recruit a Burmese singer whose vocal tone approximates that of the original singer. "I asked Zaw Win Htut to sing my *copy thachin* of a Rod Stewart song, because they sing the same way," he pointed out.

One intractable difference between original songs and *copy thachin* is the nature of the English and Burmese languages: in general, it takes more syllables to express an idea in Burmese than it does in English. Burmese singers will almost always fit their "extra" syllables to the original melody (by intoning them, very quickly, on the same pitch as the corresponding English syllable), so that the melodic contour remains the same.[19]

However, the look of Burmese *copy thachin* (including live shows and video performances) is usually quite different from the look of the original made-for-MTV model. First, Burmese pop videos are almost always released in VCD (rather than DVD) format, and the words of the song show at the bottom of the screen when the singer sings them, karaoke-style. This format makes the lyrics more clear than the lyrics in a typical American video. Second, the look of the video usually underlines the intent of the lyrics, which in Burma is less overtly sexual and often more focused on love of family and religion—in other words, more conservative. Or perhaps it is more accurate to say, more Burmese.

Burmese public culture is considerably less outwardly expressive than is American culture; sexuality is generally revealed only in private, and public actions are calmer and less demonstrative. Dating is still somewhat controversial; a remarkably well-educated and worldly-wise friend of mine said that she will not allow her daughter to go on dates when she is a teenager, and that most parents of her class and generation would not either.[20] Burmese pop music videos almost always reflect this kind of conservatism. They feature modestly-dressed young people who, in the course of acting out their love story, rarely dance together and certainly never kiss or grope each other. No doubt some of this restraint is due to the strict regulations of the censors. But some (perhaps most) of the images in the videos are obviously the reflection of an artistic vision, one which has developed in the context of Burmese society. And so we see in these videos many visuals of young lovers longing for each other, but this longing is frequently mediated by some kind of restraining agent. For example, men and women are frequently depicted looking at each other, but not directly. Rather, they look at each other through something (a window, or a camera), or in a mirror or a photograph. When characters are shown hand in hand for example, the scene is usually revealed to be only a memory of earlier, happier times.

Copying: A Rationale

Why are *copy thachin* such an important and enduring part of Burmese pop culture? I put this question to several Burmese composers, and they offered the following rationale: First, *copy thachin* offer Burmese people the chance to understand and appreciate English songs, something that many of them could not do because their English is simply not strong enough to decode the original English lyrics. In a country where many people are deeply interested in all things modern, and yet have little access to them, locally-made *copy thachin* are an entry point into international (read Anglo-American cosmopolitan) culture.

Second, *copy thachin* have served as teachers to aspiring Burmese musicians, who want to perform at an international level but have no access to American or British music teachers. By copying songs from numerous different countries across East Asia and the West, Burmese musicians have learned a wide repertoire of songs and styles.

Third, writing *copy thachin* allows Burmese composers to develop and even improve the original songs. One of Burma's most respected authors, a woman named Ma Ju, has published a book with side-by-side comparisons of original (English) lyrics and Burmese *copy thachin* lyrics. Ma Ju argues that Htin Thu's new lyrics for Aerosmith's "Angel" and Eric Clapton's "Wonderful Tonight" are *"po kaun deh"* (better) and more profound than the originals.[21]

Fourth, and perhaps most important, Burmese society values the basic idea of copying something that has already been established as valuable or success-ful. As U Ye Zaw Tun said, when we discussed the issue of imitating foreign cul-tural products, "Our Myanmar habit is, when you get the chance, you do the same [as has already been done]." For Burmese people, copying some work of art (say, a song text or a document) is not an act of laziness or theft, but rather an intelligent, sensible move. Modeling one's own work on something that has already proven its worth strengthens one's own work. For this reason, the American idea of plagiarism is almost unknown in Burma.

I recently met a young Burmese woman who is attending college in the United States. She shared that during her first year in Minnesota, she got into serious trouble for plagiarizing. She did not understand the concept, even after it was first explained to her, because during her high school years in Burma she had been encouraged by her teachers to copy sentences or even entire paragraphs from other sources into her own essays. The idea, she said, was that copying these points from established sources is a way of improving one's own writing; it is a smart and honorable thing to do. The story rings true to me, since I have read a handful of English-language master's theses in semi-nary libraries in Burma, and have noted that the authors sometimes include portions of text from other books without making even the briefest attempt to cite their sources.[22]

Not all Burmese people think this way, of course. The pop music industry, for example, includes members who are deeply committed to the idea of try-ing to create something new. Some musicians focus on creating new musi-cal genres, which I discuss below. But as a whole, the Burmese pop industry trends toward continuation of the pop music tradition rather than toward developing something innovative beyond that tradition. This seems to be true even when musicians state that they intend to be innovative. In January 2009, I attended the taping of a television show called *Living Song*. Each week, the show focuses on a different composer; the host interviews the composer and the in-house band plays "new versions" of five of that composer's songs. On the day I was there, the director arranged to have the original recording pumped through the sound system just before the "new version" of each was taped.[23] Thus I was able to compare the old and new versions of each song. In each case, the aesthetics of both were the same: the same instruments played in the same key, accompanying the same gender of singer, who sang the same lyrics in the same order. Indeed, it was hard to hear any significant difference between the old and new versions. Later, Soe Thant, the featured composer, concurred with me: the "new" versions of his songs did not sound terribly new to him, either.[24]

The nature of the pop music repertoire in Burma contradicts the linear theory of musical development articulated, or at least implied, by pop music scholar Edward Larkey.[25] Larkey proposes a four-stage model of "diffusion and tradition-formation for popular music innovations."[26] He asserts that Anglo-American pop music, once it has arrived in a Third World country, develops in four stages. First, it is integrated into the local context by being consumed as is. Second, it is imitated by local artists. Third, it is de-anglicized—that is, musicians perform in the style of Anglo-American pop bands but sing lyrics in the language of their own country. The fourth stage is reethnification, during which local musicians fuse Anglo-American pop music ideas with local ideas and approaches to create new genres.[27]

In the case of Burmese pop music, reality is not so neat. It is true that American and British pop recordings first came to Burma as consumer products, and that *stereo* music first appeared in Burma as "English songs"—Burmese performers playing English hits, singing in English, and copying the instrumental parts as closely as possible. Nearly fifty years later, we are seeing a few examples of fusion. But the reality is that for most of the history of the genre, Burmese pop musicians have been creating *copy thachin* and *own tune* songs. At the moment, most Burmese pop musicians are continuing to devote most of their energy to re-creating Anglo-American pop music in their own country, and very little energy to developing a locally-marked sound or style. For the most part, they exemplify Larkey's third stage. The Burmese pop scene, as a whole, does not seem to be moving inevitably toward "tradition-formation" as his model would have it. Notably, Larkey derived his model from his research in Austria—a Western country. As might be expected, the situation is rather different in a place where the national culture is so different.

However, the Burmese pop scene does include some notable examples of fusion genres, which I will group under the umbrella term "Burmese pop fusion" (note that this term is not used by Burmese people). In what follows, I describe three recordings that seem to me to be interesting and well-integrated, and which offer some possibilities for other artists who may pursue Burmese pop fusion in the future. The first of these, to date, has sold well and gained widespread recognition, showing that Burmese audiences are open to creative attempts to fuse distinctly Burmese sounds and cultural markers with a musical form that developed in the West. The second is known only to a select audience, because it originated in the Karen community and is being spread via the church networks that stretch around Burma and beyond; it has not been presented to the government censors and is therefore not sold in retail outlets. The third had not yet been released to the public when I was in Yangon, so it is still too early to say what kind of impact it may have.

Three Examples of Burmese Pop Fusion

Nu electro hip hop

In 2006 a pair Burmese DJs recorded a DVD called "*Yaw-thama-hmwe*," which translates as "Mix Mix Mix," signaling their intention to mix Burmese and foreign musical ideas. The album garnered such respect that when other musicians told me that they hoped to one day create some kind of fusion music, they often said, "like *Yaw-thama-hmwe.*" The producer of the album called this newly-minted style "nu electro hip-hop."

The album contains eleven tracks, all of which unfold in the context of a sonic framework of digitally-produced "house music" (or "electronica" or "dance"). The first four tracks successfully mix this sonic framework with traditional Burmese musical sounds. In three of these tracks, the music is a combination of the house sounds and sounds from the *Maha Gita* tradition. For example, the first track features a male singing a traditional *Maha Gita* melody in the rather nasal tone that is idiomatic to the genre. This melody appears near the beginning and end of the track, and the studio engineer has mixed the sound so that the human voice comes through clearly. In the middle section, the two DJs rap some lyrics.

Throughout, the video features images representing local tradition (a Buddhist spirit medium and a group of *longyi*-wearing, instrument-carrying men proceeding joyfully down a street) and modernity (young women wearing jeans while dancing in a dimly-lit nightclub and the DJs working at their mixing board). The Burmese *hnay* (an oboe-like instrument) is heard continuously, playing brief repetitive melodic ideas. In traditional performance, the *hnay* usually plays fast and wide-ranging melodies; in *Yaw-thama-mhwe*'s music, the *hnay* retains this characteristic frenetic quality, so that it fits extremely well in the context of house music. And because the *hnay* has such a distinct tone color (piercing and high-pitched), its sound never gets lost in the mix.

The third and fourth tracks also feature *hsaing waing* instruments. Importantly, the tracks have been mixed so that these instruments can actually be heard.[28] The third track begins with the clapper and cymbals that usually play the *si neh wah* pattern,[29] but here they play a fast-paced syncopated rhythm that is later incorporated into the house sound. The *pat waing* (drum circle) is also featured, and the Burmese tuning of the drums clearly contrasts with the C_6 low C of the electronic framework. The music increases in volume, with rapped lyrics and electronic sounds filling the mix. But at the two-minute mark, the DJs eliminate all of the digital sounds except for the anchoring low pitch, so that there is no competition with the sound of the *hsaing waing* instruments. At this point, the music is accompanied by images of a dancing *nat* (spirit); for a few moments, it is as if we are watching a *nat bwe* (a Buddhist religious festival). Then the composers deftly return to a composite sound, showing hip-hop dancers performing together with *Anyein* dancers. The transitions between tra-ditional and modern sights and sounds are not jarring, since the images are constantly shifting and the sonic framework remains always in place.

Karen Songs

In 2008 a young Bwe Karen man organized the recording of a number of "Karen songs," in view of making an album of "Karen music" (his terms). The tracks, which were not at the time of my research released as an album, feature a deliberate attempt to combine Karen melodies and singing style with pop instruments and recording techniques. I went to visit this artist at the home of his uncle, which includes a small recording studio. I was struck by the depth of this musician's commitment to his Karen identity; for example, he makes a concerted effort to speak Karen rather than Burmese with his friends, about of dozen of whom were present when I arrived.[30] In addition, he has a small col-lection of Karen instruments, some of which I was not allowed to touch, since he respects his elders' teaching about gender restrictions and musical instru-ments. He claims that he depended on these instruments for inspiration, if not for actual use, in his recording.

In fact, it sounds as though the instrumental tracks were played on a key-board synthesizer, using the sustained sounds of strings to outline I, IV, and V chords; a drum track to maintain a steady beat; and flute and guitar sounds for melodic fills.

The sonic framework for the nine tracks on the CD reflects the internation-ally-recognizable soft pop aesthetic. The sung melodies constitute the "Karen" component of the album. Six of the nine melodies are distinctively Karen in their pitch organization. Using solfège terminology (which many Karen people do), we would say that they emphasize, and frequently begin with the *do–low so–do* motive, and they only rarely use the pitches *la* and *re*.[31] These melodies make frequent use of *ti*, but *ti* is not usually "resolved" by moving up to *do*, as is common in Western European melodies. Rather, cadences usually consist of a *so–do* or *mi–do* melodic movement. Given these parameters, it is a rather straightforward proposition to harmonize Karen melodies with the Western tonic and dominant chords, as the composer on this album did, and as many other Karen people have done during the past two centuries. These Karen melodies are sung in the national style most commonly heard in *Maha Gita* performances.[32] This style is remarkable for its expressive power. It features a nasal tone, lots of sliding between melody pitches, frequent upward-moving appoggiaturas on melody notes, and a rhythmic freedom that allows the singer to arrive at cadence points before the instrumental accompaniment does. At times, this style can sound almost like sung speech, because the flexibility in the voice communicates a strong sense of emotional import.

New Age Myanmar

In the spring of 2009, a group of musicians in the Burmese pop music industry released the first recording in a new fusion style the composer calls "New Age Myanmar *stereo* music." The album is called *Homage to Buddha*, and it is a deliberate attempt to fuse Buddhist devotional texts and local ideas with New Age sounds. The most specific gesture toward locality is the second track, "Land of Love." The song is constructed around a melody attributed to the Pyu (the civilization that dominated Lower Burma prior to the rise of the Myanmar people) and which was documented in Chinese records in 802 CE. The seventh track is an English-language version of the same song, so foreign listeners can clearly understand the Buddhist concepts expressed in the lyrics ("The only escape from the grind of Samsara is love"). The other tracks all feature similarly Buddhist-inspired titles ("Love to All," "The Song of Peace," and so on).

All of the tracks share some commonalities, which clearly stem from the composer-producer's particular understanding of a "New Age" aesthetic.[33] A pair of female vocalists sing all of the melodies, accompanied by a synthesizer playing a variety of digitally-created sounds. The singers, who virtually always sing in unison or homophonically, use a clear open tone; they add vibrato only occasionally. Interestingly, they sometimes sing rapid turns on melody notes which appear at the ends of phrases, briefly referring to the ornate *Maha Gita* singing style.

The instrumental and vocal melodies stand out clearly in the texture, which is dominated by synth pads (long tones generated by a synthesizer, often used as background harmonies in New Age recordings). The long synth pad sounds create a sense of expansiveness, because they usually move slowly from one chord to the next, leading the ear from harmony to harmony with no changes in tone color.

Because all of the melodic and harmonic tones belong to the twelve-note Western chromatic scale, the tuning of these pieces does not sound particularly Burmese. However, the composer makes a concerted effort to avoid perfect cadences, and thereby avoids the most characteristic gesture in Western tonal harmony. Instead, he prioritizes chordal movement between the tonic triad and the triad one whole tone lower, a harmonic progression which could be analyzed as I–♭VII. In addition, he favors the melody note that is a minor seventh above the tonic (again, this could be called ♭7). In tracks 3 and 5, the melody outlines an augmented second, starting with the note one semitone above the tonic, thereby implying the Oriental scale.[34] In track 2, the bass line steps from I to V, but the chords built on these notes—A⁷ and Em—do not function as they would in Western tonal harmony. All of these sounds evoke the "Orient," if not Burma specifically.

The *Homage to Buddha* album is important because it represents, along with the two examples described above, a conscious attempt by Burmese pop musicians to create music that fuses musical instruments and aesthetics from the

West with sounds, visuals, and lyrics that evoke Burmese traditions. Along with *Mix Mix Mix* and the untitled Karen songs, this album shows that Burmese pop musicians do sometimes develop innovative musical projects. However, these examples are very much the exception rather than the rule; the Burmese pop music scene is dominated by music that sounds very much like the Anglo-American music on which it is modeled.

Scholarly Anxieties about Analyzing Burmese Pop

The academy puts an enormous premium on originality. The field of popular music studies, and cultural studies more generally, has been deeply influenced by Walter Benjamin's oft-cited essay, "The Work of Art in an Age of Mechanical Reproduction."[35] In this essay, Benjamin argued that an authentic work of art cannot be mechanically reproduced. An authentic work of art, he claims, has an "aura" because it is uniquely present in the world. Technically reproduced works of art (which Benjamin calls reproductions), such as photographs, movies, and recordings, exist at a remove from the original, authentic instance of performance. Therefore, reproductions lack the aura that originals have. Furthermore, as reproductions, they are subject to manipulations (photographs can be enlarged, recordings can be slowed down, and so on) and therefore cannot be relied upon as faithful recreations of the original piece of art. In addition, people experience such reproductions outside of the original context in which the art was created, and thereby fail to grasp their full meaning.

In Benjamin's view, a person who listens to a recording of a Beethoven symphony at home on her stereo cannot possibly experience the richness of the symphony in the way that she would if she heard the live performance of that symphony in a concert hall. To him, the act of mechanically reproducing a work of art inevitably threatens the authenticity (that is, the aura) and thus the authority of the work. The "quality of the presence [of the work of art] is always depreciated" when it is mechanically reproduced.[36]

Recently, Albin Zak provided a helpful analysis of Benjamin's theory vis-à-vis contemporary pop music.[37] Zak argues that the aura of the live performance of a rock song is not diminished, but rather transferred, when that performance is recorded. In modern pop music, it is the recording itself which has an aura: the aura is created by the recording's unique arrangement of sound elements, which is not depreciated by the fact of its reproduction. These uniquely organized sounds constitute in themselves a work of art. Cover versions of pop songs—which Zak dismisses in a single page—simply show us the importance of particular sounds to the identity of a given recording.

Ultimately, Zak's argument defends Benjamin's notion that an "authentic" work of art—whether that be a live performance or a recording—derives its authenticity from its originality. An authentic pop song, in this view, is not simply a copy of another song, but rather one that expresses something of the artist or artists who created it, who are, of course, unique individuals.[38] As pop music scholar Richard Middleton points out, rock music shows a strong "tendency to autobiography" because of its commitment to this notion of authenticity. "The aesthetic of 'authenticity' dominates mainstream rock vocalism: 'real experience,' expressed with 'sincerity,' is regarded as the indispensable basis of good (that is, 'honest') singing."[39]

Timothy D. Taylor offers a masterful summary of various understandings of authenticity in his book *Global Pop: World Music, World Markets*.[40] He explains that these understandings can be grouped into categories, three of which are important here: authenticity of positionality (meaning that musicians perform the "real" sounds of their assumed place of origin); authenticity of emotionality (musicians perform sounds that encapsulate their own emotional experiences); and authenticity as historical accuracy (musicians perform sounds in the style that the originators intended). Burmese pop musicians often become the subject of criticism when listeners invoke the authenticity of positionality (listeners like, for example, the many American undergraduates to whom I have presented examples of *copy thachin* and *own tunes*). Their reaction is most often one of amused surprise bordering on indignation. They usually sum up what they are hearing (after mere seconds) as a "rip-off." Taylor concurs: "North American and British musicians can make whatever music they want and only be viewed as sellouts if they try to make money; any other musician is constrained by the western discourse of authenticity to make music that seems to resemble the indigenous music of their place and is cast as a sellout if they make more popular-sounding music, and/or try to make money."[41]

Here I am arguing that pop music in Burma, almost all of it self-consciously copied from or modeled after original works of art created in England and America, is an "authentic" art form that deserves serious scholarly attention.[42] I do so because my analysis rests on the expressed convictions of the creators of Burmese pop music. As I explain in the introduction to this book, and earlier in this chapter, these musicians assert over and over that their music is an expression of their own ideas and emotions; they invoke an authenticity of emotionality. To them, their songs—*copy thachin* or *own tune*—are all legitimate representations of their personal artistic intentions. But at the same time, they acknowledge with pride the fact that their music is modeled closely on Anglo-American pop music. In other words, they claim the authenticity of historical accuracy.[43] "I try to make my voice sound like a singer I admire," says Nu Nu Win. "Depending on the style, I try to sound like Pink, or Avril Lavigne. . . . I watch Avril Lavingne's videos constantly and sing along with her."

Before expanding on Burmese pop musicians' perspectives on the authenticity of their music, it is important to explain that their assertions defy some strongly-held premises in both Burmese and Western scholarship. Competing understandings of authenticity, or of the relative value of various kinds of authenticities (of positionality, emotionality, and historical accuracy), lie at the root of the tensions manifest in scholarly writing from both Burmese and Western sources.

To begin with the Burmese: in their book chapter "The Musical Culture of Myanmar," two prominent performers from the *Maha Gita* tradition attempt to provide a full description of Burmese music from prehistory to the present.[44] The essay begins in nakedly ideological fashion by insisting on the historic unity of the country and defending the name "Myanmar" as a word that represents all of the inhabitants of the country.[45] The authors, Khin Maung Nyunt and U Gita Lu Lin Koko, go on to describe "Myanmar music" as the outgrowth of *nat* worship and Buddhist rituals, and they attribute most of the developments in the *Maha Gita* repertoire to the innovations of kings, princes, and ministers. They do acknowledge that Portuguese settlers, Chinese emissaries, and local *tain-yin-tha* groups provided tunes that were eventually absorbed into the *Maha Gita*, but the authors are at pains to underline that these musical developments were always the result of peaceful interactions between the Burmese court and their loyal subjects or allies. For example, when discussing the portion of the repertoire called "yodiya [Thai] songs," Nyunt and Koko claim that these songs became part of the Burmese tradition as "the result of beneficial contacts" between Burma and Siam in 1564, 1767, and 1789.[46] Historical accounts of Burma and Thailand show that each of these years was the occasion of an invasion of Siam by Burmese forces. However, Nyunt and Koko insist that each of these dates was an opportunity for Burmese musicians to exchange knowledge with Thai musical experts, omitting any mention of a bloody war.

I suspect that this omission is rather deliberate, because the current regime in Burma (whose functionaries no doubt signed off on this document) is not interested in acknowledging any kind of debt to Thailand.[47] In addition, the chapter does not mention the piano, the violin, and the steel guitar, instruments that were introduced to Burma by British colonizers and which became central to *Maha Gita* performance in the twentieth century.[48] The reason is clear: the authors are quick to point out that, while Burma has been subject to musical influences from outside, Myanmar music continues to develop and innovate while preserving its most Burmese features (like heterophonic textures). Indeed, the article insists that all of the musical ideas, instruments, and factors that originated elsewhere were "adapted to the Myanmar ambience" when they appeared in Burma.[49]

This book chapter reads like a musical version of the official history of the country as per the SPDC. In that recounting of history, the junta asserts that it is the legitimate power broker in the country because it is the heir to the Burmese monarchy, which presided over a unified and peaceful territory in its day—and of course, was not elected by popular vote. In this version, the Myanmar people are independent, both culturally and politically, from time immemorial (and thus any criticism of the status quo by outsiders who are, say, concerned about human rights abuses, are interference with the internal affairs of a sovereign state). As a self-sufficient society, the Myanmarese need no input from any outside source, and therefore the government does not acknowledge such input in any serious way.[50]

Western academics, too, are reluctant to valorize a musical culture that seems to be imported from outside, especially from the politically and economically dominant West. As Bruno Nettl points out, when Western music has come into contact with local musics, it is often the local musics that have had to react to the "impact" of the West, rather than the other way around. Sadly, sometimes the result of this impact is an impoverishment of local music, as less energy is directed toward it.[51] In addition, Western music—which arrives via technologies which allow wide market penetration—can lead to a homogenization of sound, thereby weakening local diversity.[52] Ethnomusicologists, who have historically been interested in the plurality of musics around the world, are especially hesitant to promote a musical form which has arisen from and now fosters the growth of global capitalism. Michael Hayes, writing on Western pop music in Thailand, provides one clear example of this perspective: "This music can praise materialism and/or reassert basic patriarchal and social divisions which may get blurred in the turmoil of economic development."[53] Emma Baulch summarizes: "There is a tendency to view dislocation [of Western cultural products] as progressive only in as far as it is 'oppositional'—a notion frequently measured against official (state) discourses."[54]

Western scholars of pop music are particularly uncomfortable with the phenomenon of cover songs—which are similar in some ways to the Burmese *copy thachin*—because of these songs' clear link to racial exploitation in American pop music. For example, Michael Coyle calls cover songs "hijacked hits" because, as he points out, such songs were first recorded by white singers looking to capitalize on the successful recordings made by African American artists.[55] To be fair, some Western academics have noted that there is more to the cover song art form than thievery. The May 2005 issue of *Popular Music and Society* is notable in this regard. In that journal, Don Cusic articulates a strong defense of cover song performers, arguing that when they interpret previously-recorded materials, they perform legitimate and creative music-making—just as legitimate as that of singer-songwriters who perform their own compositions.[56]

In general, though, Burmese and Western scholars are reluctant to attribute creativity and agency to non-Western musicians who copy Western pop songs. And so are laypeople.[57] I have found dozens of dismissive, insulting and even profane comments directed toward Burmese pop music on the internet. The following representative sample comes from comments on videos of *copy thachin* posted on YouTube:

From kayaliphu: i can't imagine why burmese artists can't create their songs. so, what is the point of being singers?[58]

From Xacque: Gosh! I never thought I have to be ashamed of being a burmese (at least one fourth of my blood). I am now and shame on you whoever the singer is for copying an English song and shame on the person who posted this awful video. yukkkk . . .[59]

From kokooool4: fuck u lay phyu, fucking copy guy[60]

And from someone more sympathetic:

From dminsong: everybody says that lay phyu sings just copies but nobody says of his work hards, determinations, crushed tone and high pitch voice. f..k to all of that person!! If u think singing copies r easy, just try it.[61]

These commentators are getting at one of the biggest concerns expressed by Western scholars: that Burmese pop music is not an expression of Burmese creativity, but rather a result of cultural imperialism. We must acknowledge that an originally Anglo-American art form, that is, pop music, dominates the musical culture and airwaves in Burma. And this is a serious concern, because Burma was, for more than one hundred years, a colony of Britain. During their tenure in power in Burma, the British reshaped the society. British officials exiled the last Burmese king (King Thibaw) and dismantled the monarchical system which had governed Lower Burma for nearly one thousand years. They then put their own functionaries in charge—few of whom made a serious effort to understand the language, religion, and social norms of the place—and incorporated many members of ethnic minority groups, who had long been at odds with the majority Burmans, into the national army.[62] In addition, the British treated Burma as an extension of their Indian empire, and facilitated the immigration of money-lending Indian castes to rural Burma.[63] And most importantly for this analysis, they established the English language as the language of higher education and business and cultivated among Burmese people a reverence for all things English.

And so it is beyond question that the contemporary Burmese pop scene is closely tied to the Anglo-American pop music tradition at least in part because of the legacy of British colonialism. Many generations of Burmese people were taught that European culture was superior to Asian culture, and that to succeed in society one must become fluent not just in the English language but also in the Western way of thinking. Small wonder then that some, even many, of them today conceive of all kinds of issues using a European paradigm, and appreciate Western cultural products. But there is more to the story than arrogant English oppressors and submissive Burmese citizens.

Burmese Music Industry Insiders Speak

According to all of the people that I interviewed in Yangon's pop music scene, Anglo-American pop music is a wonderful art form that is deeply appreciated by many Burmese. Rather than seeing it as some kind of manifestation of cultural domination, all of my informants described this music as being admirable, and therefore, worth learning and performing. Indeed, they often mentioned making special efforts to become involved in this music simply because they liked it so much. For example, U Hla Kyi explained how he fell in love with the sounds of Elvis, the Beatles, and other Western rock artists when he was a child: he often went to the village market to listen to pop music on the radio, since his parents did not own one.[64] Shway Nyunt, another composer of the same generation, pointed to the Beatles as a group who "changed music around the world" in the 1960s. Inspired by their use of electronically-amplified instruments, he decided to try to make "electronic music" himself. Not being able to get an electric guitar, he made his own by attaching a pickup to an acoustic guitar. And Aung Shwe talked about the Beatles, saying that because his parents listened so often to them (and to others such as Jim Reeves), he grew up with pop music and therefore likes it tremendously.

For these musicians there is seemingly no necessary link between ethnic or national identity and local musical traditions. Being Burmese, even being proudly Burmese, does not preclude embracing a musical tradition that is clearly not Burmese. These musicians genuinely like the pop music that they create and perform. Michael explained this to me in the plainest terms: "I like English songs—and Chinese and Korean songs, too," he said. He insists that for him, being a Karen Burmese composer of pop songs is not oxymoronic; indeed he was puzzled a little by my suggestion that this might pose some kind of conflict. "But I think the foreign music is beautiful. Western songs have beautiful melodies, and chords, and words." A female singer named Cherry echoed his words. When I asked her about the potential contradiction between being committed to her Karen/Burmese identity and devoting her life to American pop music, she rejected my premise completely: "Those English songs are excellent, I like them too much [i.e., very much.] There is no problem." Cho Cho Saing, who teaches European church music at a local seminary, pointed out to me that musical preference is sometimes irreducible. When I asked her why she and her students choose to learn and sing English hymns, she said, "Well, because we like it." When I asked *why* they liked it, she was stumped: "We like it just because we like it."[65]

Indeed some Burmese musicians went even further in their descriptions of American pop songs. For example, Htay Cho said to me that the ABBA song "S.O.S." has "the best fill" (i.e., piano and guitar interlude) of any song he has ever heard. He pointed out that the drum and bass guitar parts are "different, but they work together perfectly to make a good foundation for the song." He claimed that he learned the art of arranging pop melodies by listening to this and other ABBA tunes repeatedly. And *copy thachin* composer Htin Thu said that not only are Western pop songs superior to Burmese songs, but that "those [American pop] songs are *perfect*" (his emphasis). He went on to say that he spent nearly two months trying to create Burmese lyrics for Tom Waits's hit song "Downtown Train," a song that he characterized as "serious and serene." Normally, he said, he writes lyrics in an evening or two. But "Downtown Train" impressed him as such a profound work of art that he needed to spend a much longer time writing Burmese words that were equally meaningful.

Burmese pop musicians know that others, millions or even billions of others, like American pop music, too. Aye Kyi explained that she models her singing and stage performances after pop singers like Céline Dion and Shania Twain. She thinks of these world-renowned singers as "international" singers. Not only does she like their songs, she respects the role that they play on the global stage. Who better, then, to model oneself after? Nu Nu Win told me the same thing. "American music is leading the world," she said. "American singers are great—that's why I want to be like them."[66]

James Thiri, one of the most popular performers of the first generation of Burmese pop musicians explained that respect for Western pop superstars and their music is nothing new. He recounted how he and his teenage friends got their start playing covers ("English songs") of the Beatles, Cliff Richard, Roy Orbison, and other big Anglo-American pop stars in the 1960s. He explained that, young as they were, he and his bandmates immediately garnered respect because they could do "something different [i.e., foreign]." People looked up to them, he said, not because they created their own music, but because they were able to play the best-known music on the planet so well. Htet Aung, who was especially active in pop music in the 1980s, confirmed this. He affirmed that James Thiri was a "hero" to him and his friends, because of his fluency in the American pop idiom.

Similar Examples From Around the World

Scholars Alison J. Ewbank and Fouli T. Papageorgiou point out that instances of close imitation of foreign recordings—what they call "cloning"—can be found all over the world.[67] Marc Moskowitz documents the equivalent of *copy thachin* in Mandopop,[68] for example, and Keila Diehl says that one of best-loved "modern Tibetan songs" is set to the tune of "This Land Is Your Land."[69] Alexander Dent highlights another case that directly parallels the Burmese *copy thachin*: Brazilian *música sertaneja*.[70] Dent makes a strong argument against the notion that these songs are evidence of cultural imperialism and third-world dependency. He points out that *música sertaneja* (which consists of Nashville country tunes and Brazilian lyrics), despite being explicitly modeled on hit songs from America, nevertheless are "clearly communicating a Brazilian message via a Brazilian style."[71] Performers of *música sertaneja* are not signaling their alienation from their own traditions and their inability to do anything other than produce a culturally derivative product. Rather, they are showing their fans that they have the power to appropriate globally successful American music and make it their own.

Still other scholars describe cases which contest the received notions of cultural imperialism and authenticity in music. For example, Christine Yano analyzed popular Japanese songs (*enka*) which are recorded, sometimes dozens of times, by various artists, who attempt to make their recordings sound as close as possible to the original.[72] She argues that the act of reproducing a pop tune by rerecording it does not, in Japanese society, diminish the song's aura, as Benjamin would have it. Rather, covering a song is a way of conferring authenticity upon that song, because Japanese culture has long promoted the idea that learners need to be able to reproduce a model. Models—in this case, pop songs—that are covered over and over are therefore authoritative, and they gain status as they are copied by respectful newcomers. Authenticity, then, is not threatened by reproduction, and our understanding of this idea must be reevaluated when we look at pop music outside the West.

In another recent example, Jeremy Wallach describes how punk fans in Jakarta, Indonesia, are "loath to embrace musical innovations, instead maintaining their stylistic allegiance to what they perceive as a classic punk sound."[73] Like pop music performers in Burma, these Indonesian punks pose a challenge to theories about Western cultural imperialism:

> Absorbed in the documentation of the cultural particulars of specific genre-based music movements, it is all too easy for the ethnographic researcher of global music subcultures to forget the still-dominant, trivializing perspective toward such phenomena, both inside and outside the academy. For many observers, the existence of punks in Indonesia exemplifies the tragic "mimesis" of Western culture by a formerly colonized people. . . . In this view, the Indonesian punk movement is little more than a latter-day cargo cult of cultural dupes in the thrall of imported commodities and the aura of global consumer culture. Punk music in Indonesia therefore cannot be anything other than derivative and inauthentic.[74]

Indeed! Wallach does not leave it at that, of course. He goes on to point out that the "true punk" (as opposed to the "pop punk") that is loved by punks in Jakarta is a musical form that has evolved remarkably little since it developed in England in the 1970s. It is, in that sense, a traditional style, and it is appreciated as such by its Indonesian fans. The sounds and symbols of punk rock constitute "stable points of reference for identity," and therefore those in Jakarta who identify with them are not particularly interested in changing them, nor in adapting them to the Indonesian context.[75]

Punks in Jakarta are remarkably like another group of musicians who link authenticity with reproduction rather than with originality: practitioners of historical performance music (that is, historically-accurate reproductions of European classical music).[76] In the 1970s, many practitioners of European classical music in the West began to wrestle with the concepts of authenticity and interpretation with new vigor. At that point, influential performers increasingly chose to perform pieces of music on the instruments for which they had originally been written (harpsichords instead of modern pianos, for example, or baroque violins instead of the modern variant, and each of these tuned lower than modern instruments are). In addition, they rediscovered historical treatises on how to perform this music, and used these treatises to guide their musical choices.

Many classical musicians and listeners have now embraced the idea that one's performance should mimic as closely as possible the performance that the composer would have heard. And commentators designated music that was performed in this way as "authentic music."[77] The most authentically authentic music, in this view, is an interpretation which is purposely *not* innovative. An authentic performance seeks only to reproduce the mythical original performance, and to reproduce it as exactly as possible.[78] In the European high art tradition, then, committing to an ideal of authenticity leads logically to an emphasis on copying, and an accompanying lack of concern for original creation.

Like the Jakarta-based punks and the Brazilian country music performers, pop musicians in Yangon have identified themselves with a musical tradition that developed in the West. Some of them, especially those Christians who grew up in communities that still emphasize their ties to American and British missionaries, no doubt see themselves as "Westernized" (and several of them used exactly this term in interviews with me, without the least embarrassment). Others found that they had a strong preference for the sounds they heard on bootleg recordings brought into the country during the BSPP era, possibly because these sounds represented potential identities and futures that did not exist in Burma at that time. Still others—those born during the last twenty-five years—grew up hearing *stereo* songs on their parents' radios and associated those sounds with home and family, an important source of ideas about one's identity.[79] But to a greater or lesser degree, all of them consciously embraced a musical tradition that they knew had been generated in another time and place.

Like musicians from around the world, Burmese pop musicians seek to reproduce an art form that is, in some sense, foreign to them. They, too, attempt to be as faithful to history as possible, valorizing those interpretations which sound most like the original. And they, too, do this while simultaneously believing that their musical practice is an authentic expression of themselves and their community. Burmese pop musicians' commitment to imitation differs from that of other world musicians not in kind, but in degree. The amount of energy they devote to reproducing the most mainstream of the mainstream, the hit songs of the American and British pop charts, is remarkable. And it is this self-conscious modeling of local artistic expression on foreign originals, that is, ironically, the most salient "local" aspect of the Burmese scene.

Chapter Three

Learning Music in Burma Today

Ethnomusicologists prize participant-observation research. We aim to learn about musical cultures by participating in them. As I researched Burma's professional music scene for this book, I did not hold out much hope that I could actually participate in music making; after all, people earned their livelihoods at the studio sessions and performances I observed, and were unlikely to relinquish part of the process to a foreign researcher. Imagine my delight, then, when one of my favorite composers, Ko Htwe, asked me to record the keyboard part for a song on his upcoming album.

On the appointed day, I presented myself at the small recording studio owned by Soe Htun—only to discover that Ko Htwe was working on his family's goat farm that day. Luckily, Soe Htun is a friend of Ko Htwe, and was able to contact him to find out exactly which song I was supposed to record. Ko Htwe directed his recording engineer, Aye Nai, to play the *demo* for me. I dutifully sat down to write out the chord progression and melody in order to be able to improvise a piano accompaniment. When Soe Htun saw that I was working through it much more slowly than expected, he came in to help me.

At this point, the differences in our respective backgrounds became apparent. As a Western-trained classical musician with perfect pitch, I can write out a series of chords, but since I have not spent much time doing this, I find it challenging. I write the chords as I hear them—in this case, in E major, since the *demo* track was recorded in that key. Soe Htun, on the other hand, listens to and writes complex chord progressions on a daily basis, but he always writes them in C, following the standard practice in his industry. After about ten minutes, during which we tried to merge our understandings of the music, Aye Nai mentioned that Ko Htwe had already created notation. I seized on this, wondering why no one had said anything earlier.

After playing through the part repeatedly, using Ko Htwe's notation, I told Aye Nai that I was ready to record. He misunderstood me, thinking that I merely wanted to rerecord the solo section. It turned out that he had been recording every "take," unaware that I was only practicing. Although I had tried to explain this, Aye Nai seemed genuinely confused by my actions. And rightfully so: during his eighteen months of employment as a recording engineer, he had not often seen musicians rehearsing. However, we did finally realize that each of us was making incorrect presumptions about the other, and we managed to create a recording that I thought was adequate, although not excellent. I comforted myself by thinking, "Well, once the other multiples (guitar parts) are added, it will sound better."

After we finished, Soe Htun clued me in: the recording was intended to be a voice-and-piano-only performance; no other parts would be added. He informed me that the recording was now "finished" and prepared to burn a CD copy of the track for me. I protested; in my opinion, the recording was not finished, since Ko Htwe had not yet heard it. "We should wait for Ko Htwe to decide whether or not it is finished. Maybe he will want me to redo it," I said. Soe Hutn and Aye Nai burst into laughter. What an idea! They assured me in all seriousness that Ko Htwe would approve of my playing—because musicians usually work independently in Burma, and do not criticize each others' work. No producer would expect to tell a keyboardist to rerecord a part.

Of course, they were right. On my insistence, they phoned Ko Htwe and explained the situation to him. He too laughed, and then assured them (and me) that he approved the recording sight unseen—or rather, sound unheard. The recording was finished. Ko Htwe simply requested that I return once more to be photographed for the cover art.

This experience became a dinner party story that I shared with other Burmese musicians in subsequent weeks. And it always provoked laughter. The enormous differences between my own (European classical) and my interlocutors' (Burmese pop) learning and rehearsal cultures led to predictable misunderstandings. These misunderstandings were valuable, though, because they encouraged me to think more deeply about how it is that Burmese pop musicians learn and rehearse their music, and how these practices reflect the culture of their community.

Of course, one does not have to actually record music in a studio to be able to observe this culture. Just attend a typical rock concert somewhere in Yangon: it will begin with a singer walking on stage, handing a piece of musical notation to each of the instrumentalists, and then turning to face the audience as the music begins. The passing of papers is done so unobtrusively that it may be hard to spot. However, it is standard practice at virtually all the big shows, where one group of instrumentalists backs a succession of solo singers. In fact, the giving of notation to musicians is a vitally important component of the performance. The ensuing performances are always smooth, even spectacular, with coolly competent instrumental parts played perfectly in sync with the singing. The music proceeds as the participants and fans expect, with no breakdowns or glitches (other than the inevitable power surges). It would seem, then, that rehearsals are not needed.

The typical recording session I describe in chapter 1, and my own (less typical) experience both exemplify the same trend: instrumental players, hired to perform on one or more tracks, receive or create the music notation for the song when they arrive at the studio. After listening to the *demo* tape and writing the notation (or reading notation created by the arranger, who is often a

guitarist or keyboardist), they begin to record their parts. Individual performers may rehearse their parts in private (although I met only one person who
claimed to do so), but musicians generally do not rehearse as a group. Like live
performances, recorded performances are created on the spot. Naturally, in the
recording studio musicians can, and do, rerecord parts if they make mistakes.
But there is virtually no expectation that musicians doing *duty*—that is, recording tracks in studio, as described in chapter 1—will prepare for it in advance.

Singer Cherry, when confirming to me that her most recent performance
had not been rehearsed, said that this was normal, but she could not explain
why. She guessed that perhaps the "bandmaster" did not have time for a
rehearsal. She hastened to add that in the rare cases when a show organizer
does call a rehearsal, she always tries to attend: "If I don't, they [the other musi-
cians] will think of me as a proud lady" she said. Rehearsing, then, at least in
Cherry's mind, is an act of humility.

But she believes that the real obstacle to rehearsal is not her colleagues' attitudes but rather their schedules: that the reason for the lack of rehearsal is a
lack of time. Others, too, cited time pressures as the reason that group rehearsals are so rare. Professional full-time musicians often have daily performances
or recording sessions on their calendars, especially during the busy season of
October through March. Rehearsals therefore represent an investment of time
that musicians cannot afford to make; to do so would be to take time away
from paid work.

My own sense of the situation is that whether these musicians have time
for any given rehearsal or not, they generally do not plan to hold rehearsals, because they see them as unnecessary. When I wrote to Ko Htwe to tell
him that I would be returning to Yangon to conduct further research, he
responded via e-mail:

hello . . .

long time no see. i hope all of ur family members fine. i glad to hear that u
will come to yangoon again. i will inform [names of three friends who also
work full-time in the music industry] to help u in ur programm. now i am
doing my new album. so i want u to do me favour. just play piano for me,
could u? anyway see u that time. God bless all of us.

sincerely,
Ko Htwe

Ko Htwe assumed that I would be able to record the keyboard part for one
song on his *series*, despite the fact that I had been living on the other side of
the globe while all of the preparation for the *series* occurred. Although he knew

that I had never heard the song before, he felt confident asking me to record it.[1] When I arrived in Yangon, I met with Ko Htwe and explained to him that I was doubtful that I could accomplish the task, since I did not have notation and had never heard the song. He smiled and said gently that he and his colleagues at the studio had discussed the situation, and had scheduled time for me to listen to the *demo* and "write some notes." When I emphasized that I would like to have time to practice, he shrugged his shoulders and said, "Fine! You will write the notes, and then practice, and then record." Clearly, he did not anticipate that the practicing would take much time, since it was to happen during the studio session for which he had already paid.

In general, Burmese musicians prize efficiency, and they therefore aim to prepare for musical performances (and careers) in as little time as possible. Their collective attitude toward rehearsing for live shows and recordings grows out of this larger concern. If they can perform adequately after rehearsing only once, or even without rehearsing at all, then they are happy to do so. They do not see a value in spending days or weeks in rehearsal if they can sing and play successfully without rehearsing.

Of course, exceptions exist. Musicians who organize themselves into bands (like Iron Cross, for example) do sometimes rehearse their material, and therefore at their shows they do not need to pass pieces of notation to one another.[2] It is important to keep in mind, though, that in the twenty-first century many Burmese pop musicians either do not belong to bands, or do not function as if they do. Rather, individuals continually come together in various groupings for various projects, and when they come together, they usually do not rehearse. Nevertheless, I was fortunate to be able to observe three rehearsals during the course of my fieldwork.

At the first rehearsal, which took place in January 2008, a number of senior musicians—who in the past had constituted a band—worked together to create a kind of revival show. The show featured Moe Lwin, an *own-tune* composer-singer who had been very popular in the 1980s. The singer and the four instrumentalists rehearsed in a tiny room, completely unlike the stage on which they would perform the next night. It was enormously enjoyable to attend, because the "practicing" consisted of the group playing each song once, flawlessly, from start to finish. In other words, it was exactly like the show (which I subsequently attended) but in a more intimate setting. (So much like a show, in fact, that a half-dozen people stood around the room and listened at length). There were no stops, no repetitions, no obvious problems, no sense that the musicians were improving as they went along. Rather, it seemed that they were, at the moment of their coming together, completely prepared to play.

Another rehearsal that I attended in January 2009 was largely similar. This rehearsal took place in the practice room of a recording studio (the studio was unusual in that it had a designated room for rehearsals). The band was preparing for a performance the following day. They were to perform with a singer

Figure 3.1. One of the dozens of recording studios in Yangon

who had never sung with them before. Although the rehearsal was scheduled to begin at 10:00 a.m., the musicians arrived one by one well after that time, with the singer finally arriving around 12:30 p.m. At that point it was time for lunch, which we all shared sitting outside the studio at a picnic table. After 1:00 p.m., the rehearsal began in earnest.

The same casual, friendly atmosphere that had dominated the interactions all morning pervaded the practice room. The musicians played through each song once, with very few stops and starts. The instrumentalists played the notation virtually flawlessly at sight, and the singer was clearly comfortable with his entrances, with how his voice balanced with the accompaniment, and so on. Although the instrumental players did indulge in some brief discussions about timbre and form, for the most part the afternoon proceeded as if the musicians had no need to discuss or repeat sections, because they were all confident in their abilities.

I was invited to the third rehearsal, which occurred in December 2008, by U Ye Zaw Tun, a prominent member of the Yangon pop music community. During our interview we talked about my perception that Burmese pop musicians rarely practice together. A few days later, I received a surprise phone call, inviting me to come to a practice session for the annual City FM awards show (which is, in effect, a pop music concert). U Ye Zaw Tun wanted me to see that Yangon musicians do, in fact, rehearse. The rehearsal was illuminating: although singers arrived with lyric sheets and seemed to know the melodies they were to sing, the instrumentalists (who were all members of the same famous band) arrived with no prior knowledge. The first hour or so was spent waiting for the guitarist, Htay Cho, to create notation for the instrumental parts.

Like his colleagues at this highest level of pop music performance in Burma, Htay Cho has outstanding aural skills. He later guesstimated that it took him about fifteen minutes to write out the guitar, keyboard, and percussion parts for each song (which seems right according to my notes from that afternoon). He developed these skills in the context of a culture that expects him to operate at this level: although the composers of each of the songs were present, only one brought notation for his song. The other composers evidently expected the guitarist-arranger to listen to the demo and write out notation on the spot, which he did.

After all the parts had been handed out, the band settled down to play with the singers. The rehearsal was held in a studio—as I later discovered was standard practice for rehearsals, when they do occur—so the group could listen to the recording of themselves after each run-though of each song. Ultimately, they worked through four songs in about four-and-a-half hours. Near the beginning of each hour, the performers went through parts of each song, stopping and starting as needed. They worked toward complete performances, and accomplished this in each case. One singer announced at the end of the rehearsal of her song, "*Aun bi!*" ("We've succeeded!")

The performers were joined in the studio by two recording engineers; the band manager; a producer (who was to later produce a video recording of the concert) composers; studio employees; a City FM employee; and observers, including family members of performers. All of these people felt free to comment on the evolving performances. While listening to the recorded tracks, the musicians talked to each other about errors in pitch and timing and shared ideas for alternate timbral effects. In addition, they made comments to the recording engineers, who shared their opinions in return. At one point or another, all of the nonperformers made comments to the musicians, as well. The performers seemed especially interested in soliciting the composers' opinions, but they made statements to, and listened to statements from, all present.

The lack of overt hierarchy was noticeable: no conductor or director of music's artistic vision shaped the performances. As in the many recording sessions I observed, musicians operated with a great deal of autonomy, although in this context they welcomed other opinions and modified their performances based on those opinions. Furthermore, every interchange was marked with respect. The afternoon stands out in my memory as particularly enjoyable because I was part of an atmosphere of such high morale and good humor. Thuza, one of the singers who were present that day, told me later that he felt the same way: "It was like a party," he said. He added that he stayed for the entire rehearsal, although his presence was only required for one hour, because he so deeply enjoyed the opportunity to spend time with his friends.

Explaining the Burmese Approach

Why did these rehearsals occur? Numerous musicians explained to me, both then and in other contexts, that they rehearse only under certain conditions. For example, there may be a rehearsal if the instrumentalists have no experience playing with a particular singer. In many cases, live shows link instrumentalists with singers with whom they have previously made recordings, so that they know and have performed the repertoire before the show takes place. Some of the most prominent bands make a practice of regularly appearing with the same singers, so they know those singers' songs particularly well. If the band plans to rehearse with a new singer, they will rehearse with this singer once only, usually on the day before the performance, as in the case of the second rehearsal described above. In the case of the City FM rehearsal, half of the featured singers were not in fact professional singers, but actors who had been invited to sing for this prestigious event. (One of the concert organizers explained that they hoped that the inclusion of actors with singers would increase the audience for the show, which would be broadcast on national TV sometime after the awards show.)[3] Therefore the band needed to rehearse with these singers.

In addition, musicians rehearse for "big shows." A big show is one intended for an audience of some thousands; at least two thousand, according to Aung Shwe, or four thousand, according to Thet Htaw Mya (manager of one of Burma's busiest bands). In addition, the audience must consist of ticket-holders, that is, people who have paid to see the show. Therefore, Htay Cho dismissed a recent concert which attracted thirty to forty thousand people as not being a "big show" because it was a free New Year's Day concert, open to all members of the public. He added that he and his band did not rehearse for this show. By contrast, the City FM show was a "big show" in all of the musicians' minds, because it would be televised to a large segment of the population on government TV and because it was to be performed before a by-invitation-only audience.

How is it possible that Burmese pop musicians are able to perform so well without rehearsing together? When I asked musicians about this, most pointed out that when they come to perform music, whether live or in a recording studio, the music is already familiar to them. The musicians develop their familiarity with the repertoire in a number of ways. If the song to be recorded is a *copy thachin*, for example, the musicians are likely to have heard the original Western-made recording. If it is an *own tune* song, musicians always listen to the *demo* tape before recording; one or two hearings are sufficient to render them familiar with the song. And as I explain above, in the case of live performances, musicians often find themselves playing music that they have already played in the studio. Live shows, therefore, are not usually first-time performances, and thus the instrument players need only to glance at the notation in order to play it successfully for the audience.

James Thiri, who attended the January 2008 rehearsal described above, explained it to me this way: "All of the people here have twenty years experience, or more. And they have worked together before on recordings." For James Thiri and his colleagues, the idea that familiarity with the material makes rehearsal unnecessary pretty much settles the matter. However, it seems to me that there is more to the story: Burmese pop musicians are able to operate this way in part because the songs they perform are rather formulaic. North American readers will recognize the idea that pop songs usually have a verse-chorus-bridge-chorus form. In Burma, this is equally true. Songs generally have the same overall structure, with an instrumental (usually lead guitar) solo occurring two-thirds of the way through the song, and a coda to end it. (The most common song structure I encountered was verse-verse-chorus-solo-verse-chorus-coda).

Songs are almost always in common time, and the introduction to the first verse is almost always eight measures long. The verses and choruses usually consist of four phrases of eight measures each. In addition, the instrumental solo always lasts eight or sixteen measures. Chord changes always occur on the first beat of a measure (and sometimes on other beats). The instrumental accompaniment is almost always the same: one drum kit, one bass guitar, one lead guitar, and one set of keyboards. The instrumentalists do not have to coordinate their playing with singers' movements, since singers usually do not dance while performing. And shows do not feature elaborate light shows or revolving stages or other infrastructure that might affect the players' performances.

Therefore, once a musician has developed the skill of playing a pop song, he can apply this skill to almost any song he encounters. He is unlikely, as a professional in Yangon, to have to deal with many deviations from this norm. Thus he is able to fully master it. Also, he works with others who have mastered this norm. A new song is unlikely to hold any musical surprises for them.

Furthermore, these musicians have excellent aural skills—the ability to rapidly re-create (on paper or in performance) sound that they have heard. To be sure, none of the musicians I interviewed said anything like, "We can perform with little or no rehearsal because we have very good aural skills." Burmese musicians simply do not talk this way, in part because it would be perceived to be self-aggrandizing (more on this in my discussion of musical talent, below), but also because they have no vocabulary for this kind of skill. For instance, I discovered that a number of the instrumentalists I interviewed have absolute pitch—that is, they were able to listen to pitches that I sang, and without resorting to any reference pitch, to immediately play them on their own instruments. I asked them about absolute pitch, and either they did not recognize the term, or they thought it meant "ability to sing in tune."[4] Htet Aung, a music teacher who was educated abroad, told me that there is no term in Burmese for this particular skill; after pondering the idea for moment, he said that the closest equivalent would be "*na kaun teh*," which means, "The ears are good." Those pop instrumentalists who do not have absolute pitch have very strong relative pitch, and all have an excellent ability to re-create rhythms and identify timbres.

These tremendous aural skills are especially apparent among guitarists (and note that many Burmese pop musicians play guitar, although they work professionally as singers, drummers, or keyboard players). Guitarists often work as arrangers, writing the notation for the songs that bands will play. It was when I observed guitarists working on arrangements that I saw most clearly how skilled they are in listening to and understanding musical sound. Here is one incident out of many that I observed. In December 2008, I watched Htay Cho at work in a recording studio. He was writing out the lead and rhythm guitar parts for a song he was about to record. The *demo* of the song was actually an earlier commercial recording of the same song, made by Iron Cross. Knowing that Htay Cho had a strong relationship with the Iron Cross guitarist, I asked him why he did not just phone his colleague and request the notation from him. He laughed in surprise, and then gamely tried to answer. He said that the guitarist would probably have difficulty finding the part, since he does not keep his scores in well-organized files. Therefore, he said, it would take "too long." I thought it over. Travel time from our location to the guitarist's home, plus twenty minutes or so to locate the notation, would add up to about one hour. "Yes!" Htay Cho pronounced. An hour was longer than the time it would take him to create his own notation from scratch. And indeed this proved to be the case. Htay Cho managed to write out both parts and record them in less than an hour.

In this culture, no master scores exist to be passed along to whoever will learn the repertoire. Composers simply give *demo* recordings to arrangers, who create new notation very quickly, relying on their finely-honed aural skills. Having watched a number of keyboard players and guitarists do this, I can verify that they are generally able to create notation for the instrumental parts of a song while listening to it once or twice. They write chords (in C, always), numbers indicating melody notes where instruments play solos, symbols representing rhythm (especially rests), and indications to outline the complete form.

Arrangers say that they are able to work so quickly and accurately because they have had so many years of experience doing this work, and this is undoubtedly true. But it seems to me that they are able to do so also because they are expected to do so. People live up to what is expected of them, and Burmese pop musicians are no exception. It simply does not occur to them to rely on notation generated by others when preparing for recording. When I suggested that Htay Cho call his friend to get a copy of the notation, he laughed. For him, the idea was absurd. And the recording engineer, who overheard our conversation, found it equally laughable.

During another encounter with another professional Burmese pop musician, I saw similarly strong aural skills at work. While interviewing Myine Myat, I asked him to show me what it means to "follow" a song. Musicians frequently use this word to describe how they learn music, and I wanted to observe it in real time. Myine Myat, who works as a guitarist but who makes bamboo flutes in his leisure time, picked up one of his flutes and said, "Well, if you sing a song for me, I'll play it." Nonplussed, I pressed him: "Any song?" He smiled, serenely self-confident. I decided to sing a song that he could not possibly have heard before, a Canadian folk song called "Land of the Silver Birch." The melody is in Dorian mode and is therefore a little less predictable than a melody using a major scale. I launched into the song, and after I had sung the first five or six notes, Myine Myat played them, exactly as I had sung them. As I continued to sing, he continued to play, imitating my voice with perfect accuracy. Importantly, he did not wait until the end of each phrase to repeat after me, but rather played the notes I sang, remaining three or four pitches behind me for the duration of the melody. The best way to describe what happened is that Myine Myat "followed" the melody I sang. What is more, he did so perfectly on his first exposure to the new melody. After we finished, he grinned at me and said, "See? My hands just follow!"

How do these musicians develop their advanced aural skills? Musicians often referred to the idea of "talent" when I queried them on this point.

Contrasting Notions of Musical Talent

In Burma, as in the West, the ability to learn music is closely linked to the notion of talent. Western scholars have discussed the concept of talent at length.[5] The most complete account from an ethnomusicological point of view comes from Henry Kingsbury.[6] To begin, Kingsbury points out that the North American musical establishment generally holds the idea that "rock music requires little or no talent" and therefore believes that rock music does not need to be taught.[7] In Burma, among the music teachers and musicians that I interviewed, the view is precisely the opposite: to be a successful rock or pop music performer does indeed require talent, but talented people do not need extensive teaching, and that is why Burmese pop stars mostly learn on their own.

Burmese pop musicians believe in the idea of talent, and they assert that some people are more talented than others. Although there are a few Burmese words that approximate the English word "talent" (one is *pa-ra-mee*, a Buddhist concept meaning "accumulated virtue"), most of the people I interviewed used the English term or at least recognized it. They differed, however, from their Anglo-American counterparts in their beliefs about where talent comes from and how it manifests itself in the lives of musicians.

Most Burmese musicians—Buddhists and Christians—believe that talent has a supernatural origin. Christian singers and instrumentalists not only agreed on the concept, but were almost unanimous in the way they worded their idea: "Talent is a gift from God," they said, over and over. They tended to say this not only when I asked direct questions about talent, but also when I expressed admiration for a musical performance. For Christians, this belief about talent is part of a larger belief that "everything [we have] is a gift from God," as Myo Myo Thant put it.

Like talent, success in musical endeavors is a gift from God, and so Christian Burmese musicians say that they and their families pray to God for sustainable careers and even for specific performances. For example, Julia (a young singer from a devoutly Christian family), who performed at a live show without having rehearsed, explained that she was not nervous during the show because "I trust in Jesus; I put my trust in God for a good performance. I always pray before I go on stage." The one Muslim performer I was able to interview also affirmed without hesitation that "God gives talent."[8] Buddhists also believe that talent originates with the supernatural, but that it is the direct result of an individual's righteous behavior during a past life. In that sense, the Buddhist notion of talent is equally as inscrutable as is the Christian idea: just as gifts given by God are unpredictable, so is the good karma that was created by some past, unknown, action. However, in Buddhist belief the relationship between one's past and current lives is a direct cause-and-effect relationship, and it is the responsibility of the individual soul to regulate this relationship.

Chit Nyein, a Buddhist pop singer who subscribes to this notion, theorized that perhaps his talent comes from having performed and taught music for free in a previous life. Although he is not certain of this, he says that he is committed to performing live shows "FOC" (free of charge) for charity in this life, so that his accumulated meritorious deeds will redound to his benefit in his next life. Thuza, another successful Buddhist singer, said that because he believes so firmly that past lives influence future lives, he is careful to follow the teachings of the Buddha in the present. He says that he does his best to do good to others, to honor his parents, and to pay homage to the Buddha and to Buddhist monks; in this way he hopes to ensure that he will be blessed in his next life.

For many Buddhist musicians, the idea that one's past deeds account for one's present circumstances extends beyond the idea of having talent. This belief system helps them to account for material prosperity and for success in their careers. For example, as we discussed musical talent, Thuza said to me that his good deeds (in his past and present lives) explain why he is able to live comfortably in a poor country, and why he has been able to start a business. And a record producer—one who has been able to hang on during the recent developments which have eliminated most music producers in the Burmese market (see chapter 4)—claimed that his substantial material success was due to "luck" and "decided by fate."[9] This luck is, of course, not random fortune as Westerners understand it, but rather the logical result of the producer's actions in his past lives.

The one substantial difference between Christian and Buddhist views of musical talent seems to be that Buddhists are more likely to say that one's talent derives from one's "genes" or one's "DNA."[10] For example, Shwe Nyunt, a senior Burman Buddhist musician, told me that talent really boils down to identifiable, natural causes: "A gifted singer is a person who is born with a body structure that can create a good vocal tone," he said, mentioning that the shape of one's mouth and one's lung capacity affect this tone. This does not necessarily negate the idea of past lives and accumulated virtue. As Ko Chit Min said to me, "I think 'talented' means 'gifted.' It is something you are born with. My religion says it comes from a previous life. I think it's in your DNA. I believe in Buddhism *and* science."[11]

There are some dissenters, of course. A small minority of Burmese musicians and music teachers, both Buddhist and Christian, say that either they have no explanation for musical talent, or that musical skill is primarily the result of an individual's hard work and practice.[12] Cho Cho Saing, a Karen Christian music teacher who has decades of experience mentoring younger musicians, told me that "talent is a gift from God," but then immediately followed that up with, "You have to use your common sense. God gives this gift but you have to exercise your own resources." Interestingly, Cho Cho Saing describes herself as "Westernized." She speaks perfect English, is highly educated, and is conversant with many Western ways of understanding the world. Perhaps this is why she articulates what Kingsbury claims is a Western notion: musical talent as a "potential" or a "gift" which nonetheless has to be developed, through years of rigorous work, by the talented individual.[13] But this view is not widely held among professional Burmese musicians. Indeed virtually all of them, be they Buddhist, Christian or Muslim, agree on one crucial point: being talented means that one does *not* have to work hard to learn music and by extension, to achieve professional success. Some expressed this idea as a clear opposition, saying that it is possible for untalented people to achieve success by exercising extreme effort—that is, by practicing a lot.[14] Most simply said that being musically talented means that a person is able to learn music quickly, that he or she does not have to work particularly hard to master it. Composer and performer Khine Ta Htun stated it flatly: "You cannot practice your talent."[15]

Specifically, Burmese musicians frequently said that being talented means that one does not need many, or any, formal lessons in music. In fact, a number of them explained that they knew they had talent precisely because they had been able to learn a lot about music despite having no access to formal lessons. R Zani, a well-known Burmese pop singer, is aware that he was quoted in the Yangon press implying that musical success is entirely due to *san* or luck.[16] He took pains to emphasize to me that he "never spoke against training [taking music lessons]."[17] He added that people "who are interested [in music] but don't have talent should get training."

When I asked Burmese musicians and music teachers to explain how one can know that one or another person is talented, most said the same thing: talent manifests itself as the ability to learn music by ear, quickly. Talent is particularly evident in people who can reproduce a melody they have just heard (either by singing it or by playing it on an instrument). Because most Burmese pop musicians teach themselves by listening to and following along with recordings, talent is often described as the ability to perform what one hears on a recording.[18] James Thiri described his cousin, a lead guitarist, as a "genius" because the man could listen to a recording ten times (or so), turn it off, and play the lead guitar part flawlessly. Ko Htwe said that he was sure that God had given him talent because he can listen to a recorded song only once and then sing the tune himself. And Theingi Zaw, a Buddhist composer, said that talent means being able to hear a song on the radio (or on a recording) and to understand it "immediately—like knowing how many bars [in the phrase.]"

To contrast this understanding, once more, with Western notions of talent: scholar Joanne Haroutounian sums up two thousand years of Western theories about musical talent by describing it as a "spark" that can be fanned into a flame by the diligent work of the talented, guided by their teachers.[19] But in Burma, musical talent is an ability that is given to or is born into a person, fully fledged. When a Burmese person has talent, it is understood to be a mature, ripened talent that needs little or no nurturing from a teacher in order to be useful. It is not a spark that needs to be coaxed into a flame, but rather a brightly burning fire. In scholar Susan O'Neill's terms, Burmese people subscribe to an "entity theory of talent" ("the notion that people only have a certain amount of musical ability") rather than an "incremental theory" (the idea that "anyone can improve their musical ability though effort and practising musical skills").[20] Talent, coming as it does from the supernatural, is not partial or in need of development. Rather, it is a divine gift that frees the recipient from the need to practice, and it grants to him or her the most important skill in Burmese pop music culture: the ability to learn by ear.

For Burmese pop musicians, talent has nothing to do with the ability to sight-read notation easily, or to play one's instrument with virtuosity (two ideas that were emphasized in my classical music training in Canada). Instead, talent means that one is able to easily learn and reproduce music that one has heard. However, both Burmese and Western musicians usually experience the recognition of their talent in the same way: the talent of a "talented" musician is usually proclaimed by someone other than the musician.

In the West, this person is often a music teacher, adjudicator, or master class instructor.[21] In Burma, the person who most often affirms to a young person that he or she is talented is a member of the family. Nu Nu Win shared that she recalls her parents (one of whom was a professional guitarist) saying, "She will be a famous singer!" when she was only five years old. Ko Htwe said that he believed his prayer for musical talent was answered when his older brother, who was already working as a professional musician in Yangon, wrote to him, inviting him to come to the city to play in a hotel band. Ohnmar Tun said that the leading nun (the "Mother") in her convent school insisted that she had a good voice and made her join the choir. And composer U Hla Kyi said simply that he realized he had talent when he was a teenager, because his grandparents told him so.

Although Burmese pop musicians are happy to talk about theories of talent, and about how their talent was initially recognized, they are markedly less willing to verbally claim that they themselves are talented. Approximately two thirds of my respondents basically refused to answer yes to the question, "Do you have talent?" Despite my prodding ("Surely you must be talented! Look at how successful you are in music!"), even the biggest stars in the country ducked their heads in shyness when I asked them to affirm their own talent. Young Julia did finally agree that she is "a little talented." Saw Leh Dah, a composer in training, admitted that he was simply embarrassed to make such an assertion.[22]

I came to believe that these musicians are in fact comfortable with the idea that they are talented, but reluctant to say so out loud, especially to an interviewer who is writing down their statements. In Burma, as in many other countries, it is considered self-aggrandizing to claim that one is talented, and socially appropriate people usually do not do so. But when I proposed this theory to Ko Chit Min, a very successful and self-confident musician, he flatly denied the possibility. No, he said, he was not feigning humility; he simply did not believe that he had any talent.

While talking about one's own talent was difficult for many Burmese musicians, talking about learning music was not. Indeed, virtually everyone I interviewed spoke at length about what he knew and how he had learned to do it.

Knowledge about Music: Notation, Meter, Harmony, and Vocalization

Notation

When I broached the topic of learning music with Burmese pop musicians, we usually began by discussing notation—although, as I discovered, most of these

musicians do not read or write Western staff notation. Their ideas about notation, however, reveal other interesting aspects of their musical culture.

At least three different types of notation are known and used in Burma.
Some choral conductors and singers use a solfège system, in which letters representing the tones *do, re, mi, fa, so, la,* and *ti* are written to show pitch, and
dots and lines are set above these to show rhythms. Pop musicians use a second
method of music notation known variously as "1234 notes," "number notes,"
"Chinese notes," or "Oriental notes." In this method, the numbers 1 through
7 represent the solfège pitches, and lines below and dots between the numbers represent rhythms. Students studying traditional Burmese music at the
University of Culture, for example, use this method to notate melodies from
the *Maha Gita,* and a specialized form of it is used throughout the Yangon pop
industry. Musicians who play European art music (usually instrumental) use
staff notation, in which notes are written on five-line staves. The government of
Burma is now using this notation to notate the high art repertoire of their own
country, publishing books of *Maha Gita* repertoire in piano score. When pop
musicians talk about notation methods, they often refer to Western notation
as "staff notes" and less frequently as "professional notes" (these English words
are used in the context of Burmese sentences). Charmingly, it is also known
as *paka* notes, which means "bean sprouts," because the notes, with their long
stems and round heads, look like bean plants growing up among the lines of
the staff. But most frequently, and most tellingly, this kind of notation is called
"international notes." Staff notation is understood to be the universal standard
or norm for writing notation, while the number notes system—the most locally
prominent system—is clearly understood to be the product of a particular
bounded geographic area.

I would not put a great deal of emphasis on these names for notation systems if it were not for the fact that they seem to reflect their relative status
in the eyes of many Burmese people. Musicians and music teachers I interviewed consistently valorized "international notes." Michael, for example,
pointed out that he believed that this notation, which he cannot read with
any fluency, must be important, since it is used worldwide. Ko Htwe and Myo
Myo Thant independently shared with me that one of their life goals was to
learn how to read and use international notes. And in June 2007, when I was
asked to teach a week-long class on music at one of the local music schools,
the students (most of whom were music students either at private music acad-
emies or at the University of Culture) asked me to focus on explaining how
to read this notation.

Burmese musicians' low opinion of their own local notation vis-à-vis European notation is part of a larger tendency to express some degree of humility,
if not fatalistic acceptance, about their own version of worldwide pop music
culture. Doubtless this attitude is in part a legacy of the colonial era, when
all things English were considered to be more worthy than anything that was

locally made, including the Burmese language itself.[23] Sometimes this attitude manifested itself in slightly defensive statements in interviews, as when composer Htin Thu told me that Burmese *own tune* songs "are not world standard, but okay for Myanmar." Pee Paw, the country's most prominent impresario, said it the most clearly. When I asked him about some stage practices that struck me as being unique to Burma—such as stage hands being on stage during the performance and singers leaving the stage before a song is over—he assumed that I was criticizing local norms as being inferior to the international standard. "My own goal is that each show I organize will be the best. But in Myanmar, sometimes it is not possible. So we settle for what is acceptable [by local standards]."

To be sure, some pop music composers and instrumentalists were less in awe of "international notes." They pointed out that this system is very limited, because a note on a staff represents only one absolute pitch. Their own system, a modified form of "Chinese notes," is much more efficient than international notes, they claimed, because it is more flexible. This system, which was apparently invented by a Yangon guitarist named Zar Lian in the 1970s, is called "C Rule."

In the C Rule system, the focus is on notating chords rather than notes *per se*. The chords are written using capital letters of the Roman alphabet separated by bar lines, as in the chord charts used by session players in the American recording industry.[24] The difference is that in the Burmese C Rule system, "C" indicates the tonic chord of the song, "G" the dominant chord, and so on. The letter C does not represent the chord C–E–G unless the song is in the key of C major. Accordingly, the key of the song must be prominently indicated at the top of any C Rule notation.

Of course, this system requires pop musicians who play harmony instruments (guitars and keyboards) to be able to transpose at sight into any major key, which they do handily. For the most part, however, they do not conceive of the process as "transposing." During interviews, few of them recognized the word. They take it for granted that professional pop musicians can play any song, in any key, at sight, and they attribute this reality to the "easiness" of C Rule notation.

C Rule notation seems to have originated as a way for Burmese musicians to capture the chord progressions they heard in Anglo-American recordings. Now, the arranger often adds significant information to the sheet, indicating, for example, where recording musicians ought to play solos. Composers and arrangers use slash notation (with a slash for a beat and a circle for a rest) to fill in measures after the initial letter indicating the chord. In addition, they use the "1234 notes" system, with its numbers, lines and dots, to write in melodic fills for piano, bass, or lead guitar. English words ("verse," "chorus," "solo," etc.) are used to indicate where sections begin, and *segno* and *coda* symbols to mark repetitions. Some arrangers create more detailed notation than

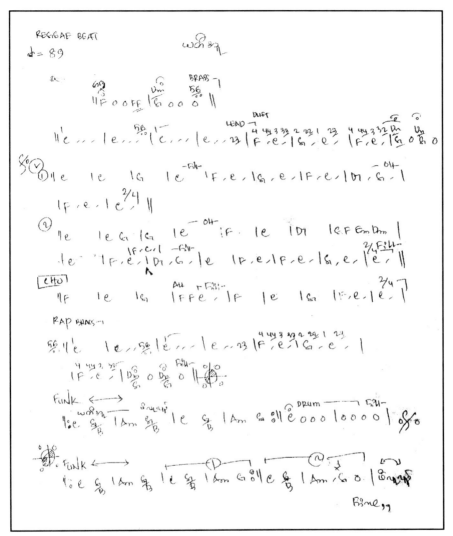

Figure 3.2. Example of C Rule notation

others, of course. The sample of C Rule notation shown in figure 3.2 was written by a composer who subsequently arranged his song for a band: he had very definite ideas about how the piece should sound, and so his page has rather more symbols on it than many others I have seen.

One thing that does not usually appear in C rule notation is any marker for meter. When I asked musicians about this, they explained that there is a very simple reason: all songs (or most songs) are in $\frac{4}{4}$ time. I did see one example in which Johnson had written $\frac{3}{4}$ in front of two measures in the bridge section of a song—but this was clearly an exception.

Interestingly, when Burmese musicians talk about this issue, whether they are speaking in Burmese or in English, they use the English expression "four-four time." In fact, all of the music vocabulary used in the Burmese pop industry seems to be in English. When listening to musicians work in the studio, I often heard them using a kind of industry lingo that combines Burmese grammar and context with technical terms in English ("Chorus *hma sa*," for example: "Start at the chorus"). Sometimes, Italian terms were used, but pronounced as they would be in English (so *fine* rhymes with "mine" in the mouths of some musicians). The constant use of English to refer to music emphasizes the fact that in Burma, pop music is a foreign import. There are literally no words in Burmese for the concepts embedded in the music. Therefore the musicians, coming to it as outsiders, have had to make sense of it for themselves, and in so doing, they have developed theories about it.

Meter

One of these theories, as I just mentioned, is that all pop songs are in $\frac{4}{4}$ time. This makes sense, since so many songs are indeed in common meter. And others can be counted as if they are. A song in the compound meter of $\frac{12}{8}$, for example, can be counted as having four beats in a measure (each beat subdivided into three), and songs in $\frac{2}{4}$ and $\frac{6}{8}$ can be counted that way if the musician combines measures into pairs. Indeed, most musicians that I met were aware that music can be organized into other meters, but did not have a good understanding of those meters. (Those who had had formal lessons had learned about the various meters, but they were in the minority.)[25]

Some musicians seemed to believe that all songs are in $\frac{4}{4}$. This may be because the high art music of Burma is always performed with a steady beat pattern, called *si neh wah*.[26] The *si* beat is played by a pair of hand cymbals and the *wah* beat by a wooden clapper. These instruments outline the structure of the music, which is organized into phrases of eight beats.[27] The *si neh wah* pattern is ever-present, underpinning the music and providing a steady pulse over which the melodic lines flow. Some pop musicians believe that this *si neh wa* pattern is analogous to the accented first and third beats in $\frac{4}{4}$ time. As Shway Nyunt told me: "They are alike. The *si* is like the first beat [in common meter] and the *wah* is like the third beat."[28]

Shway Nyunt went on to say that his music teacher had explained meter this way when he took lessons in the 1960s. Evidently the theory is spreading. When I visited one of the campuses of the State High School of Fine Arts in Yangon, I discovered that the music teacher advances exactly this theory in her music classes. Furthermore, she equates the pitches of the traditional Burmese scale with the notes of the Western major scale—though these pitches are not the same.[29] In fact, the principal at this high school explained to me that the goal of the class is help students understand how to equate Burmese and Western music theory concepts.

For Burmese pop musicians, the idea of meter is ultimately an unimportant issue, because they know what they need to know: that is, the "beats." "Beats," or "rhythm patterns" as a Western musicologist might call them, are foundational because they determine the genre of the music. Musicians label the various beats according to the musical genres in which they are used. For example, when Ma Khin Sein explained to me the development of her career said, "First, I asked friends to explain to me about the beats—like reggae, slow go-go, cha-cha, and rock." Ohnmar Tun explained that when she works with accompanying musicians, before she begins she must always tell them the key of the song, the tempo (or speed) and "the beat—like rock, cha-cha or beguine." C Rule scores show the link between beats and genre. These scores often include a beat indicator in the spot where a tempo marking is placed in Western notation. In figure 3.2, the marking "reggae beat" is given at the upper left.

When musicians create studio recordings, the drum track is always recorded first, and establishes the style for each song. People in the Burmese recording industry call the drum track "the body"—the core on which the clothing of the other tracks (the guitar, keyboard, and vocal parts) is hung. Pop instrumentalists in Yangon claim to know all the beats and therefore to be able to play in a variety of styles, because to them, beats are the distinguishing feature of style. (They do not talk about styles being associated with different timbres, for example.) The same group of instruments is played in the same basic way for all songs, whether those songs are in bossa nova style or heavy metal. This linking of beat patterns with genre explains, at least to some degree, why Burmese pop songs all tend to sound much the same to Western ears. At pop concerts in Yangon, my Burmese friends have identified various singers or songs to me as being "alternative," "rock," "reggae," and so on. Without their guidance, I would not have been able to distinguish these various styles, since the the same techniques and musical approaches were used in all of them.

Harmony

Probably the most widespread theoretical concept in the Yangon pop music community is the idea of chords and chord families. Knowing chords is considered to be foundational for pop musicians, so much so that when interviewees talked about how they learned to play pop music, they often began, "When I learned the chords . . . ." In fact, one guitarist said that the most important thing that one needs to know about "American" music is "the chords."[30] This makes sense, since one of the most immediate differences between Burmese art music and European-derived musics is that Burmese music is heterophonic, while European music focuses on chordal harmonies.[31] But Burmese musicians differentiate the idea of chords from Western classical music, also. For example, Esther explained to me that she took piano lessons as a child, but doesn't play European classical piano repertoire anymore: "Now I play chords. Chords are better for hearing and singing."

Burmese musicians say that chords belong to "chord families." These chord families are not groups of chords based on the notes of a diatonic scale, as students in the West learn. Rather, they are common chord progressions, successions of chords that occur so frequently that they are understood to constitute a kind of family. As Myine Myat explained to me, "With C Rule, you have to know every key. And you have to know the chord family for each key." When I asked him to give me an example, he named the tonic, submediant, subdominant, and dominant chords in C major. I then asked him to give me the chord families for a few more key signatures, and each time, not needing a moment to reflect, he named the same chords in the same order.

Michael expanded on this theory, saying that chord families are related to genre. Writing rapidly on a piece of paper, he showed me the chord family for rock tunes:

$A^7 D^7 E^7$

The verse of a pop song, he says, uses the following chord family:
C Am Dm G Em Am
Dm G C

And, Michael says, the chorus in a pop song always follows this pattern:
$F^{maj7} Em^7$ Dm G C
$F^{maj7} Em^7 A^7$ Dm G Em Am Dm G C

It is clear that chord families are not understood in the exact same way by all Burmese pop musicians, but the general theory—that certain chords typically follow other chords—is common to all. These musicians do not possess a widely-agreed-upon, systemized listing of chord families, but they do all assert that chords make up families.

Vocalization

Burmese pop musicians also theorize vocal performance. The general consensus is that there are at least two distinct ways to approach singing in pop music. It seems that a lyrical, unforced sound is considered "sweet." A sweet sound may or may not be desirable. A woman named Tulip, who recorded a hobby album and spent her career working for the Burma Broadcasting Service, explained the terminology to me. She said that she herself has a "sweet voice."[32] I listened to her VCD and heard a vocal tone that I can best describe as gentle, quite the opposite of the forcefully projected chest tone (sometimes called "belting") that is often associated with Western pop singers.

Tulip distinguished her own sweet sound from a "heavy voice," which she demonstrated by singing in a loud, high tone. She said that she had been invited to record an album because members of her community like her sweet voice. Pressed to give more examples of sweet and heavy voices, she listed Cliff Richard (the British pop star) and Elvis Presley as singers with sweet voices. She identified Lay Phyu (the former lead singer of Iron Cross) and "hip-hop singers" as examples of heavy voices.

Aye Kyi used some of the same terminology when she spoke to me about vocal tone. She explained: "My mother and her sisters were singers. But I wanted to sing like American singers, like Céline Dion, so I forced myself to sing in high keys like them. Normally, here [in Burma], the songs are easy to sing, not high. And they have to be sung sweetly." When I pressed her to explain what a "sweet" sound is, she demonstrated by singing a short phrase with a soft, diffuse, head tone. She then contrasted this with a "Whitney Houston style" of singing—a loud chest voice.

Like most of the Burmese musicians I spoke to, Aye Kyi correlates loud volume and high pitch with foreign singers. Julia, who shares this notion, sings with a well-projected chest tone. She says that her voice is "loud by Myanmar standards." Cho Cho Saing, who has some connections to members of the pop music industry, underlined this point. Her students do not like to sing high notes, she says, because they are difficult to sing loudly; she has noticed that even her professional friends prefer to sing in middle or low ranges and often request that songs be transposed down. Overall, this seemed to be a common perception; high melody notes are associated both with foreignness and with difficulty.

Experienced professionals claimed that the highest extent of the vocal range for female singers is usually D_5. Singing notes higher than this is considered to be very difficult, and those who can do it are respected. Aye Kyi, who is well-known in part for being able to sing high notes, says that this is one way that singers can "show their talent." On the other hand, male singers routinely sing up to G_4. Again, Burmese audiences appreciate the few male singers who can sing higher than this, but singing above middle C—well into what Westerners understand as a "high tenor" range—is quite normal.

In effect, male and female Burmese pop singers often sing in approximately the same range. This is evident in one recently-released VCD called "U Saw Nu: Vocal Lesson." In this recording, a famous Yangon-area singing teacher works through some vocal exercises first with a group of young men and later, with a group of young women. The teacher uses most of the same exercises, in the same keys, for both groups. Interestingly, the students sing up to the exact pitches that my informants told me were the typical high notes for Burmese singers: D_5 for women, and G_4 for men.

While conducting research in Yangon, I heard out-of-tune singing rather more frequently than I would expect to hear it among professional musicians in the West. But in-tuneness did not seem to be a big concern for my interlocutors. For example, after sitting through a choir rehearsal in which Cho Cho Saing played a dreadfully out-of-tune piano to accompany the singing, I queried her about it. Did she feel the piano was out of tune? Yes, she said, the piano goes out of tune frequently because of the intense heat and humidity in the city. She said that the normal procedure was to call a piano tuner when she had time to do so, and that she had not had time recently. She was also unsure how often, on average, the piano got tuned, although she was the person responsible for making this happen. Another example: in the U Saw Nu video mentioned above, at the beginning of Lesson Six, the assembled male and female students sing very sharp—so sharp that the sound is a semitone higher than the keyboard pitch. U Saw Nu does not comment, but continues with the exercise.

In another telling incident, I interviewed an organizer for the TV show *Melody World.* He told me that the judges on the show evaluate the competing singers according to the "five components of good singing: pitch, timing, tone color, performance, and diction."[33] He went on to explain that pitch problems are by far the most common weakness that the judges encounter in contestants, and that only those who can sing consistently in tune make it to the final rounds. However, when I watched the final episode of the second season (aired on January 4, 2009), I noted that the judges picked the most out-of-tune singer as the winner for the evening. Her opening pitches (A♭–G–F above middle C) were terribly flat, and she struggled to hit other notes as the song progressed. At the end of the show, the four finalists performed a group number, and the other woman in the group could clearly be heard singing flat on her highest pitch, a B above middle C.

Of course, it is understandable that these singers might have problems singing at the top of their range in a nerve-wracking, nationally televised event. And it is worth noting that I subsequently heard both women perform live, and both sang well in tune at that time. However, it is striking that during this culminating episode of a national singing contest, the judges' professed concern for in-tune singing clearly did not weigh heavily in their evaluation of the singers.

Intrigued by the striking opposition to my own Western experience, where singing in tune seems to be the *sine qua non* of good singing, I repeatedly asked my interviewees to either describe good singing or to give me a quick lesson in singing. "What do I need to know or to do to be a good singer?" I said. As I discovered, Burmese musicians only rarely focus on issues of technique. Not one person, for example, mentioned in-tuneness, vibrato, vowel shaping, or vocal projection.[34] A few talked about health practices—avoiding alcohol or fatty foods, for example, or getting enough sleep. But the main thing to know about singing, according to Burmese musicians, is that a good singer communicates the mood of the song. As with much of their musical vocabulary, my Burmese informants used an English word to elucidate an important concept. The "mood," or emotional affect, of a song is so important, in fact, that most people mentioned it first when we discussed the issue of good singing, and some mentioned nothing else.[35]

Burmese musicians believe that mood is an identifiable property located within a song. Beyond that, the concept is somewhat amorphous. Mood is clearly not a function of lyrics, since *copy thachin* composers repeatedly say that they can sense the mood of a English-language song even when they cannot understand the lyrics. Further, they say that when composing government songs, they virtually always write *own tunes*, since the "mood" of preexisting English-language songs would never match the lyrics required by the SPDC.[36] Mood cannot be directly linked to performance styles or to timbral effects, either. As arranger Theingi Zaw explained to me, the "mood" of a song determines what kind of arrangement he will create. For him, then, mood is already present and distinguishable when a song exists in *demo* form—that is, when only the basic lyrics, melody, and harmonies have been recorded. Presumably, then, the mood is independent of the timbres and textures contributed by professionals who improvise large portions of their parts for the final recording.

Mood may be hard to pin down, but this in no way reduces its importance. Indeed, professional performers insist that they must be able to enter into the mood of the song, and to share that with an audience, in order to be successful in their artistic endeavors. Indeed, producer Kaung Lin Lin complained that singers' focus on "mood" causes all kinds of problems, because they frequently refuse to show up to recording sessions until they feel they are in the mood of the song.

Learning Music in Private Lessons and Institutions

As I mentioned in chapter 1, the majority of people working in the Yangon pop music scene served long apprenticeships in the city's tourist hotels and restaurants, where they developed their abilities to learn and remember large numbers of songs in order to be able to play them on request. Three musicians currently working in such venues told me that they know hundreds of songs from memory.[37] Furthermore, they say that it takes them roughly one half-day, maximum, to learn a new song.[38] These musicians are representative of Yangon-based pop musicians as a group. Their experience shows that they and their colleagues are able to familiarize themselves with (and then confidently perform) songs in short order, because they have been required to do so by the institutions where they developed their performance skills.

Interestingly, though, none of the musicians I interviewed for this project described their hotel experience as a kind of "training" or "apprenticeship," as I am doing here. Rather, when I asked them how they learned to play and sing at a professional level, they pointed to times and places where they had learned music in their youth. According to these informants, Burmese musicians usually acquire their skills in one of three ways: in private lessons, at institutions that offer music instruction, or by teaching themselves.

Private lessons

Some musicians take individual lessons with music teachers in their home communities. Lessons usually take place weekly, in either the teacher's or the student's home. In every case that I was able to identify, the teacher belonged to the same ethnic group as the student. This may be simply a matter of geography (students usually take lessons in their own villages or urban neighborhoods, and these communities are, even today, often ethnically homogeneous); but it partially explains why members of some ethnic minority groups are so overrepresented among Burmese pop musicians.

Music is not one of the subjects taught in public schools in Burma, so Burmese children are not learning the basics of one musical language or another. In "mixed" (predominantly Burman Buddhist) areas, where the monastery is the most important focal point for the residents, Burman teachers often teach the heterophonic structure of traditional Burmese music. In areas centered around churches, Christian *tain-yin-tha* teachers usually teach European classical and pop styles. Chin, Karen, or Kachin teachers tend to teach fundamental concepts such as melody and accompaniment. Because this training is so directly applicable to the performance of pop music, *tain-yin-tha* youngsters often have a more direct path to success in Western pop music than do Burmans.

In their individual lessons, Burmese music students usually learn the basic theoretical concepts that I outlined above (chord families, beats, and in some cases, notation). At least this is what all of the adults who recalled their lesson experiences for me remembered. Musicians said that their teachers taught them how to read both "Chinese" and "international" notes, and explained to them how chords and rhythms are organized. Now grown up, students did not recall learning much beyond these foundational ideas from their teachers. Indeed, most said that they took lessons for only a matter of months at most— presumably because it does not take much more time than that to cover this material. Shway Nyunt, though, proved to be a notable exception. He shared that his teacher, a Burman Buddhist like himself, was fluent in "English, Burmese, and modern music." This teacher taught the music theory (the different rhythm styles and melody structures) for each of these traditions. In addition, the teacher taught composing styles, singing techniques, "emotion in music," and even Burmese literature. Shway Nyunt acknowledged that his teacher was "great" by local standards, and that he had received a richer education than many of his colleagues.

Some Burmese pop musicians have received institutional training of some sort, though many members of the community told me that "there is no music school in Burma."[39] This is not accurate, as I will explain, but the fact that so many professional musicians believe it to be true reflects their tendency to think of music education institutions as being restricted to formal conservatories and the like (of which there are very few). In fact, during my fieldwork in Yangon I discovered that formal musical learning takes place in a number of institutional settings, and that some members of the pop music scene point directly to this training as centrally important to their development as performers. These settings include schools dedicated to music instruction, churches, and parachurch organizations.

Music Schools

Yangon is home to number of music schools, founded and directed for the most part by teachers who trained outside of Burma. Some are small storefront operations in which a single teacher offers private and group lessons. If the business grows large enough, the founding teacher may deputize one or more of the senior students to teach beginners. Cherry explained that she developed her pop music chops in a little school like this near her home. She had some previous knowledge about Western musical concepts, and so, she says, it took her only three months to "learn the chords." After mastering the various chord families, she began to work as a teacher in the school.

Ma Khin Sein's path was more circuitous. She first began working as a clerk in a well-known Yangon musical café called "Mr. Guitar." Seizing the opportunity, she prevailed upon a fellow worker, a young man who already knew how to play, to teach her how to play drums. When the store was not busy with customers, he taught her the basics by rote. Today she works full-time as a drummer and is becoming well known in the Yangon industry.

Two of the best-known music schools in Yangon at the moment are the Art Music Academy and Gita Meit. Each was founded in the past decade by an energetic, charismatic teacher, using a conservatory model to deliver music education to committed young adults. At each school, students range from eight or nine to thirty years of age, with the core group of students being in their midtwenties. This core group usually attends multiple classes per week for years at a time. Though neither school, as yet, offers a formal diploma, the reality is that the students are experiencing post-high-school intensive training in one subject area, rather like students taking undergraduate degrees at universities.[40] At both schools, the founding directors are determined not to limit the instruction to Western music theory and performance, although, at this point, such instruction comprises the bulk of the lessons.

Kit Young, the founder of Gita Meit, says that many of her students arrive saying that they want to study there so that they can become "famous," although this is an unlikely outcome for most students.[41] To date, one of the school's graduates has embarked on a promising career as a pop music pianist, and the school's choir, the Gita Meit Voices, has become very active. The choir performs at many events around the city, including at some live shows, and participates in some pop music recordings. It has even been featured at the annual Yangon City FM awards banquet—effectively cementing Gita Meit's place in the Burmese pop music scene.[42] The Art Music Academy, which is a little older, has now produced a handful of veritable stars. The two DJs at the center of *Yaw-thama-hmwe* (described in chapter 2), for example, trained at the AMA, as did the two young singers known as No.

The founders of the Art Music Academy and the Gita Meit school both insist that their schools aim to inculcate not only an understanding of Western music, but also other, more fundamental, "foreign" ideas. Kit Young says that her school's first goal is to encourage a mindset that she believes is largely missing from contemporary Burmese culture. In fact, she states bluntly that her school "is not a music education project." Gita Meit, she says, focuses on teaching young adults two things: to develop self-confidence and to be socially responsible—that is, to develop skills and then to use those traits to work with others to build a stronger society. She says that she senses an identity crisis among aspiring Burmese musicians: "They think we are not good musicians because we are not good *Western* musicians." She hopes that the school will give the students the tools to master Western classical music, but more importantly, that it will offer students the chance to succeed in a tradition that is associated with high-status (foreign, white-skinned) people.

Ultimately she hopes that her students can deploy their newfound self-confidence in the wider Burmese society, where hierarchical relationships between "upper" and "lower" people have, in her view, made it difficult to sustain mutually beneficial relationships between people. She points out that her school is not intended to be a conservatory, but is deliberately modeled after the community music school concept articulated by Dr. Herbert Zipper, the classically-educated conductor who survived the Holocaust and went on to be a leader in the community music school movement in the United States.[43] Therefore, Gita Meit emphasizes social service projects rather than competitions, exams, and rankings. Gita Meit students have undertaken tasks such as teaching music in one of the poorest neighborhoods in Yangon, delivering supplies to victims of Hurricane Nargis in the delta region, and presenting free performances for audiences as far away as Mandalay.[44]

Ko Doo, the leader of the AMA, was quoted in the *Myanmar Times* in 2005 saying that his school aims to change the thinking of Myanmar people, who [are] used to spoon-feeding and parrot-style learning methods. International music-teaching techniques focus on creativity and improvisation. But in Myanmar, most people are reluctant to do something new. That's why I always drive my students to change their attitudes. I want them to be music creators, not imitators.[45]

Accordingly, he teaches composition and encourages his students to write songs and to share their work with others. (And two of his students did exactly this when I visited the school in 2007.) For Ko Doo, fostering innovation is primary—more important than teaching all of the formal theory and performances classes. Interestingly, he sees innovation as an "international" rather than a local way of thinking.[46] Ko Doo emphasizes that he is trying to teach his students to have an "open mind," that is, to cultivate the "mental flexibility" that is necessary to think new thoughts and create new music. He bemoans the fact that many older Burmese people are still interested in maintaining social hierarchy and are therefore unwilling to share their knowledge with younger people. (He cites a Burmese "tradition" that a teacher never teaches all that he knows, so that the student will never supersede the master.) In addition, in the wake of Cyclone Nargis, he is starting to combine his ideas for a music school with his desire to do social service work. Accordingly, he recently initiated a new project, Green Island Education, which grew out of the free music classes he is now offering to young people affected by the cyclone.

Churches

Christian churches and parachurch organizations offer significant amounts of musical instruction, both in Yangon and in other urban centers. In fact, such organizations are probably the most overlooked factor in the broader context of Western musical learning in Burma. Some of the most prominent Burmese pop stars point to church-based music instruction as their main source of training.

In churches, formal musical instruction, mostly focused on choral singing, often takes place during the time designated for Sunday school. In the few Sunday school classes that I observed, approximately fifty percent of the class time was devoted to singing, not just for fun or worship, but in preparation for performance during an upcoming service. During Sunday School classes, the teachers instructed the children on part-singing, diction, posture, and other technical points.

One of the most important learning opportunities that churches provide to young musicians is the late-afternoon youth-oriented service that takes place each Sunday at churches all across the country. The format for this service (which was always held at 4:00 p.m. in the churches I visited) is roughly the same as that of other services: opening prayer and announcements, followed by singing and a sermon. However, during youth services, the singing portion is open-ended, and all congregants who wish to come to the front to share a song or musical performance are "warmly welcome" to do so, as Soe Htun says. Performances usually consist of soloists or groups of singers presenting the gospel song of their choice to the accompaniment of whatever guitars, keyboards, and percussion may be available. Performers are not usually greeted with applause (this being forbidden in most churches), but each and every one gets an attentive listening. The youth service represents a chance for aspiring pop singers to become familiar with the use of microphones, the feeling of being on stage, and the necessity of performing without having spent much (or any) time rehearsing with the instrumentalists.

Importantly, the "youth" service is open to people of any age, and frequently very young children sing solos at this service. Every congregation I visited included at least a couple of five-year-olds who belted out pop standards, singing flawlessly from memory.[47] Seeing these kindergartners perform at such a high level, without much or any prior rehearsal with the band, made it clear that churches' youth services represent a valuable learning experience where up-and-coming musicians can hone their skills weekly. It also helped me appreciate the statements of people such as Nu Nu Win, who said, "I started singing in church when I was three years old." To have repeated opportunities to perform pop music in a supportive environment is to have a chance at future professional success. Thus churches are contributing to the training of pop stars in a tangible way.

These youth services can become so musically engaging that they draw an audience beyond that of the church congregation. For example, I attended the 4:00 p.m. service at a nondenominational church in North Yangon where, as many city residents know, Chit San Maung, the lead guitarist for Iron Cross, plays guitar every Sunday. Although I arrived before the appointed time, the sanctuary of the church and the overflow space were already packed to bursting. Chit San Maung and two other professional musicians (whom I recognized from my time spent in recording studios) provided exciting accompaniment for two young men who sang solos, and then to a tiny girl who sang "Free of Charge."[48] Best of all, from the point of view of the many young men who attended church that day in order to take in a free live show, the musicians improvised a blistering instrumental postlude while the ushers were stacking chairs.

The most consistent explicit musical instruction in churches takes place in choir rehearsals. In all the churches that I either attended or inquired about, the choir is open to all interested teenagers and adults. The choristers always sing from hymnals (or books of choral anthems), and therefore the choir leader must explain to the members how to read staff notation. In some cases, such as in the church I attended most often, the explanation is cursory at best.

Choir rehearsals often resemble rehearsals in the pop music scene: that is, they are used as an occasion to sing through the repertoire once, with no time given to practicing or repetition. However, in other churches, the musical instruction given during choir rehearsal is so helpful that now-famous professionals point to their church choir experience as foundational to their success. Aye Kyi exemplified many others by saying that her church's choir conductor taught her about meters, singing in parts and reading "1234 notes"—skills that she uses now in her professional career in pop music. Cherry went even further, saying that the choir conductor at the church she grew up in is her "hero." This woman provided choir members with a "remarkable experience," because she taught the complexities of vocal tone, English pronunciation, and dynamic expression, eventually leading the choir in performing a complicated cantata.

Churches also facilitate other, more focused, opportunities for musical learning. Some of the largest Yangon churches, for example, run two-week-long summer music camps for teenagers from across the country. I attended one of these camps and was impressed by the rigorous training on offer. The one hundred or so enthusiastic young people in attendance worked through a theory textbook and participated in choir rehearsals each day. The program consumed most of the working day. Parachurch groups also coordinate music education opportunities. For example, in 2008, the Karen Baptist Convention organized a week-long song-writing seminar for interested members. The convention invited three Nashville-based songwriters to come to Yangon to instruct aspiring Burmese composers in the art of the pop song.

In February 2008, I attended a meeting of the Church Music Institute of Myanmar to get a sense of how such programs come to be. The CMIM was founded in 2003 because, as the chair of the meeting explained, "There is no music school in Myanmar," and the Myanmar Baptist Convention saw a need for young people to get training in order to sustain the tradition of choral singing in Burmese churches. During the three-hour meeting, the committee members planned their annual monthlong music training course. The subjects to be taught, they decided, would include ear training, sight-singing, music theory, conducting, how to lead a choir,[49] vocal development, hymnology, church music history, music ministry, piano, keyboard, violin, guitar, and vocal lessons. They decided to use the textbooks they have used in the past: a Burmese translation of a theory book published by the Associated Board of the Royal Schools of Music, and an English-language ear-training textbook.

At the end of the of course, the committee decided, each student must sit for a juried exam; this aspect of the course is likely an attraction for many Burmese students, since those who pass the exam will receive a certificate attesting to their achievement.[50] Interestingly, the CMIM committee is interested in branching out into teaching other musical subjects. The committee members discussed the possibility of adding classes called "Eastern Music" (which would focus on the basics of Burmese traditional music, using the recordings of Burmese piano master U Ko Ko as a starting point) and "Computer Music" (which would focus on learning to use recording and editing software).

The meeting revealed the breadth of educational opportunity that para-church groups in Burma are able to provide. It also illuminated the truism that many Burmese people shared with me: members of *tain-yin-tha* minority groups are prominent in the pop music industry because "they learn to sing in church." The group of people at the CMIM meeting united under the umbrella of "Myanmar," and they conducted their meeting entirely in Burmese, but all seven of them were in fact Sgaw Karen. Four of the seven are employed full-time as music instructors at Karen seminaries. Although musical leadership in the Burmese Christian community is theoretically open to Christians of any ethnic background, the reality is that the overwhelming majority of that leadership is provided by non-Burmans. This makes sense, since the large majority of Christians in Burma are not Burman, but rather members of *tain-yin-tha* groups.

In addition, the church tends to focus on Western forms of music education, teaching sound concepts organized according to paradigms developed in the Western academy, and even relying on textbooks developed in the West. (Unsurprisingly, given that Burmese music teachers often rely on Western expertise, I was treated as a kind of resource at the CMIM meeting. The chair told me that the committee has in the past recruited guest teachers from the United States, and asked me to recommend individuals who might be available for the 2009 course.) Therefore, *tain-yin-tha* Christians do, in many cases, have more access to Western musical education than do Buddhist Burmans, and so a larger percentage of these groups are able to proceed with careers in Western-style pop music.

Burmans who wish to learn about Western musical traditions often study privately with *tain-yin-tha* Christians. I saw for myself how this situation develops: a Burman Buddhist friend of mine, who lives in downtown Yangon, attempted to find a piano teacher for her daughter in late 2008. She said that all the teachers she had been able to find were members of the "national races."[51] One day when we were together, I saw her approach a mutual acquaintance, a professional keyboardist, for advice. He turned out to be a Christian Sgaw Karen, and he recommended another Christian Karen piano teacher: the pianist from the biggest church in the downtown area, who was apparently accepting students.

What do aspiring musicians learn in Christian institutions? First, they learn how to read "international notes." In fact, all of the institutional music education programs I encountered emphasized note-reading and introductory music theory, and indeed this facet of their programs seemed to be one of the features that drew students. Second, choral singing seems to be a central focus of music training programs both in churches and in music schools. Indeed, Kit Young of Gita Meit told me that thrice-weekly choir rehearsals are compulsory in her school because one of her goals is to counteract "the stereotype that

Burmans can't sing." By attending choir rehearsals at the Gita Meit school, a music camp, and two seminaries, I discerned some common trends. For example, choirs are usually not formally conducted. The conductor often serves as pianist and vocal coach, but rarely stands in front of the group to keep time during the performance. Nevertheless, I will use the word "conductor" here to distinguish this person from the choir leader.

At all of the choir rehearsals I observed, the conductor's focus was on note learning. He or she led the choir in singing their parts using solfège syllables. Without exception, all of the choirs I saw demonstrated high levels of competence in sight-singing, and so the parts usually came together in a short amount of time. Conductors also talked about posture, projecting one's voice, and the importance of pronouncing English words correctly. I was fascinated to note, however, that conductors almost never spoke about the importance of dynamic expression or word painting. The lack of focus on expression was so glaring to me (coming from a "Sing it with feeling!" background) that I began to question conductors about it.

All the conductors I spoke with affirmed the importance of using expression (and especially of varying the dynamics) in singing. They acknowledged that their choirs do not usually sing with the amount of dynamic variation they might wish for.[52] One conductor joked, "My choir only knows how to sing three different ways: loud, louder, and loudest!" Others were a little defensive, saying that the singers in their choirs know that they are supposed to pay attention to dynamic markings in scores, but fail to do so. When I asked one conductor why he had not talked about this during the two-hour rehearsal I had just observed, he said that he simply had not had time to address the issue. This after a session in which he had had time to rehearse four songs, give a fifteen-minute break, and allow numerous choir members to try out their conducting skills by directing one song each! I began to wonder if my questions were off-base, since there seemed to be such a disconnect between what conductors told me they expected and what they asked of their choirs during rehearsal. Ultimately I decided that these conductors simply have other priorities.

Like the musicians in the professional pop scene, choir conductors value efficiency, and expect singers to learn large amounts of repertoire quickly. Choir rehearsals often—not always—resembled the January 2008 rock band rehearsal that I observed: generally, the group would sing through each song from start to finish, with no glaring mistakes, using solfège syllables. After some verbal pointers from the conductor, the choir would sing the same song once more, with the words, and then move on to another song. Given the time constraints imposed by this kind of rehearsing, there is indeed not enough time to focus on the details of dynamic variations, articulations, tempo changes, and so on. And it should be said that even without these kinds of niceties, Burmese choirs do generally sound wonderful: they sing correct pitches and rhythms, creating a uniform ensemble sound, and they always do it with full-throated enthusiasm. Concern for stylistic subtlety is, for Burmese choir conductors, a little beside the point. As Cherry told me, "I only recently realized that people in foreign countries think more about expression and take much longer to learn a piece [of music], when I saw the movie *Shine.*"[53]

Self-Teaching: Learning by Imitating

Among Burmese pop musicians, by far the most common way to acquire musical knowledge is to teach oneself. Burmese people do not usually describe this process as "teaching myself," however. They sometimes say that they "learn by hearing" or "learn by looking" or "learn by heart." Most often, they use the lovely Burmese expression *kya-saya-myin-saya* which, literally translated, means, "Teacher that I hear, teacher that I see." We might call them "role models." For example, Myo Myo Thant said, "I didn't have any formal lessons (other than Sunday School), but all of the shows I attended and all of the singers that I heard were my *kya-saya-myin-saya.*" Others who used the same expression used it in the same way, as shorthand for the concept that one learns by observing and imitating others who are not intending to serve in a formal teaching role.

Aspiring Burmese pop musicians most often look to performers on Anglo-American recordings as their *kya-saya-myin-saya*. In fact, in the course of my interviews, I only rarely heard Burmese musicians cite other Burmese musicians as teachers or role models.[54] Htay Cho, for example, remembered his *kya-saya-myin-saya* with great specificity. He recounted how, when he was a young aspiring musician, he approached Burma's two most famous guitarists for counsel. They did not advise him to follow their own example, but rather to listen to well-known rock guitarists from the West, including Joe Satriani, Vinny Moore, and Eddie Van Halen. They also recommended that he use specific Anglo-American recordings as teaching tools, including the guitar solo from "Hello," by Lionel Richie, and albums made by Deep Purple and Pink Floyd.

Burmese musicians look to Anglo-American recordings as their teachers even when they have an outstanding Burmese model close at hand. Khine Ta Tun, whose mother is one of the most prominent pop singers in Burma, cited the Ramones and David Bowie as his first musical "heroes." Nu Nu Win's father had a long career as a guitarist and composer; but when I asked her about her role models, she said that she loves Avril Lavigne and Pink and tries to sound exactly like them, omitting any mention of her father.

I asked my informants to describe how they learn from their *kya-saya-myin-saya*. The musicians consistently said that they learned by listening to the recordings, over and over, eventually singing and playing along with the recorded sounds. For many of them, this kind of learning began in childhood, when they listened repeatedly to songs they enjoyed. At this point, young musicians become aware of a developing passion for pop music ("*wah-tha-na bah-deh*," or, "It is my hobby.") Over time this kind of listening became more purposeful, as young people began to picture themselves as performers. Htay Cho described his approach as the "pause-and-rewind method." He said that he listened to short sections of recordings, attempted to play them, and then repeated this as needed. He added that he was able to slow down the speed of the tape using a control button on his cassette player.

Musicians who teach themselves in this way usually do it when they are alone. Thus, although groups may not practice together, individuals certainly practice for long hours by themselves, particularly when they are teenagers and still developing their craft. Of course, sometimes musicians do listen to recordings together, particularly when they are working professionals who need to be able to imitate a specific song for a performance or a recording. However, musicians did not cite these experiences when they talked about "learning" music. Instead, they referred to the time period they associated with their musical training—their teenage years—and recalled how they had learned the basics of the art.

One might be tempted to explain the tendency for Burmese pop musicians to teach themselves by referring to notions of Burmese individualism. Certainly, other anthropologists of Burmese culture have remarked that Burmese society is marked by factionalism rather than collective unity.[55] Burmese people themselves sometimes sarcastically explain the nature of their politics (even the idealistic prodemocracy movement is marked by infighting and the continual creation of new splinter groups) by joking that "when you have two Burmese people in a room together, you have at least three different opinions." The fact that many pop musicians work primarily as individuals, coming together with others for one performance only, may be one manifestation of the Burmese preference for individual activity. But I do not think that their tendency to rely on self-instruction stems from the same root.

Burmese pop musicians do not primarily learn by self-teaching because they are Burmese; rather, they tend to learn this way because they are pop musicians, and pop musicians around the world learn their skills this way. Lucy Green, who studied British pop musicians in order to discover how it is that they learn to perform their music, has written the most substantive piece of scholarship describing this process. She discovered the same tendencies among British musicians that I am identifying here as common to Burmese musicians: that is, they learn to play their instruments primarily by listening to and copying recordings,[56] usually in solitude.[57] Although aspiring British musicians have much more access to private lessons and institutional training than do their Burmese counterparts (music is taught in government schools in the United Kingdom), they, too, mostly learn informally. For British pop musicians also, notation is used as a "supplement" and a "memory-jogger" rather than as the principal source for learning new music.[58]

Interestingly, Green found that in the United Kingdom, informal learning practices are not considered true learning, even by the musicians themselves.[59] Therefore British pop musicians often feel somewhat embarrassed about their learning methods. In Burma, by contrast, the musicians I met were proud of their history of self-teaching, in part because their society valorizes learning from *kya-saya-myin-saya*. For Buddhists especially, the notion that one relies on oneself is deeply respectable, in one's spiritual work of making merit as well as in daily activities. Therefore, during interviews Burmese musicians were glad to tell me about their experiences of teaching themselves.

Indeed, recording engineers and band managers in the Yangon pop music industry also said proudly that they were self-taught in their respective professions.[60] While they regretted the paucity of music schools in their country, they were happy to depend on themselves for musical training. As Thuza, who has reached the pinnacle of success in Burma's pop music scene, explained: "I am still learning from *kya-saya-myin-saya*. Every time I go to a recording session, I watch the others to learn more about singing in harmony, about music notes, and about guitar chords."

The Scarcity of Formal Criticism

It is important to note that Burmese musicians usually do *not* learn in one important way: they do not learn from formal, public criticism. By and large, they do not have the opportunity to receive comments from a music critic, nor to read such comments directed at their peers. This is because the profession of music critic is virtually nonexistent. Now, the Burmese do have a word for "critic" and they do sometimes use this word to describe journalists who write about music, film, literature, or other forms of cultural production. However, as far as I can determine, these "critics" generally do not write analytical opinion pieces about artists' work. The writing may be descriptive, and it will give facts about the subject of the article, such as a new *series*, and it may include the writer's opinion—but that opinion will always be a positive one.

This is the recollection of all of the musicians I queried about this. Aung Shwe, who has nearly thirty years' experience in the Yangon pop music industry, said that he can not remember ever reading a negative review of a concert or a *series*. Kyaw Naing Oo, whose experience is nearly as extensive as that of Aung Shwe, said that journalists sometimes do (negatively) criticize a famous singer's songs in print. However he instantly added that such comments are the result of petty conflicts. "Like maybe they [the singer and the interviewer] didn't get along during the interview," he offered. From this perspective, any negative comments about music are seen as deeply biased, and therefore are unlikely to be taken seriously by musicians.

I continued my search for a music critic until the next-to-last week of my time in Burma, when I met a Yangon-based pop culture journalist, Daw Khin Soe. She understood instantly why I was unsuccessful. "Journalists don't want to be called critics," she said bluntly.[61] She said she was unsurprised that I had been unable to find anyone who would consent to an interview, since people in her field don't see themselves as critics and might be offended to be approached as such. Daw Khin Soe acknowledged that sincere criticism was more common in the past (in the 1970s, she hazarded) but that even then, all music and movie critics, like most Burmese journalists, wrote under pseudonyms. Now, she said, these kinds of reviews are extremely rare.[62] Instead, articles about pop culture celebrities tend to be based on interviews with those celebrities, and the questions usually go along the lines of: "When is your next *series* going to be released? Who is the songwriter on that *series*? How do you personally feel about the *series*?" She noted that Burmese magazine readers tend to be interested in the stars' personal lives, and so her responsibility as a journalist includes asking about the famous person's family, for example.[63] However, the average interview lasts only fifteen minutes, she said. Evidently there is hardly time to go beyond basic facts, and certainly not enough time for a wide-ranging discussion.

It is important to point out that on rare occasions, Burmese music and musicians may be publicly criticized. In the TV show *Melody World*, for example, three judges comment regularly, and often negatively, about performances. And at one point in the midseason, the format of the show allows members of the live audience to voice their opinions of the performances. Another example of musical criticism occurs weekly during the New Song Class on Yangon City FM Radio. During the broadcast, a pop music composer of great experience, U Htun Naung, plays an unreleased recording made by an aspiring singer or group, and then comments extensively on the work. However, these kinds of formal, public criticisms are few and far between in Burma. Therefore, developing musicians do not often have the opportunity to read or hear criticism of their own and others' ideas and to reflect accordingly.[64]

Generally, Burmese pop musicians do not benefit from criticism they might receive in private, either. Rehearsals are few and far between, and when they occur, the participants usually do not spend a lot of time discussing how to improve their performance. I think that explicit, articulated criticism is uncommon because musicians are committed to maintaining an egalitarian social structure in the studio. To criticize another person would be to imply that one is somehow more knowledgeable or more competent than that person. Therefore, critical comments are rare in studio and in rehearsals.

During interviews, industry members confirmed my own limited observations about this. They said that global criticisms of performances (e.g., "That wasn't good") are virtually never spoken. Aung Shwe told me (and I observed it to be true) that he sometimes spends hours digitally correcting out-of-tune singers; evidently no one tells singers while they are recording tracks that they should alter their pitch. Guitarist and recording engineer Myint Oo confirmed that criticisms are almost never voiced in studio. He said that with the exception of a composer giving directions to musicians about how to play his composition, musicians do not comment critically on each other's performances. He did say that if a musician's playing is "*very* bad," then others in the studio might say something like, "Why don't you take some time to practice?" His comment reveals that practicing, as well as criticism, is the exception rather than the norm in Burmese pop music culture.

The Link between Belief and Practice

Burmese musicians' culture of learning and rehearsing developed in the context of their religious beliefs. Whether they are Buddhist, Christian, or Muslim, almost all of them believe that their ability comes from some supernatural source. And this belief leads to a kind of fatalism, an attitude that says: An individual has no control over his talent, because talent comes (or does not come) from God. And if one does have talent, then of course one can learn quickly and well; extensive training and rehearsals are not necessary. At least, this is the argument of some of the influential music educators mentioned in this chapter. A 2005 *Myanmar Times* article sums it up:

> Many of Myanmar's most famous singers have had no training whatsoever. Famous pop diva, Htun Eaindra Bo, said she believed her success as a singer was due to "san," a god-given gift, and she did not need to take any lessons. Popular rock singer R Zar Ni said he also believed he owed his success to "san" and had no interest in formal training. This is the mindset Ko Du, U Saw Nu, and the Gitameit team said they are struggling against.[65]

Indeed, it seems that progressive music teachers must continue to struggle if they intend to counter religiously rooted beliefs and practices that hold sway among the most influential musical figures in Burma. Furthermore, they will need to acknowledge that the current norm is the norm in part because it has certain advantages: it fosters strong aural skills among musicians, and it allows them to maximize their earnings, since they do not spend much time in unpaid rehearsals. Of course, the musicians who are operating according to this norm would benefit from considering how a change in their learning and rehearsal culture might be for the better. Spending more time working in groups and experimenting with music would probably lead to more innovation in pop musicians' creative output. And creating new music may shortly become not only an artistic but an economic imperative—as I will explain in the next chapter.

Chapter Four

Six Facets of the Burmese Pop Music Industry

The Myaynigone junction, one of the biggest and busiest intersections in Yangon, is located on Pyay Lan (formerly Prome Road). This junction is well known to all city residents in part because in 2007 a huge electronic billboard, the first in the city, was installed there. The "big TV," as it is called, plays an endless loop of advertisements for locally owned businesses. Of the two ads I remember best—probably because I saw them so often—one was for a brand of iced tea (during which a supple tenor sang the praises of said tea to the tune of John Denver's "Take Me Home, Country Roads") and the other for a photography studio (accompanied by the theme from *Mission Impossible*). The combination of current technology, brash capitalism, and American hit music tempted me to think of this junction as the Times Square of Yangon; but I resisted using the label, because Burmese people do not, and I was committed to understanding their city, as best I could, on their terms. What my friends often mentioned was that this junction is the site of the famous Dagon Center, an upscale shopping mall where one can buy musical recordings and concert tickets. Accordingly, I headed off toward Dagon Center on my first afternoon in the city, and I returned frequently thereafter.

Entering Dagon Center is no uncomplicated task. The junction is the site of a major bus stop and a sidewalk market. During shopping hours, public buses, private chauffeured cars, taxis, trishaws, pedestrians, and even the odd man on horseback all compete to arrive at the entrance. The noise is almost deafening: the bus conductors holler their vehicles' destinations, taxi drivers call out to potential customers, beggars plead for money, and parking attendants blow furiously on whistles while directing the never-ending stream of cars and SUVs entering the parking lot. Crossing the street is tricky; the traffic is mostly uncontrolled, with no lanes marked on the road, no speed limit, and aggressive driving on the part of most drivers. Adults often hold hands when they attempt to dart across this particular junction, as much for mutual reassurance as for safety. But it's worth the trouble to make your way there. Once you finally make it to the front steps of the shopping center, you can feel the blast of air conditioning, a relief from the year-round tropical heat.

At the top of the steps, all customers have to pass through a metal detector, submit their bags to be searched, and then allow themselves to be patted down by security guards. The security system was installed after Dagon Center was bombed on May 7, 2005. The bombing occurred within minutes of explosions at two other locations that symbolized power and affluence: another well-known shopping center, and the Yangon Trade Center. Government reports at the time indicated that 11 people were killed and 162 wounded in the bombings. The state-controlled newspaper, *The New Light of Myanmar*, immediately blamed the bombings on "terrorists," pointing the finger at their perennial enemies—the ethnic insurgents that operate in the border states and urban prodemocracy activists.[1] The government offered no proof to back this assertion, and never brought any suspects to trial.

Burmese citizens had their own opinions. I was told, for example, that "everyone knows" that the bombings were the result of internecine fighting among members of the army: one faction, perhaps those loyal to the recently deposed prime minister and chief of intelligence, was attempting to undermine the authority of another faction, presumably that of the head of state, General Than Shwe.[2] The fact that fire trucks, normally parked in a station nearly a mile away, were observed in front of Dagon Center an hour before the bomb exploded lends some credence to this theory.[3] What the government does not say is that the 2005 shopping mall bombings are part of a pattern. During the last decade, civilian targets all over Burma have been bombed at the rate of nearly one per month.[4] The bombings regularly remind the public that the country is unstable.

However, there was no sense of impending doom hovering over Dagon Center in 2007 when I first began to visit it. The mall was flooded with well-heeled customers—youth wearing blue jeans and sporting dyed hair, young mothers wearing modest yet fashionable dresses, and middle-aged professionals in business attire. Their affluence was evident in the foreign-made goods that they were able to acquire—sunglasses and jewelry, ExerSaucers, imported peanut butter and chocolate. The security procedures seemed lax. The guards performed their duties perfunctorily, barely glancing in the bags they checked.

At the Star Mart, the Burmese pop music industry is represented by a small retail shop that sells the latest releases of all of the biggest stars in the Burmese pop scene, as well as foreign-made recordings—cassette tapes, CDs, DVDs, and VCDs—on floor-to-ceiling, wall-to-wall shelves. When I visited the store, music was booming over the sound system. I noticed a "Top Twenty" list, at the entrance, listing the recordings sold there, separated into the categories of "English" and "Burmese."

Customers did not seem to consult the list, though, and the sales clerks had difficulty answering questions about it when I asked. As a foreign researcher, I was interested in the way the list organizes information: the "English" category,

Figure 4.1. Retail shop selling recordings in Dagon Center

for example, includes all Western-made recordings, including an album by the Columbian-born artist Shakira. (In Burma, "English" songs are songs sung in English, and singers of English songs are almost always believed to be Americans.[5] Every time I informed Burmese friends that some of their favorite "American" singers—such as Céline Dion, Bryan Adams, Shania Twain, and Avril Lavigne—are actually Canadians, they expressed surprise.) On the "Burmese" albums, most of the album titles and artists' names are written in Burmese. Group albums—*series* to which a group of solo artists have contributed songs—predominate in this category. On these *series*, the singers do not sing together, but rather perform as soloists, with a backup band. One singer usually contributes one or two tracks; on an average group album, the listener can hear twelve or fifteen different singers. Duet albums are a subset of group albums: on a duet album, two singers sing six or seven songs each—but rarely sing a duet.

The average price of a CD at the Dagon Center Star Mart in 2008 was 1,600 *kyat*, or a little more than $1. To put this in context: the average daily wage in Yangon that year was 1,000 *kyat*. To earn this amount, workers often put in twelve-hour days.[6] Despite the government's protestations that this amount is an adequate living wage, the fact is that it is barely enough to feed an adult for one day.[7] This helps to explain why, when the government raised fuel prices in the summer of 2007, causing bus fares to double in price (up to an average of 200 *kyat*), thousands of people took to the streets. People faced the impossible choice of either paying for transportation to work or having enough to eat. The demonstrations of September 2007, which began with demands for affordable fuel, reliable electricity, and other quality-of-life issues, quickly expanded to include calls for democracy. The international media labeled the events as prodemocracy demonstrations. In reality, Burmese people were protesting not only their country's seemingly intractable political situation, but also the current regime's inability (or refusal) to provide a reasonable standard of living to the majority of its citizens.

The fact that many Burmese people, perhaps the majority of people in Yangon, have little or no money left over after paying for the bare necessities of life (food, clothing, shelter, transportation) helps to explain the significance of a CD at the Dagon Center Star Mart: it is clearly a luxury item that can be purchased only by the economic elite. Indeed, the appearance of the customers that I saw there during my visits supports this notion. Star Mart customers tended to be young adults (under the age of thirty) and they were always dressed in the latest Western fashions. They were free to shop during business hours, suggesting that they were not obligated to hold regular jobs. It was impossible to tell by looking at them, but the conventional wisdom would suggest that these customers are the children of international (Chinese, Thai, Korean, Singaporean) businesspeople or of Burmese military officials.

If only a privileged few can shop at Star Mart, can we then say that Burmese pop music is truly popular, that is, that it is appreciated by a wide swath of the population? The answer is yes, and the proof lay just a few steps away, beyond the front entrance of Dagon Center. There, among the sidewalk vendors selling fresh food, sunglasses, locks, and a thousand other items, was a pair of men hawking pirated CDs, VCDs, and DVDs. The discs were not in jewel cases, but their paper covers featured vivid graphics, making it easy to see what was what. Here, customers could find virtually any of the *series* being sold inside at Star Mart—and pay far less for them.

The sellers were engaging in what is known as "piracy": selling cheaply duplicated recordings and pocketing the profits. It is a widespread phenomenon; on this one street corner alone, six different groups of pirates set up shop on a daily basis, and they did a brisk business selling the latest pop music recordings, often with cover art identical to that of the originals. Ohnmar Tun ruefully recounted to me the story of her most recent *series*, a Christmas disc released in December 2007. It was delivered to retail stores at 9:00 a.m., and she celebrated the official release at that time. By 2:00 p.m. on the same day, a relative of hers found a pirated version for sale on the street. She points out that some *series* have been pirated even before they have been officially released, so it is clear that at least one industry insider, employed perhaps in a legitimate recording studio, is working with pirates.

Figure 4.2. Pirates selling musical recordings and films on the sidewalk outside Dagon Center

Burma's Music Distribution System

As a consumer, I participated in the system that I describe in this book as the Burmese pop music industry. I purchased pop music *series* at both the Star Mart and at one of the ubiquitous stalls on the sidewalk outside. Both the legal vendors and the pirates are important to the distribution of Burmese pop recordings.

To organize my description of distributors of pop music in Burma, I will rely on a theoretical framework developed by sociologist Richard Peterson, who has spent his career developing ideas about how cultural products (books, films, paintings, musical recordings, and so on) come to be produced,[8] articulating what he calls the "production-of-culture perspective."[9] According to this perspective, cultural products take the shapes they do in part because of the nature of the system that produces them. Certain kinds of books are published, for example, because the nature of the book publishing industry facilitates their publication.[10] Though it is helpful (and convenient) to privilege the ideas of the author in this process, the production perspective argues that the author's work is fundamentally shaped by the reality that her ideas must be presented in such a way that the existing industry will be willing to publish them. This perspective takes the focus off individual initiative and creativity, and places it on the institutions and organizations that work together to make cultural products. As Diana Crane, another prominent sociologist, asserts, "It is impossible to understand the nature and role of recorded culture in contemporary society without examining the characteristics of the organizations in which it is produced and disseminated."[11]

In his masterful review of the literature on the production perspective, Peterson presents a "six-facet model of production."[12] The six facets are: industry structure, the market, organizational structure, technology, law and regulation, and occupational careers. Changes in any of these six facets, even seemingly minor changes, lead to changes in the kinds of cultural products that are created by the system. And "a major change in one of the facets can start a cycle of destabilization and reorganization in the entire production nexus."[13] In this chapter, I will use Peterson's six-facet model to analyze the processes by which Burmese pop music is distributed. As we will see, recent changes in some of these facets have already resulted in a restructuring of the industry, and further looming changes promise to affect, and even remake, the music itself.

Industry Structure

One of the most immediately noticeable features of Burma's pop music industry's distribution system is its lack of lack of formal institutions. This is, of course, a "lack" only from the perspective of the field of popular music studies, which has developed its models and theories based on Western norms.[14] In Burma, most pop musicians do not belong to bands, or at least, do not work exclusively with a stable group of colleagues. In addition, there is no Ticket-master-like entity; concert tickets are sold through beauty salons and upscale retail shops. Furthermore, in Burma, there is no such thing as a record label. The individuals (or very small groups of individuals) who create and produce albums have no long-term relationships with businesses that fund their work. Instead, these individuals, known as producers, raise private funds to cover the costs of making a *series*.

Producers pay composers for songs, musicians for performances, studio owners for *duty* (time spent recording music), and the City of Yangon for advertising space on billboards. These costs add up to anywhere from 150 *lakhs* (approximately $12,000) to 400 *lakhs* ($30,000) per album.[15] Producers are also required to submit recordings to the Press Security Board (PSB) for censorship. When I asked Aung Shwe (who has produced three albums) what producers do, he smiled and said, "Everything!"—noting that sometimes producers who are musicians like himself also create the arrangements of the songs on the *series*. They also liaise with music distribution companies, who send copies of the recordings to retail shops around the country.

There are three main distribution companies in Burma: Chokyithar, Manthiri, and Yadana Myaing. All three are headquartered in downtown Yangon,

on or near Thirty-Sixth Street. These distribution companies are private entities whose owners are solely concerned with making a profit. Therefore, they
ship their wares only to major population centers, where they can be sure that
enough customers will purchase recordings to make the shipping costs worthwhile. They hedge their bets when dealing with producers: if the distributor
believes that a *series* will sell well, the company will accept one master copy
of the recording from the producer and then arrange for retail copies to be
made, packaged, and shipped. However, if the company predicts that the disc
will not sell many copies, the producer must supply for-sale copies to the distributor, and provide further funds if more copies need to be made. The distribution companies send representatives around to retail shops to collect profits
generated by the sales of recordings. The profits are split with producers.

Importantly, producers trust distribution companies (who trust retail shop
owners) to calculate profits honestly and to pay the correct amount owed.
These business deals do not operate according to written contracts. Rather,
like other aspects of the Burmese pop music industry, the distribution of
recordings seems to depend largely on personal relationships, friendships of
long duration, which provide the basis for entering into an unwritten financial
agreement.

Just as the producers and distribution companies work together without
written contracts, there are usually no formal agreements made between
other industry members. Typically, a producer and a composer (for example)
will verbally agree to work together for the duration of one recording project
or concert. However, it is true that certain producers fund multiple albums
by the same musicians. In addition, well-established bands tend to appear in
live shows with the same singers. For example, band manager Thet Htaw Mya
explained to me that when he organizes a live show for his band, he routinely
asks five singers—individuals whose names he rattled off—to participate. He
says that he always invites these particular singers, because the band has performed with them many times before and likes to work with them. Likewise,
show organizers (or "contractors") may focus on promoting the same few
singers and bands. Composers often end up writing songs for a handful of
singers or movie directors, and some musicians routinely record in only two
or three studios.

So while the Burmese industry is marked by individual rather than institutional activity, the reality is that individuals know each other and, over many
years, evolve working relationships that are as stable as (or more stable than)
those governed by legal documents or formal business arrangements.[16] In fact,
in Burma professional relationships tend to be like family relationships, where
unwritten but extremely powerful expectations of loyalty govern behavior.

Among the many stories that my Burmese friends told me how these expectations had come to bear on their working lives, two exemplify the informal
yet deeply familial aspect of the Burmese pop music industry—the stories of

Htay Cho and Moe Lwin. Htay Cho worked as a recording engineer in a studio in North Yangon while simultaneously building a performing career as a guitarist. Eventually he realized that his guitar playing was taking so much of his time that he needed to quit working for the studio. He asked the studio owner's permission to quit—it was inconceivable that he would simply write a resignation letter—but the owner refused. Htay Cho had to find a replacement to work in the studio before he could honorably leave the job. So he recruited his younger brother. The brother had never previously worked in a studio, but because the business atmosphere was (as in many Burmese businesses) somewhat akin to that of a family, the new employee was welcomed: he was, in a sense, a relative.

Moe Lwin began his recording career very young. A family friend funded his very first *series*, since he was unknown to professional producers. (And knowing people, or being known by them, is essential to getting anything done in Burma.) The album was a success, and Moe Lwin was able to attract a professional producer for his second *series*. However, before embarking on a new project with the new producer, he asked permission to do so from the original producer. He shared that, nearly forty years later, he still visits this now-elderly friend regularly, to show his respect and gratitude. As these two stories illustrate, professional relationships in the Burmese music industry are sustained by personal relationships rather than by formalized agreements. This system is problematic, and a system of written contracts would no doubt be problematic in other ways, if Burmese musicians chose to adopt it. But the "honor system" has worked well enough until now that they are loath to see it change.

The industry does not pay royalties to composers and performers. Rather, these musicians receive a flat fee for their services (usually the equivalent of a few hundred US dollars) from the *series* producer when they either compose the song or record the *series*. I asked a number of full-time professionals if they recognized the word "royalties," and none of them did. The one exception was Thida Zay, who has been active as a singer since the early 1980s. He recalled that in 1996 a large group of professional musicians met to discuss the possibility of establishing a system of royalties. After the idea was explained, the group took a vote. Thida Zay rather bitterly named off the five people (including himself) who voted for the idea. Since the large majority was not interested— either not understanding the concept, or preferring a bird in the hand to two in the bush—the proposal died. Thida Zay was the only person I met who remembered any such proposal. Indeed, most of the others (who are younger) had only the vaguest notion that pop musicians are paid differently in Western countries, and that these payments have historically been the source of their wealth. When I asked Ma Khin Sein, for example, about payment methods, she seemed a little surprised: of course she always gets paid once, up front, for her work, she said. "It's the rule of Burma."

The Market

As I discovered during my shopping trips to Dagon Center (and other places where commercial music recordings are sold), the market for pop music in Burma prioritizes group albums. Group albums are so dominant now that they constitute the majority of the recordings made by famous singers. Indeed, when I interviewed some of the most famous singers in the country, each said that while they knew how many solo albums they had made (usually a handful), they had lost count of the dozens of group albums in which they had participated. According to Pee Paw (the impresario we met in chapter 1), the fact that their musical culture takes this form can be traced back to a marketing decision.

In early 2001, Pee Paw was working as the manager of one of Burma's best-known rock stars, Zaw Win Htut. Pee Paw decided to promote him by presenting him in concert with a band and some guest singers. This was a strategic choice: Pee Paw was determined to turn a profit, and figured that the way to do so would be to sell "a package" rather than an artist. He believed that if a potential ticket buyer was not interested in hearing Zaw Win Htut, but did want to hear one of the other singers on the program, the buyer would be likely to buy the package, and thus the manager could maximize ticket sales. Pee Paw's prediction came true; he sold many tickets for his show, in which multiple singers appeared one by one accompanied by the same band, and determined that the group performance idea was viable. The show was the first live show of the new millennium and the first large public concert in many years. It marked the beginning of a new era in Burmese pop music history, one in which the format of that first show predominates.

Of course, a few shows do feature only one singer, and most of the successful singers do record a few solo albums. However, there is a general consensus among musicians that since the year 2000, it is getting harder and harder to sell solo albums, and that fewer of these are being produced because they often do not *paut* (or "burst," meaning "to succeed commercially"). Instrumentalists pride themselves on being able to accompany any singer in virtually any popular style, and of course they need to be able to do this in an industry where most recordings feature a variety of singers and styles. But I think that this situation may change, and that if it does, it will likely be due to marketing practices.

Until very recently, market research was unknown in Burma. The Myanmar Marketing Research and Development Company (MMRDS), which began operations in 1997 and is headquartered in Yangon, now has eight branch offices around the country. MMRDS provides social, consumer, and business market research to paying customers who want to strategize about selling their products.[17] Its founder, Peter Thein, says that he got into business in Burma by publishing Yangon's very first City Directory (or Yellow Pages).[18] He and his employees now address questions such as the incidence of owning home appliances, watching television, and listening to the radio. During their years of operation the company has interviewed more than two hundred thousand Burmese households on these and other topics. Thein began collecting information on musical preferences not for a client, but because he hoped to establish a Billboard-type chart which would document the popularity of Burmese pop singers, songs, and *series*. Although this project did not come to fruition due to lack of financing, Thein discovered that he could sell this information to Yangon City FM, as well as to a spate of entertainment-oriented magazines and journals, all of which began publishing during the past decade. As of 2008, two data collectors from MMRDS visit sixty-five retail stores around Yangon, pen and paper in hand, every week. They ask the store managers how many copies of each album currently in stock were sold during the past week. The data are entered into a computer and tallied, and then used to identify the best-selling *series* in Burma.

Clearly, these data are reasonably accurate. However, they are beset with limitations. For example, MMRDS employees do not have a particularly consistent way of knowing when new albums are released. They rely on seeing new advertisements on billboards around Yangon and on the recollections of store managers. In other words, the big three music distribution companies do not communicate directly with MMRDS—nor do they post new release information on the Internet—and so market researchers have to backtrack to find it. In addition, most retail shops do not have computerized cash registers. Vendors use a calculator (if needed) to figure out the price and then announce it verbally to the customer, only rarely handwriting a receipt. Store managers rely on their memories and (possibly) written sales orders to establish how many copies of a given *series* were on the shelf at the beginning of a week, subsequently subtracting the number remaining to find the difference. Again, this system is roughly accurate, but not perfectly so: discs can easily be misplaced on the shelves and then miscounted.

Most importantly, MMRDS data (like data collected by any market research firm) are selective. MMRDS workers survey more than five dozen shops weekly—but there are 284 retail stores that sell music recordings in Yangon alone, not to mention the hundreds (possibly thousands) of shops in other cities.[19] Claims about sales numbers based on MMRDS research must be evaluated in light of these limitations. And conclusions about which music is the "most popular" in Burma must be understood to be provisional.

However, Burmese media outlets that purchase the MMRDS data do not treat it in this way. Yangon City FM, for example, instituted the first-ever national music awards beginning in 2002. At its annual awards banquet, the radio station hands out prizes for the Best-Selling Album of the Year (Male), Best-Selling Album of the Year (Female), Best-Selling Group Album, Most-Requested Singer of the Year, and a number of similar prizes. The station consciously awards prizes on the basis of objective data (sales numbers and tallied requests) rather than for subjective criteria such as Best Album or Best Singer.[20] And the prizes go to the usual suspects, the most famous artists who are widely-believed to have the highest sales numbers.

During the two years that I spent researching this book, the prizes were given to some of my interviewees, singers who command the highest performance fees in the Burmese industry (approximately $1,500 for one live show) and whose faces appear on billboards around the city. Were it possible to document every sale of every disc in Burma, we would likely discover that the prizes were in fact given to the best-selling artists of the year. But given the widespread sales by pirates and the fact that the market research on which the conclusions are based is rather limited, it is impossible to claim that Yangon City FM is accurately identifying the best-selling singers and albums.

Yangon City FM does make this claim, though, and publicizes it widely by televising the awards banquet on national television. For the past few years, recordings of the television broadcast have also been sold, and tabloid-style reporting about the banquet is common, so that a message (in January 2009) such as "R Zani is the best-selling male singer in the country" is widely inculcated. Giving this kind of prestigious recognition to R Zani virtually guarantees that he will become more famous and that potential consumers will become more interested in buying his albums. This claim, then, can have a tangible effect on sales; it can become a self-fulfilling prophecy. The net result could be that already successful artists become even more financially successful as a result of marketing practices. At the same time, the sales numbers of new artists with poorly advertised albums, who may be very popular with customers outside of Yangon, can be undercounted or even overlooked.

It is impossible to definitively claim, at this time, that MMRDS market research is influencing or even distorting the consumption of Burmese pop music. But Aung Shwe, at least, is sure this is the case. Speaking of *mono* music (that is, the *kalabaw* style featuring classical melodies and singing styles accompanied by modern instruments) he asserted, "the *mono* market is much bigger than *stereo* music" and that "many people" buy these recordings. He has no way of confirming this, though. And distribution companies, those who decide in advance whether a *series* will be popular or not and provide copies to the public accordingly, have no way of confirming this, either. They do know, thanks to MMRDS, that *stereo* music is the "best-selling" music in the country and that they can rely on selling this music to make a profit. They are therefore less likely to distribute *mono* recordings—so *mono* music is less likely to reach the general public, and may therefore decline in popularity. If Aung Shwe is correct, this trend has already begun. I visited the retail store operated by Manthiri Music Distributors in early 2009 and perused their inventory. Although they do sell *mono* music and some other, more marginal, *tain-yin-tha* recordings (such as recordings of traditional Mon music, for example), the reality is that the large majority of their wares are pop music *series* (solo and group albums).

Yangon City FM, and a new, similarly conceived radio station called Mandalay FM Radio, also use MMRDS marketing research to make programming decisions. Programmers and advisors (who often work as on-air personalities) are now creating shows such as the weekly *Yangon Top 20* (the best-selling Yangon-produced albums) and *Star on Line* (during which listeners can call to speak to a "star" singer). Every week announcers on Yangon City FM announce the title of the best-selling VCD on the market. Insiders at both of these stations say their goal is to provide programming that is appreciated by the public.[21] The advisors see themselves as responding to the audience by playing recordings that the audience has already indicated that it likes—as documented by MMRDS.

These radio stations are influencing their listeners by presenting to them singers who are "stars" and albums which are "popular." By playing these recordings, the radio stations help to promote them, and thereby likely help to increase their sales. Again, by prioritizing the "best-sellers," the stations leave less air time for new artists and innovative projects, thereby effectually depressing their sales potential. The stations contribute to a sales spiral in which the rich get richer (or, the popular albums become even more popular) and the less established, poorly funded projects have less chance to become popular.

In addition, these two radio stations are developing niche shows (for example, an hour of hip-hop music, an hour of *mono* music, etc.). Again, the goal here is to serve a broad swath of the listening public by targeting a variety of tastes. However, what may happen is that innovative music that crosses stylistic boundaries will be played less often on air, since it cannot be categorized as belonging to one style or another. Take, for example, the *Homage to Buddha* album described in chapter 2. The composer-producer of this album has worked for his entire career in the pop music industry. With this new album, he is attempting to establish a new genre, which he calls "New Age Myanmar." The music on the album is unlikely to be programmed on a pop-music-focused show, but then again, it does not neatly fit into any of the other categories used by radio stations either (such as "oldies," "traditional," and so on). If it does not receive extensive radio airplay, the album will not make it into the "Yangon Top 20," and the producer, who funded the recording privately, will not earn a profit that could be used to finance a second album in the new genre.

The marketing of Burmese pop music may be directly impacting its consumption, and therefore, transforming the nature of the repertoire, since producers are unlikely to fund "unpopular" projects that may not turn a profit. This is conjecture at this point, but history teaches that it is a strong possibility: a similar phenomenon has been documented in the United States.[22]

Just two radio stations, Yangon City FM and Mandalay FM, together play an enormous role in the Burmese pop music industry. They are both semi-independent stations dedicated to entertaining the public, rather than to serving the state's interests. Indeed, the four radio station employees I interviewed were adamant on this point: they insisted that their stations are *not* like the government stations; they play what common folks want to hear, rather than what the government commands them to play. They point out that the new radio stations play music and traffic warnings and public health messages, but not news and commentary from the SPDC perspective. And Yangon City FM is the first radio station in Burmese history to permit listeners to call in and express their preferences on air. The station seems to be widely appreciated: I heard Yangon City FM frequently in public spaces when I lived in Yangon, and friends told me that the station was the "only one" to which Yangon residents now listen.

Many Burmese pop musicians say that their earning potential decreased after the advent of pop radio, because listeners could hear their music for free on the air and therefore stopped buying *series* in stores. One organization, the Myanmar Musicians Association, successfully advocated for musicians' interests by negotiating an agreement with the government vis-à-vis the radio stations. This organization is the most important entity to consider as we turn to the next facet of the industry's distribution system: organizational structure.

Organizational Structure

The Myanmar Musicians Association (or *Gita Aseeayon*, hereinafter the MMA) is the only formal organization that exists to protect and promote the interests of musicians in Burma. It is an umbrella group that aims to represent not only pop musicians but also studio owners, recording engineers, music producers, and composers. It was created in 1991 by the then-new SPDC regime,[23] and was widely viewed by musicians as merely a front for government interests. However, in 2005, the MMA was reconstituted. It now has twenty-five board members, fourteen of whom are elected by the membership at large, and the balance of whom are appointed to their positions by government ministers. None of the board members receive any pay for their work. In the course of my research, I interviewed three elected board members and two appointed members of the MMA board. They all said—and their actions indicated—that they wanted to "help musicians" and therefore were glad to serve, whether they had come to their positions voluntarily or not.[24] And they asserted that this new, more democratic version of the MMA can and does help musicians.

Unfortunately, this viewpoint does not seem to be widespread among musicians themselves. U Hla Kyi was flatly contemptuous ("I will never join") when I asked him about belonging to the MMA. Moe Lwin told me that he had been "forced" to join by a highly placed government official. Many other musicians said that their membership in the MMA means almost nothing to them, because they do not believe that the group is truly helpful. In the eyes of these men and women, the MMA is an empty symbol, a government-organized group that does nothing but implement the government's agenda. A few cautiously said that the MMA can support, or should support, musicians, and that the new MMA may be providing some limited advantages to their community.

MMA insiders point to a number of tangible benefits that the group provides: clerical support, dispute resolution, and serving as a buffer between musicians and the Burmese regime. The MMA aids producers as they prepare their submissions to the PSB, essentially providing a precheck for spelling errors or offensive language, thereby helping the producer to avoid being fined by the censors. The MMA also organizes a dispute-resolution committee that meets weekly and renders judgments on disagreements between members. For example, if a movie director uses a recording for a soundtrack, and the composer or performer of the song alleges that the director did not pay for the song, the MMA committee will arbitrate the dispute. Ohnmar Tun, a member of this committee, says that she has seen substantive progress made on behalf of musicians through the work of this committee: prior to its formation, she says, musicians had to approach movie directors individually, and (lesser-known musicians especially) were frequently ignored or victimized.

Another member of the committee, Ko Chit Min, says that while the committee is making a good-faith attempt to render justice, they have not yet developed a "mature" system for dealing with conflicts. Decisions are not based on precedent or informed study of the situation, he claims. Since the industry does not use written contracts to document financial agreements, and the evidence consists of competing verbal accounts, it is difficult for the committee to make fair decisions. The MMA has not been working in this way for very long, and so it is certain that their dispute resolution committee functions rather imperfectly. However, this is the one aspect of their mission that musicians—even those who have nothing good to say about the organization—seem to know about and grudgingly appreciate.

MMA board members also claim that their organization helps defend musicians when their rights are encroached upon by the government. James Thiri even described the group as "an NGO," emphasizing that the MMA is not a branch of the SPDC apparatus. In chapter 5, I tell the story of how the MMA refused a direct request for public support from the government. But here I offer another story as an example, one I heard from an elected member of the MMA.

In 2001, when Yangon City FM began broadcasting, station employees went directly to the three big music distribution companies and asked for complimentary copies of their latest releases. They then played these recordings on the air. The composers, performers, and producers of the albums received no compensation from the radio station, despite the fact that the station was earning good profits by selling advertising time on shows that featured their music. After a couple of years, musicians began to express their discontent with this situation in interviews and op-ed articles. In response, the general manager of the Yangon City Development Committee (which owns and operates Yangon City FM) stated publicly that the station played only the recordings of artists who had agreed to allow them to be played for free. At that point, a group of about twenty of Burma's most popular musicians jointly sent a letter to City FM saying, "Why are you playing our music on air? We never consented to this!" The YCDC retaliated against these musicians (including Lay Phyu, one of the signatories to the letter) by banning them from appearing on city billboards, which the YCDC controls. This was a major blow to the musicians because, as we have seen, billboards are an important way for them to advertise their new *series*.

After the international media began asking questions about the situation, the government minister responsible for media agreed that Yangon City FM would in future play only the recordings of musicians who had explicitly consented to this by signing an agreement.[25] More importantly, the government delayed the planned opening of Mandalay FM (which began operating in 2008) in order to negotiate the issue with MMA board members. Ultimately, the government agreed that each time a song is played on Mandalay FM, the station will pay 1,000 *kyat* (a little less than $1) to the MMA. The MMA is then tasked with distributing the money to the musicians who participated in creating that recording. As of early 2009, Mandalay FM had paid for three months worth of broadcasting fees (about 4,500 *lakhs*, or $450,000), but the MMA had yet to disperse the money. No doubt the organization will have some difficulty determining who (composer? performer? recording engineer? studio owner? producer?) should get the money, and what proportion of the 1,000 *kyat* that he or she will receive. And it has yet to be seen how accurate the station's record-keeping will be.

Nevertheless, the beginning of a royalties system is now in place. The financial benefits will redound to musicians, and the MMA can take credit for helping musicians in the face of government pressure. Kyaw Naing Oo, who was the first to tell me this story, signed the original protest letter and subsequently worked to negotiate the payment system. He asserts that he is respected by the rank and file MMA members who elected him for precisely this reason.

The change in the organizational structure of the MMA may very well contribute to a significant change in the larger Burmese music industry. Now that a significant proportion of the board is elected by musicians, the board undoubtedly believes that is has an increased mandate to represent musicians' interests. In pursuing this mandate, MMA board members have already won a significant victory for musicians whose music is played on Mandalay FM. Once the radio royalties begin to filter down to musicians, these musicians will have money at their disposal to pursue their own interests (for example, to self-produce new *series*). If the MMA can convince a critical mass of its membership to actively support the organization, Burmese musicians may be empowered as never before to pursue their own agendas.

MMA board members do often talk about "helping" and "supporting" musicians. However, the issue they say that they are primarily concerned with is the problem of piracy. This problem, as I explain below, exploded in Burma because of a technological change.

Technology

Arguably the most significant recent change in the Burmese pop industry was provoked by the advent of new technology. After the turn of the millennium, personal computers and CD burners became available in Burma. As many of my informants pointed out, this single addition to their market sparked a revolution in the distribution side of the industry, and may ultimately lead to its destruction. This technology allows small groups of people to copy thousands of CDs very quickly. Thus it is directly responsible for the explosion in piracy that marks the contemporary scene.

Of course, piracy was always a problem in Burma, as it is in many other countries. As James Thiri said, when we discussed the issue of piracy and copyrights, "Many people here use the copy and they neglect the right." However, in previous decades would-be pirates were obligated to create copies of recordings using tape cassette machines. Recording a copy of a tape took as long as playing the tape itself (usually approximately one hour). One machine could therefore only create a dozen or so copies of a tape in one working day. CD burners, on the other hand, create durable and accurate copies of CD recordings in a matter of minutes. Enterprising people who invest in multiple CD burners (which are now standard equipment on most personal computers) can produce thousands of copied recordings in a day.

Khine Ta Tun, who like so many others in the Burmese pop music industry has spent his career filling a number of different roles, told me about his experience working as a supplier for one of Burma's best-known "music production companies," as duplicating businesses are called. From 2002 to 2005, Khine Ta Tun traveled monthly to Bangkok, where he purchased original recordings, thermal printers (to print CD covers), and burner machines "of the highest quality." The company owners, he said, were teenagers when they got started, and they lost money during their first two years of operation. Eventually, as they matured and learned how to track their own sales, they became financially viable and ultimately very successful. However, by 2005, another technological advance, high-speed Internet access, made the role of supplier obsolete. At that point, the company owners found that they could download entire albums from Internet sites such as iTunes, and could sell them to well-heeled Burmese customers who are increasingly buying iPods and mp3 players.[26]

Such music production companies are distinguished in the minds of Burmese people from pirate companies. I will discuss this distinction in greater detail below, but suffice it to say that a "music production company" duplicates and sells recordings (usually English-language recordings) made in the West, whereas "pirates" duplicate locally-made Burmese-language recordings. Both kinds of enterprise use the same technology, however, to create their duplicate copies. And both became much more successful after the turn of the millennium because they acquired high-end, imported CD burners. However, professional creators of music in Yangon reserve all their anger for pirates, and say that piracy is a "huge problem"—if not the biggest problem—they face.[27]

In an interview, Ohnmar Tun described pirates as "parasites . . . because they prey on others to survive." Shway Nyunt, who has written articles and spoken on government TV about the piracy problem, says that for every legal copy (of a local artist's *series*) that is sold in legitimate shops, pirates now sell approximately one hundred copies. I quoted this ratio to a number of Shway Nyunt's colleagues in subsequent interviews, and most agreed that the proportion sounded accurate. (Aung Shwe estimated thirty pirated copies for every legal copy, and Moe Lwin estimated fifty.) In fact, a number of musicians said that, because of piracy, the very future of their industry is in serious danger.

Burmese musicians explain that piracy endangers their livelihoods because it discourages potential producers from investing in the production of new *series*. And this is a serious problem because, for most of four decades during which the pop music industry has existed in Burma, the system has been structured around producers. Producers are business people (almost always men) who provide the funds to pay for the creation of a new *series*, and then reap the profits when the *series* is sold. In legal shops in Yangon, a *series* usually sells for between 1,200 and 2,000 *kyat* (most often for 1,600 *kyat*). Until recently, a successful *series* (one that *paut* or "bursts") would sell approximately fifty thousand copies.[28] A producer who backed a top-selling *series* could count on a significant profit, since the cost of producing a *series* is usually around 200 *lakh*, or 20 million *kyat*. Indeed, producers did succeed financially, and some numbers of them, until quite recently, devoted their entire business lives to producing pop music. Producers apparently represented the entire ethnic spectrum in Yangon; musicians remember producers of Burman, Indian, and *tain-yin-tha* descent. (At no time did foreign nationals ever constitute a significant percentage of pop music producers; music producing has always been a locally controlled phenomenon.)[29] However, producers are hard to find these days, as I discovered when I attempted to interview a producer for this book. Most have ceased working as music producers because it has become a money-losing proposition.

Pirates, that is, networks of men who sell duplicated copies of recordings on the streets and along the highways and byways of the country, sell one *series* for 400 *kyat*. Most often, they sell three *series* for 1,000 *kyat*, lowering the price per copy even further. Burmese people of all economic classes value a bargain, and are happy to buy the latest *series* from their favorite singer for one quarter of the retail cost. The pirates' networks are now large enough that they employ traveling salesmen who journey to rural areas, where per capita income is even lower than in Yangon, to sell recordings on credit. They allow poor customers to make monthly payments of amounts as small as 100 *kyat*, or 10¢. They are well-organized; as Ohnmar Tun explained, they are able to offer cheap, pirated versions of new *series* on the very same day that those *series* are released, and sometimes even before they are released. And they even create new products, of a sort: pirates sometimes compile popular tracks from a variety of *series* to create "best-of" recordings.

By undercutting the legitimate market, pirates have effectively monopolized the business. They sell the large majority of the copies that are sold, leaving producers to shoulder the recording costs without being able to earn much, or any, profit. Producers, therefore, have turned away from the music industry, leaving musicians struggling to find financial support for their new recordings. This is deeply troubling to musicians, most of whom have matured in their careers knowing only the system as it functioned in the 1980s and 1990s, and who find it hard to imagine other possibilities. Decrying the growth of piracy and the increasing rarity of producers, Htay Cho said that this is "not natural." To him, as to many of his colleagues, the idea that musicians should be able to rely on individual producers to fund their work is simply the way of things, and to change this system is to tamper with the natural and inevitable social order.

After repeated queries, I did manage to locate and interview a producer in Yangon in 2008. By all accounts, Kaung Lin Lin is one of only a handful now working full-time as a music producer. He was introduced to me by composer Htin Thu, who called the producer "a hero" for continuing to fund new *series* in spite of widespread piracy. Kaung Lin Lin immediately pointed out that his family owns a very successful construction business, and it is this financial cushion that has allowed him to pursue his work as a producer. He has produced eight *series* to date, including some of the best-known recent *series*. He says that as late as 2003, he and his colleagues were able to earn five to fifteen times what they invested in a *series*. He recalls that at that time, *series* featuring the most popular singers in the country could sell as many as 150,000 legal copies. Now the norm is roughly 10,000 legal copies—too few to create a profit for the investing producer. Kaung Lin Lin says he is currently losing a little money on his musical projects, and anticipates losing more in future. But he is hanging on, hoping that he can maintain a viable business long enough to pass it on to his children when they come of age. He places his hope in the government's antipiracy campaign.

This campaign has been featured in the state-run media on a number of occasions during the past two years. For example, the state-owned newspaper *The New Light of Myanmar* periodically runs stories about how police have arrested pirates for selling copied *series* on the streets. Quite a few musicians said, when I asked them about how this problem might be solved, that only the government can stamp out piracy—the problem is too big and too persistent for anything other than a national entity to solve. However, very few of them are holding their breath. The government of Burma is, as all Burmese people know very well, fundamentally inept and corrupt. It devotes very little of the national budget to services that aid the general population and, as a result, fails to help its people on many fronts.[30] Music industry insiders have no more reason than any of their fellow citizens to trust that the government will help them with their greatest need. Indeed, they have good reason to believe precisely the opposite, that the government is aiding and abetting pirates because members of the government are in fact profiting from piracy.

This is a logical deduction even if one does not have insider information about the situation. Pirates sell their wares on the busiest corners of the biggest city in the country, in broad daylight, on a daily basis. It would be a simple matter to arrest them red-handed, if police officers were empowered to do so. (For example, the six pirate stalls at the Myaynigone junction described at the beginning of this chapter are located only one block from a continually manned police post. Needless to say, the police officers at that post never venture outside their small shelter for any reason except to direct traffic during rush hour). There are laws on the books protecting intellectual property, but they are not enforced, with the result that many Burmese people are not even aware that such laws exist.[31]

The fact that the police hardly ever take action against a crime that is being committed constantly, in public, indicates that they are willfully ignoring it. And this, of course, indicates that they have been ordered to ignore it, as the totalitarian rulers of the Burmese state do not encourage individual initiative in their employees. However, some of the people interviewed for this book went farther than this, asserting that they "know" that the government has a vested interest in sustaining piracy. For example, Thida Zay relayed the story of another singer, who, along with her producer, created a *series* that was supposed to be tamper-proof. The producer arranged to have a virus installed on the recording, so that if someone attempted to copy the disc, his or her computer would be infected with the virus. Days after the release of the *series*, the IT specialist who had created the virus got a telephone call from a government official, warning him never to do such a thing again.

Burmese musicians do not hold a uniformly pessimistic view of the piracy problem. I was surprised at how many of them expressed nuanced and even sympathetic opinions about pirates and piracy. For example, the owner of a legal shop said that pirates are doing Burmese pop stars a favor, since they help to spread their recordings around the country and contribute to their popularity.[32] Thuza said that although it would be best if piracy did not exist, he understands that those who sell pirated *series* on the streets do it in order to survive. Thida Zay said that piracy is, at its heart, a problem of poverty: many music fans in Burma are simply too poor to pay for legal copies. Still others said music consumers in rural Burma have no option but to buy pirated copies, because the legal distribution companies do not stock the shops in small towns and villages.

In this sense, pirates are filling a gap in the market, bringing products to customers who cannot access legal copies, either because they are too highly-priced or because they are sold only in distant locations. Indeed, some musicians who have toured throughout Burma claim that many rural Burmese folk do not understand the difference between original and pirated recordings, since they have never seen a legal *series* and therefore cannot make the comparison. Khine Ta Tun grimly recounted the story of how, when he was on tour in northern Burma, he was approached by a fan who presented a pirated copy of his *series* and asked him to autograph it. "I won't sign that shit," Khine Ta Tun told the fan, who was shocked by the refusal, since he did not understand how his request could possibly be offensive. Khine Ta Tun concluded that the ultimate solution to piracy will be a public education campaign. Currently, the average Burmese person simply does not perceive the copying of recordings to be a moral issue.[33]

Here we must acknowledge that the notion of intellectual property (admittedly a modern construct) is almost unknown in Burma. Moreover, it has been undermined by pop musicians themselves. Taking the long view, the music community in Yangon has been its own worst enemy. Composers and performers have, for decades, presented *copy thachin* to the public, thereby valorizing the idea that an artist can take an entire tune from another artist, write new lyrics, and then proclaim it a new song, without ever offering payment to the original creator of that tune. In addition, they have, like millions of customers over the years, purchased duplicated copies of original English-language recordings for pleasure or for learning. These duplicated copies are, as we have seen, sold in legal shops for fair prices (or at least, for the same price as a Burmese-made recording, about one-tenth of the price in the United States).

When I spoke with Khine Ta Tun (the touring singer who was so offended by the autograph request) about this, he acknowledged that from a Western outsider's perspective, it does seem hypocritical for local stars to insist that their own recordings not be pirated while they themselves purchase duplicated American recordings in order to create *copy thachin*. But, he says, "in Myanmar and in other Asian countries" duplication is not considered to be theft. It is not illegal; it is not even questionable behavior. "It's like they [the music production companies] are doing the public a favor," he claims, since the average Burmese person could never access original copies of American or British albums, and if they could, could not afford to pay for them.[34] Khine Ta Tun says that he himself took a long time to adjust to the idea that buying duplicated recordings is tantamount to stealing from the original artist. Since 2000, he has made it a practice to buy only original recordings, which he obtains when he travels to Japan or Thailand—but he knows that he is rare, even among his worldly-wise peers in the Burmese pop music industry.

Figure 4.3. Duplicated copies of American recordings (including Snoop Dogg, Leona Lewis, Britney Spears, and Hilary Duff albums) for sale in a legal retail shop in Yangon

One amusing incident from my research illuminates this way of thinking: I was spending the day in a recording studio. During my conversation with Aung Shwe, a well-educated man of high moral principles, he articulated a strong complaint about piracy and government inaction. At the very same time, he was making duplicate copies of the movie *Rambo IV*.[35] He gave these copies to a line of grateful customers who dropped by the studio that day. He embodied the simultaneous concern about local theft and disregard for, or ignorance of, foreign laws that I encountered many times among Yangon musicians.

It is clear that piracy will be a difficult problem to solve in Burma. For all kinds of reasons—financial, organizational, and cultural—this will be a hard row to hoe. However, the SPDC claims that it is going to solve the problem, and rather quickly, by changing the regulations that control duplication of intellectual property. How might this proposed change affect the production of Burmese pop music?

Law and Regulation

The government of Burma has given the MMA a mandate to join the World Intellectual Property Organization by 2014. WIPO is a United Nations agency that is "dedicated to developing a balanced and accessible international intellectual property (IP) system."[36] The organization has a mission "to promote the protection of IP throughout the world." To this end, WIPO administrates twenty-four treaties which govern the use of intellectual property, including those which specifically outline the issues of copyright and the payment of royalties.

The history and work of WIPO are too detailed to explain here, but suffice it to say that WIPO membership should signify that a member state is serious about developing legislation to protect the owners of intellectual property and then enforcing that legislation. Member states cooperate to protect the use of intellectual property across national boundaries. In many countries, collective management organizations (CMOs), operating under the auspices of WIPO, administrate the use of musical works and coordinate payment to the owners of those works.[37] Generally, CMOs communicate on an organization-to-organization basis. For example, the CMO representing a purchaser in the United States will pay the CMO representing a rights-holder in Brazil, and the Brazilian CMO is responsible to funnel that payment to the rights-holder. In Burma, the Myanmar Musicians Association is specifically tasked with forming a CMO. Once a CMO is in place, the country can join WIPO and begin participating in the international system of exchange that governs payment for intellectual property. It is a huge task, to be sure: the CMO must represent all creators of intellectual property—not just musicians but also authors, movie-makers, and so on.

If the MMA is able to form a CMO, and if the government takes seriously the responsibility of enforcing WIPO rules (both debatable prospects), then the Burmese music industry will see two effects: first, it will likely produce many fewer *copy thachin*. *Copy thachin* have historically been and continue to be an important part of the Burmese pop music repertoire. If Burma were to become a compliant member of WIPO, *copy thachin* composers would have to obtain permission to write their *copy thachin* from the person holding the rights to the original tune. According to WIPO:

> The original creators of works protected by copyright, and their heirs, have certain basic rights. They hold the exclusive right to use or authorize others to use the work on agreed terms. The creator of a work can prohibit or authorize: its reproduction in various forms, such as printed publication or sound recording ... and [importantly] its translation into other languages, or its adaptation, such as a novel into a screenplay.[38]

Rights-holders may be unwilling to sell their rights. Most Burmese *copy thachin* are based on English-language songs, which originate in Anglo-American culture, where most artists have rather different ideas about artistic integrity, originality, and copying (or "ripping off" someone else's work). As WIPO points out, "Copyright protection also includes moral rights, which involve the right to claim authorship of a work, and the right to oppose changes to it that could harm the creator's reputation."[39] It is entirely possible that a Western songwriter would object to the idea that a Burmese composer could assign to their music an entirely different meaning by creating new lyrics. But even if they are willing, since the original songs are usually very financially valuable to the rights-holders, they will demand a high price for their intellectual property. Given the exchange rate between the Burmese *kyat* and the American dollar or the Euro, it is unlikely that most Burmese musicians, even the very richest, could amass enough money to pay for the rights. Therefore, they will not able to continue to legally record *copy thachin.*

WIPO membership would have a second, less immediate, effect on the current Burmese pop music industry: it would codify and strengthen the notion of intellectual property among Burmese musicians and their fans. WIPO insists on the idea that "a created work is considered protected by copyright as soon as it exists."[40] Creators of works have inherent rights concerning the distribution of their property, and they need not formally register those works with WIPO or with a national body in order to obtain copyright.

In Burmese society most people—including creators of music, who depend on selling their intellectual property for their livelihood—do not understand copyright in this way. Rather, they believe that "copyright" (a word that virtually all of my interviewees used, even those who had never heard of "royalties") is a right that will be granted to them only when their country becomes one of WIPO's member states. Over and over, musicians said to me "We have no copyright here," or "We need to get copyright." The establishment of a CMO which operates according to WIPO principles could help to shift this way of thinking, effectively empowering musicians to defend the use of their property. For example, if Burma began to govern copyright according to international norms, musicians would not only become educated about royalties, but might begin to insist on them, rather than signing a form allowing Yangon City FM, the most influential radio station in their country, to broadcast their recordings for free.

However, it is equally likely that in the short term at least, WIPO membership could increase conflict between music industry members. WIPO regulations are based on the idea that a work of art (say, a recording of a song) has an identifiable "original creator." This notion is immediately problematic in the case of pop music. Hit songs are colloquially identified by fans as belonging to the famous singers that perform them, and indeed, performers do generally believe that their recorded performance is part of the creation of the song, and therefore that they are in some sense the creators of the music. Most CMO's rules say that fifty percent of any royalty fee should be paid to the song's composer and lyricist.[41] And of course other people involved with the creation of a recording can also make a legitimate argument that they contributed to its creation and are therefore entitled to a portion of the money. It is a tricky thing, in any country, to identify the "original creator" of a recorded song. If Burma joins WIPO, music industry members will be obligated to join in this debate, and it is likely to be a contentious one.

Indeed, this has already begun to happen. Because the MMA is now operating a dispute resolution committee, industry members have a forum in which to assert their rights. As Ko Chit Min, an active MMA member, explained to me, "In the past, singers did not share their income from live shows with composers. [Composers accepted this state of affairs because] they could earn extra income by selling their songs again to movie directors. But now, when a song is used in a movie, everyone, the singer, the recording engineer, the studio owner and others all want to be paid for it." Ko Chit Min says that he has become quite pessimistic about the work of the MMA committee, since it does not seem to be producing good results. Complainants, he says, often argue with the mediators even after they have pronounced judgment. Ultimately, he believes that the problem stems from the fact that industry members do not understand each other's work and therefore do not appreciate it. A movie director, for example, may believe that songwriting is very easy, and therefore not accept the idea that a composer should receive a substantial sum of money when his song is used in a movie.

Ko Chit Min argued passionately that Burmese people in general are poorly educated and self-interested, and that this accounts for the MMA committee's lack of substantial progress. Whatever the case—and numerous other community members have much more positive views of this committee—it is clear that the MMA, in trying to standardize norms and dispense justice, is causing industry members to reconsider their own and others' rights. If the MMA creates a CMO, I imagine that this debate will increase dramatically, as many people with opposing interests try to decide who exactly is entitled to payment for a song.

I wonder if, in the brave new world of copyright and royalties, some Burmese musicians may wish they had maintained the old system (the "rule of Burma" as Ma Khin Sein put it, above). As we have seen, when a Burmese pop recording is being made, producers pay flat fees to composers, performers, arrangers, recording engineers, and studio owners for their services. Creators of music are virtually guaranteed to get a reasonable amount of money for their work at the time it is recorded. However, if Burma switches to a system of copyright and royalties, musicians will create recordings in the hope that they will eventually be reimbursed for their work with future royalty payments. As Roger Wallis and Krister Malm discovered in their grand survey of recording industries in twelve small countries, the existence of a CMO and national support for intellectual property rights does not guarantee that rights-owners will be fairly reimbursed. As they point out, CMOs often have an easier time collecting money than dispersing it.[42] And when they do disperse it, they cannot do so perfectly precisely. CMOs usually pay rights-holders when their works are performed—but "it is virtually impossible to keep track of the actual works performed."[43] CMOs usually rely on samples of radio playlists, missing all of the songs that were performed in night clubs, for example, and all of the songs that were not included in the sample.

The parallels with the Burmese case are clear. As we have already seen, the market research firm which provides the only music sales data available in Burma renders an incomplete picture of the true situation. And although the MMA has begun to collect royalty payments for members whose songs are performed on Mandalay FM, they are experiencing difficulty dispersing the money to their members after only three months. It may well be that by receiving payment at the time they complete their work, musicians are better off. They are more likely to collect what they are owed under current norms than if they wait for potentially bigger royalty payments.

At this point, though, no members of the Burmese pop music industry are expressing any concerns about the advent of enforced copyright law. Quite the contrary: they are virtually unanimous in hailing this possibility (and I emphasize that they see it only as a possibility, not a certainty). They welcome the idea of enforced copyright because they believe that the new regime will lead to the eradication of piracy. When I asked musicians to predict what the effects of joining WIPO might be, they all focused on the prospect of ending piracy, which they linked directly to "having copyright." In addition, they seem, as a group, to be markedly optimistic about the other possible consequences.[44]

For example, when I pointed out that copyright would protect not only Burmese musicians but also artists from whom they regularly copy (like Shania Twain, Bryan Adams, the Eagles, and so on), several people asserted that they were not worried. Htin Thu, who has made a career of writing *copy thachin* and by his own count has written only a handful of *own tune* songs, said that he will simply switch to writing nothing but *own tunes* when Burma joins WIPO. "It won't be world standard, but it will be okay for Myanmar," he offered. And Chit Nyein said that he was confident that local composers would still be able to rewrite and adapt foreign recordings.

Khine Ta Tun asserted that multinational record companies should be prepared to "do business differently in a country like this [i.e., a poor country with a widespread practice of duplicating foreign recordings.]" He suggested that such companies should not bother trying to sell individual copies of recordings in Burma, but should rather sell a license to copy the master recording an unlimited number of times, for a flat fee. Others hoped—and claimed there is good reason to believe—that after joining WIPO, Burmese musicians will not be held to international standards with regard to the intellectual property of others. Htin Thu claimed he had been told by an MMA official that, in future, the Big Four record companies will charge less than normal for permission fees to Burmese composers who want to buy songs to make *copy thachin*, because they will be sympathetic to a developing country. And I heard about a book publisher who said that a WIPO official has already made an informal agreement with Burmese publishers, allowing them to photocopy English-language original books and sell them. Apparently this official expressed deep sympathy for the Burmese situation, acknowledging that if WIPO rules were to be followed to the letter, most Burmese people would lose all access to English books.

Members of the Burmese pop music industry are optimistic (and possibly naïve) about their government's efforts to join WIPO and enforce copyright law. If such a move does result in the lessening or elimination of piracy, then WIPO membership will provide a tangible benefit to musicians. Legal sales will likely increase if consumers lose the option to buy a pirated version. In addition, Burmese customers will likely buy more locally made recordings, because duplicates of foreign-made albums will no longer be for sale in legal shops. On the other hand, as I have pointed out above, pirates do offer a service to Yangon-based musicians: the pirates are the only vendors selling pop music in any form in many rural communities. Even if piracy were to be eliminated, the three major distribution companies in Yangon would probably not expand their sales networks into impoverished townships where few people can afford to pay nearly two days' wages for a disc. Therefore, pop musicians would lose some of the rural audience that piracy has helped them to acquire.

Occupational Careers

Changes in the first five facets of the distribution of Burmese pop music (that is, industry structure, the market, organizational structure, technology, and law) have already begun to spark changes in the sixth. The nature of industry members' occupations are beginning to change. As I discussed in chapter 1, industry members have long functioned as generalists, rather than specialists, with individuals filling several roles simultaneously. Because this pattern of behavior is so well established, I believe that expanding their career repertoire will be well within the reach of most Burmese musicians. As a group, creators of Burmese pop music are resourceful, energetic, and adaptable. Despite the gloomy predictions that many expressed to me ("In two or three years no one will produce any albums," said Kenneth), there is good reason to believe that they will find ways to continue to make and sell music in their continually changing industry.

Indeed, some have already begun to do so. Creators of music are moving into the distribution realm. This phenomenon is manifest in two main ways: first, music creators are becoming distributors of their own music, and second, they are developing new relationships with other entities to aid in the distribution of their music.

Because of the almost-total disappearance of professional producers during the past five years, many Burmese composers, arrangers, and performers are now self-producing their *series*. In some cases, musicians rely on savings or family money to fund their projects. In other cases, they solicit sponsorship (more on this below). I met very few people who were enthusiastic about this way of operating, but certainly some people are making a success of their self-produced *series*.

Others are going one step farther and taking charge of the physical distribution of their latest albums. For example, Moe Lwin told me of his "plan to combat piracy": he intended to spend the month of February 2009 touring around Burma, stopping at all of the major cities and as many of the small towns as possible. At each stop, he planned to give a short performance and then sell autographed original copies of his latest album. The sale price, he decided, would be 500 *kyat*: more than what pirates charge for an illegal copy, but not so much more that average consumers would be dissuaded. He was able to price it this low because he planned to drive himself and to sell his discs in plastic pockets rather than regular CD cases. Moe Lwin hoped that if his tour was profitable, other musicians would follow his lead. "Right now, one hundred percent of people are losing money on their albums," he said frankly.

There is nothing to be lost, and perhaps much to be gained, by offering one's wares directly for sale to the public, rather than sharing profit with distribution companies and retail store owners. Hpone Thant, a younger musician (who produces his own *series* in his home recording studio) articulated a plan very similar to that of Moe Lwin. He, too, intended to do a "CD release tour" in early 2009, with the aim of getting his recordings into as many little villages as possible. Like his older colleague, he hoped to bypass both the legal and illegal distributors of music in order to take charge of the distribution himself.

In order to be able to afford to distribute their own music, Burmese pop musicians are increasingly developing relationships with corporate sponsors. In less than a decade, sponsors have become such an important part of the scene that, as Aung Shwe put it, "now sponsors have replaced producers." Looking at some of the typical billboards at junctions in Yangon, one could be forgiven for thinking that sponsors have replaced musicians themselves. I passed one billboard multiple times before I realized that it was advertising a new *series*. The huge lettering for the name of the sponsor, and the picture of the sponsor's product, a watch, led me to believe it was promoting watches.

And one ubiquitous billboard that went up in December 2008 was intended to promote Lay Phyu's highly anticipated return album. But the sponsor's name was bigger than Lay Phyu's name! This was strange enough. Later, friends explained to me that the sponsor's name (BOB, for Bay of Bengal Hotel) was so big because Lay Phyu actually named his recording after the sponsor, so the sponsor's name was in fact the title of the *series*.

Figure 4.4. Billboard advertising a live show

Figure 4.5. Billboard advertising Lay Phyu's BOB album

Sponsorship is mutually beneficial for both musicians and sponsors. Musicians approach Yangon-based businesses and ask them to cover the cost of producing a *series*. In return, the musicians promise to feature the businesses' logos on the cover art of the recording and in the video portion of a VCD. (Frequently now, when watching a VCD, the viewer is treated to the sight of the logo for a bottled-water company scrolling across the screen at the beginning of, or even during, a song). The corporate sponsors I saw most often were beverage sales companies (coffee, tea, and so on). Myanmar Beer and Dagon Beer, for example, are frequent sponsors of live shows. These companies gain a tangible advantage by advertising at pop music concerts: since they are not allowed to promote their stock on television in Burma, they seize the opportunity to do it in front of large crowds of well-heeled consumers. They also maximize their profits by supplying all of the surrounding restaurants with their products, and then announcing at the show that customers can get a discount if they buy three or more drinks.

It can be difficult to find a sponsor, just as it was challenging in the past to find a producer. However, those that have been able to do it report that it is a relatively straightforward transaction. Chit Nyein, a well-known singer, says that he routinely goes to his sponsors' corporate offices in person, asks for the money he needs, and receives it about one week later. Local brands provide seventy to ninety percent of the sponsorship that pop music currently receives, so Yangon-based musicians are dealing with Yangon-based business people. Corporate sponsorship, then, would seem to be an increasingly important part of the Burmese music industry. But insiders are dubious about how helpful sponsorship really is.

They point out that, first, corporate sponsors do not pay enough to defray all of the costs associated with recording a *series* or presenting a live show. Typically, corporate sponsors pay thirty to fifty *lakhs* (or one-quarter of the cost) to get their logo onto a VCD, and twenty-five to one hundred *lakhs* to hang their banners at a live show.[45] Producers (nowadays, usually musicians who are self-producing) and contractors must approach multiple sponsors to completely cover their costs. This becomes very time-consuming. In addition, producers must deal with the challenge of organizing the space available on the stage to present all of the sponsors' logos while still preserving the visual aspect of the performance.

Second, pop music industry insiders say that a sponsor is not equivalent to a producer because a sponsor only provides financial support. A producer, on the other hand, commits to the whole project. He or she helps to organize all of the different stages of the recording and distribution process. A producer, ultimately, is personally present and invested in the production of music in a way that a corporate entity simply is not.

And while my interviewees did not mention it, it is of course true that corporations and musicians have dissimilar goals. While musicians aim to "share their hearts" with audiences, corporations want to promote their brands. "The goal of the corporation . . . is to support art that is decorative, entertaining and safe, as befits a vehicle for public relations."[46] Musicians may find themselves at odds, then, with their corporate sponsors, particularly if their songs are perceived to be provocative. (And Buddhist musicians may have strong objections to being linked with a sponsor who sells alcoholic drinks). But since musicians are financially dependent on their sponsoring companies, they may have difficulty staying true to their artistic goals, or else they may find that they cannot disseminate their music at all, since no business will sponsor it.

It is possible that if corporate sponsorship continues to increase in importance for both musicians and sponsors, yet another occupational career shift will occur. At present, sponsoring companies do not employ people specifically to act as go-betweens with personnel in the music industry. The arrangements are made directly between musicians and company managers. However, activity may increase to a point where companies need to employ public relations officers (or something of the sort) and musicians need to delegate their search for corporate money to experts (such as agents).

Other occupations may arise, and other significant changes may occur as the other five facets of the Burmese pop industry continue to evolve. For example, a seemingly small technological change could have major ramifications. Just after I concluded the research for this book, Burma's Press Security Board (the government entity responsible for censoring all publications including musical recordings) announced that it would soon begin accepting submissions in digital form.[47] Industry members are cautiously welcoming this prospect, because it will mean that they can submit an alterable document, rather than a hard copy, to be censored, and incur much less expense if the censor demands a change. But digital submissions could provoke other changes. For example, the flash drives and computers that producers will need are very expensive, much more expensive in Burma than in the United States or in the rest of Asia.[48] Musicians who are bearing the cost of producing their own *series* may not be able to afford this technology. Some marginal musicians may be completely shut out of the industry, meaning that their artistic contributions will be lost.

Possibilities abound. Whatever new occupational careers do come to the forefront of the Burmese pop music industry will inevitably affect other parts of the industry. A change in one of the six facets of the production of culture provokes changes in the other five. And as the industry changes, so do the cultural products it creates.

Revisiting Peterson's Theory

Burma's pop music recording industry is undergoing a period of marked transition. It remains to be seen how current changes will affect the future structures of the industry—the market, organizations, technologies, laws, careers, and musical products. But the Burmese case, analyzed according to Richard A. Peterson's six-facet model, ultimately brings into question one of his major assertions. Throughout his career, Peterson observed, and then stated as a "regularity," that the presence of oligarchic organizations tends to stifle innovation.[49] He claimed that when an industry is dominated by a handful of large, hierarchically structured companies, those companies will tend to produce standardized, homogeneous products.[50] The corollary to this theory is the idea that when an industry is composed of a multitude of small, flexible, and independent organizations (for example, indie record labels), that industry will tend to produce a diverse array of innovative cultural products. "The greater the number of competing firms in the popular music industry, the greater the diversity in types of music presented."[51]

Peterson developed this theory during three decades spent studying the American popular music industry. He argued that, for example, rock and roll music developed in the 1950s in part because the nature of the popular music industry, which until then had been dominated by four firms that produced recordings by swing bands and crooners. Technological innovations made it easier for smaller independent firms to compete in the marketplace. These small firms were responsible for promoting rock and roll and the diversity of popular music styles that followed.[52] Peterson's theory is now so well known that the idea of "the ground-breaking independent record company—the 'indie'—imbued with connotations of a radical, alternative and more sincere way of producing music, has become part of the everyday theory of rock fans."[53]

In Burma's pop music scene, the industry is almost atomized. Individuals collaborate for the duration of a common project, which is often just one song on a group album. In the recording studios, performers work independently. Groups virtually never record their tracks at the same time. On stage, instrumentalists often form a band for the duration of just one concert. And that band backs a rotation of six or seven singers. Since they rarely rehearse together (more about this in chapter 3), musicians ultimately spend very little time creating music as a group. Since there are no record labels, musicians rely on producers to fund their recordings, and producers commit to funding only one album at a time. (And now musicians are increasingly relying on their own fund-raising abilities and limited agreements with sponsors to raise money for their *series*). While long-term relationships do exist, and do tend to regulate interactions between individuals, the fact remains that individual members of the Burmese pop music industry operate as quasi-free agents. Musicians, especially those at the top of the earning bracket, are fundamentally flexible, since they often own their own recording studios, are capable of doing many of the varied tasks needed to produce an album, and do not have to answer to publicists or agents. The Yangon industry is virtually the polar opposite of the Nashville industry, where Peterson spent so much time and on which he based his conclusions.

And yet Burmese pop music is not marked by innovation. Burmese pop musicians tend to be focused on preserving the pop music song tradition rather than on creating significant variations on that tradition (see chapter 2 for more on this). One might expect, given the regularity claimed by Peterson and other sociologists, that Burmese pop musicians would be creating an intense diversity of musical forms and frequently advancing new ideas. After all, the Big Four[54] record companies have no presence in Burma, and the informal groupings that do exist are small, egalitarian and flexible. However, these musicians create music that is largely standardized. Oligopoly may stifle innovation, as Peterson and others have shown in Western societies, but my analysis shows that its opposite does not necessarily foster innovation.

Because Burmese pop musicians, functioning as individuals, have limited resources, they want to minimize the financial risk that they face. They therefore prefer to repeat a successful formula; that is, they prefer to create music that sounds very like music that has, in the past, sold well. If one of the Big Four multinational recording companies were to establish a business presence in Burma—that is, if it were to operate as an oligopoly—it would offer Burmese pop musicians much more financial stability than the musicians currently enjoy. Oligarchic companies would likely give musicians contracts and pay them large advances and royalties. The musicians would therefore have more time to experiment in the studio and would likely be more willing to take artistic risks. In Burma, the presence of an oligopoly might very well foster innovation. Certainly the lack of one is doing little to encourage creativity. The Burmese pop music industry, analyzed using Peterson's production perspective, suggests that his "regularity" should be reconsidered.

Chapter Five

Musicians and the Censors

The Negotiation of Power

Observers of international affairs consistently identify Burma's military government as a totalitarian regime, which manifests its cruelty toward its citizens in a myriad of ways, including the restriction of public expression. The titles of two of the best-known recently published books about Burma exemplify this characterization, *Living Silence* by Christina Fink and *Karaoke Fascism* by Monique Skidmore.[1] The titles evoke the dangers of making sound, literal and figurative, in Burmese society. Reporters Without Borders, which releases an annual report that "reflects the degree of freedom that journalists and news organisations enjoy in each country, and the efforts made by the authorities to respect and ensure respect for this freedom," ranked Burma number 164 out of 169 in 2007.[2] Upon releasing their 2007 list, the group made a statement of special concern about Burma:

> We are particularly disturbed by the situation in Burma (164th). The military junta's crackdown on demonstrations bodes ill for the future of basic freedoms in this country. Journalists continue to work under the yoke of harsh censorship from which nothing escapes, not even small ads.[3]

As the Reporters Without Borders website implies, journalists' freedom to speak and write is reliant on the degree of censorship they must endure.[4] Some scholars of Burma have already written helpful accounts of censorship in that country. The best of their writing, to date, has focused on the government's treatment of written texts and their authors.[5] The Fink and Skidmore monographs mentioned above treat this subject,[6] and Anna J. Allott's *Inked Over, Ripped Out: Burmese Storytellers and the Censors* focuses exclusively on it.[7]

Aung Zaw's book chapter "Burma Under Siege" is the only comprehensive scholarly treatment of the censorship of music in particular.[8] (The chapter is a compilation of the research he performed and supervised during his tenure as editor of the *Irrawaddy* online magazine, which has an ongoing interest in music and censorship in Burma.) In total, the literature about censorship of artistic expression in Burma is remarkably brief, given the importance of this issue to artists and their audiences—millions of Burmese people.

In order to learn more about how censorship impacts musicians, and how they respond to it, I interviewed many Yangon-based creators of music. In an effort to understand how the relationship of power between musicians and censors works, I also interviewed music censors. In this chapter, I examine the interactions between Burmese pop musicians and their censors. Censorship always occurs on multiple levels.[9] In Burma, the most widespread level of censorship occurs at the level of the individual. Composers and performers censor themselves as they write and perform music, in order to conform to the government's requirements. In addition, their work is edited by others who control the public performance of music, such as radio disc jockeys, stage show organizers, and official government censors. My perception of these interactions is, of course, influenced by the scholarly debate about popular music and power relations.

Popular Music, Resistance, and the Scholarly Debate

The field of popular music studies has, since its inception, been deeply concerned with the notions of power, political change, and musical performance. Theodor Adorno, the mid-twentieth century philosopher and musicologist, may be identified as the founder of the discipline, for his writings about popular music, capitalism, and fascism are lodestones to all who have come after him.[10] Briefly, Adorno (and his colleagues who formed what came to be known as the Frankfurt School) questioned the value of cultural products for "the masses," particularly pop music. In the 1940s, Adorno began arguing that the Western popular culture industry is solely concerned with making a profit.[11] The industry values and continues to produce whatever has been profitable in the past. The result, in the case of the pop music recording industry, is stasis, a paralysis of imagination and critical thought: "No independent thinking must be expected from the audience: the product prescribes every reaction."[12]

According to Adorno, pop songs are insidious not only because they are formulaic, but also because they are pleasurable, and therefore a distraction from the daily reality of social injustice. After being subjected to pop music on the radio, on television, and seemingly at every turn, "the masses" lose their ability to question the status quo. They become politically impotent, unable to challenge the capitalist economic and social hierarchy that controls their lives: "Capitalist production so confines [consumers], body and soul, that they fall helpless victims to what is offered them."[13]

Adorno's grim vision has been contested by numerous scholars of popular music, particularly those who were born during or after the 1960s, when rock music became the soundtrack for a youth movement that challenged many social norms in the Western world.[14] Some of these authors argue in direct opposition to Adorno: popular music provides a locus of resistance, they say, precisely because of some of the characteristics Adorno vilified. Craig Lockard, for example, argues that the mass nature of popular music is its strength: its distribution through the mass media enables it to reach large audiences. His detailed study of popular music in Southeast Asia documents numerous songs from various countries whose lyrics enunciate resistance. He argues that "as one of the most accessible media, the popular music industry inevitably became one of the few possible venues in which protest and criticism could be presented, and the major practitioners inevitably became important voices in their own right."[15] Timothy Ryback's book about rock and roll in the Soviet bloc, finished just before the fall of the Berlin Wall, triumphantly concludes:

> [Rock and roll] transformed the sights and sounds of everyday life in the Soviet bloc. In a very real sense, the triumph of rock and roll in Eastern Europe and the Soviet Union has been the realization of a democratic process. . . . In the course of thirty years, rock bands have stormed every bastion of official resistance and forced both party and government to accept rock-and-roll music as a part of life in the Marxist-Leninist state."[16]

Another more recent example is Jeff Chang's work on hip-hop, which he characterizes as "revolutionary."[17] Chang's study points out how rappers such as Public Enemy managed not only to articulate a message that was sharply critical of the economic and cultural marginalization of Black people in the USA, but also to sell millions of albums. Hip-hop artists actually transformed society, setting fashion trends for middle-class white youth and empowering hundreds of inner-city teens who became well-respected and affluent artists, producers, and label owners.[18] Michael Bodden says that rap's association with social protest is well understood by youth in Indonesia, and that Indonesian musicians began using it to express rebellion against their own authoritarian government in the 1990s.[19]

Both Robert Walser and Richard Middleton assert that pop music is, if not a site of resistance, at least a locus where fans and consumers ("the masses") exercise agency. Pointing out that pop songs emphasize stories, characters, and feelings, these authors say that pop music is "where [people] find dominant definitions of themselves as well as alternatives, options to try on for size."[20] People construct meanings for the songs they hear, and for their own lives, and they are able to do so in part because of the very nature of this kind of music: the conventional musical ideas, or hooks, that are ubiquitous in pop music (and were so despised by Adorno) carry tremendous social meaning, because they have been so often reused.[21] Pop music, therefore, in the eyes of Walser and Middleton and their colleagues, offers the *possibility* of social change on a broad scale.

To be sure, the discipline of popular music studies has not completely rejected Adorno's thesis; in fact, a number of scholars who study not only the songs but the global industry that produces them make compelling arguments that resemble Adorno's. Roger Wallis and Krister Malm, for example, have spent decades examining the production and consumption of popular music around the globe. They point out that the dissemination of sounds and production methods that originated in America resulted, by the 1970s, in a "transnational music"—a popular music using the instrumentation and performance practice of American rock and roll bands, now well-known in many countries.[22] This transnational music is created and sold by a global recording industry controlled by only a handful of record companies. The so-called Big Four record companies (Sony BMG, Universal, Warner, and EMI) constitute an oligopoly that controls more than 80 percent of the commercially available music recordings worldwide. Independent record labels, which often support new and experimental artists, do exist. However, virtually none of them outlive their founders. Indie labels are inevitably purchased by one of the Big Four or disappear when they are no longer financially viable.[23] As Marcus Breen points out, the convergence of entertainment and information technology in the digital age means that the Big Four now deliver music to consumers as part of a music/telecommunications/software package; the influence of these few companies is therefore increasing in ways that even Adorno could not have envisioned.[24]

In the face of this pervasive control by a tiny group of companies, some scholars are skeptical of claims that pop music affords any opportunity for resistance. How, they ask, can people envision and effect significant social change when the context for such change, the very field in which they might operate, is sharply limited by the forces of capitalism? Keith Negus, for example, states flatly, "Making meanings, actively using technologies and interpreting texts is not the same as having the power and influence to distribute cultural forms."[25] And Michael Hayes is equally blunt: "Regardless of the cultural value placed upon pop music, its fundamental allegiance to corporate structures . . . must lead to a reconsideration of the transgressive ability of this form."[26]

Clearly, the debate about the political potential of pop music is central to the field.[27] It is important to note that the debate usually focuses on the musical artifact (a song, or less commonly, the complete oeuvre of an artist). Scholars usually ask: Is this piece of music politically progressive, or not?

After interviewing both Burmese pop musicians and government censors, I decided that, in this case, the question should be framed somewhat differently. Scholar James Scott's work provides the frame. In his book *Domination and the Arts of Resistance*, Scott elucidates the idea of public transcripts and hidden transcripts. In another of his widely read works, *Weapons of the Weak*, Scott describes the many ways in which seemingly powerless groups resist state power. Ultimately, I found that the ideas outlined in these two books shed the most light on the Burmese pop music industry.

Public Transcript and Hidden Transcript

Scott defines the public transcript as "the open interaction between subordinates and those who dominate."[28] In other words, the public transcript is the story about society that the most powerful in that society wish to tell. It is the "truth" that elites promote, since it justifies their own continued dominance. And because this story is told by the most powerful in the society, it becomes the accepted story, the narrative that is proclaimed publicly. The hidden transcript, on the other hand, is "the discourse that takes place 'offstage,' beyond direct observation by powerholders."[29] This is the story that subordinates tell each other when they are out of the spotlight. It serves to uphold their own dignity and autonomy, and it differs from the public transcript in significant ways. "While the hidden transcript cannot be described as the truth that contradicts the lies told to power, it is correct to say that the hidden transcript is a self-disclosure that power relations normally exclude from the official transcript."[30]

Occasionally, subordinates succeed in inserting a disguised form of the hidden transcript into the public transcript.[31] In these cases, the message of the hidden transcript is cloaked in euphemism: "While it is surely less satisfying than an open declaration of the hidden transcript, it nevertheless achieves something the backstage can never match. It carves out a public, if provisional, space for the autonomous cultural expression of dissent. If it is disguised, it is at least not hidden; it is spoken to power."[32]

In Burma, the power holders are the leaders of the Tatmadaw, the national army. Unelected, they have controlled the government of the country since 1962. While the population at large has descended into poverty, they have enriched themselves by virtue of their control over business and trade.[33] They have repeatedly shown their willingness to deploy the power of their arms against the citizens of the country. Of course, they maintain control over all forms of media with the aim of ensuring that the public transcript—the story that justifies their refusal to cede power to a democratically elected government—remains the only "truth" available to the Burmese public. In short, the public transcript is: The Union of Myanmar is just that, a united country that is happily developing itself. Citizens may experience interpersonal problems (the kind that pop songs tend to speak about), but they have no complaints about the SPDC's "disciplined road to democracy."[34]

Longer versions of this transcript appear in state-run media constantly. Here is one that appeared in *The New Light of Myanmar* in 2009, just over a month before the annual Union Day:

> Myanmar is a country where national races reside in unity. All the national people have been living and consistently safeguarding their own nation, sovereignty and national prestige and integrity from time immemorial.

Myanmar regained independence and sovereignty through national solidarity. The Union Day is observed every year with the aim of keeping Union spirit alive and upholding fine traditions in the history among the people. . . . Nowadays, the government is building a new modern developed discipline-flourishing democratic nation with the participation of all the national people. Brilliant achievements have been made in political, economic and social sectors. The national objectives of the Union Day for this year indicate the national duties to be discharged by all at present or in the future. Therefore, all the national people need to discharge the national duties in accord with the Union spirit and noble traditions so that there will be peace, unity and prosperity nationwide.[35]

The hidden transcript is of course, hidden, and therefore no convenient summaries of it are ever published in the state media. However I heard excerpts from it almost daily when I lived in Yangon. During informal conversations with clerks, taxi drivers, and other working-class Burmese, people told me that "our government is terrible" and that they hoped to one day emigrate. Members of *tain-yin-tha* groups were especially caustic in their criticism; many of the older people in ethnic minority neighborhoods recounted stories of government oppression (such as the takeover of a local school) that dated back to the early 1960s. One young lady begged me for the t-shirt I was wearing, which had a photo of Aung San Suu Kyi on the front—a garment she could never wear in public. After hearing these kinds of complaints and frustrated hopes expressed dozens of times, I developed the following précis of Burma's hidden transcript:

Burma is home to groups with deep historical, ethnic, and religious differences. Many of these "national races" (most of which are non-Burman, non-Buddhist groups) mounted armed resistance against the central government shortly after Burma achieved independence, and many members of those groups cherish dreams of self-determination. Furthermore, the large majority of all Burmese voters voted for democratically constituted political parties in the 1990 elections, when Aung San Suu Kyi's National League for Democracy won 83 percent of the seats in the Hluttdaw, or People's Parliament. The SPDC, which held Suu Kyi under house arrest until 2010, is unjust and corrupt.

This hidden transcript is indeed an offstage narrative, and many Burmese people, while acceding to it, deeply fear it being spoken aloud. Like other visitors to Burma,[36] I have participated in numerous conversations in which my Burmese interlocutor has resorted to whispering words like "democracy," "refugees," "Aung San Suu Kyi" and "KNU" (the acronym for the largest armed ethnic insurgent group). Twice, I was reproved for saying "Burma" rather than "Myanmar" (the SPDC's official name for the country).

The Burmese pop music industry as a whole and individual musicians who work within that industry manifest a variety of responses to the government's ceaseless promotion of the public transcript. I will explain these responses below, but I begin by describing the Press Security Board (PSB), the organization charged with upholding the monopoly of the public transcript.

Visiting the Press Security Board

On January 30, 2008, I went to the PSB office to request an interview. The office, a large white building built around a quadrangle, sits on a recessed lot in a narrow, dusty street directly across from Kandawgyi Park in central Yangon. I did not know then that the building had served as the headquarters for the Japanese Secret Police during the brutal World War II occupation, but had I known I would have found it hard to believe.[37] There were no ominous vibrations in the air as I approached the front door.

The building was a hub of activity that day, with vehicles entering and leaving the small parking lot, and businessmen crowding the halls. Upon arrival, I was asked for my name, address, and six other identifying markers (none of which I could provide, since I do not hold a Burmese identification card). Clearly, I was an oddity—a foreigner in a government office—but the innate courtesy of Burmese people toward visitors won out, and despite the fact that I could not adequately account for myself, a young woman showed me to an office room where workers censor music. The office held ten desks, and the walls were covered by floor-to-ceiling shelves that contained stacks of dusty files, all encased in identical dark green covers. There were literally piles of work in evidence. Not much work was being done, though, at least at that moment. Most of the desks were empty, the computer screens were dark, and the ceiling fan was motionless.

When a worker queried me about the purpose of my visit ("Do you want to publish an album?"), I explained that I would simply like to interview someone who works for the PSB. Immediately, a young man who spoke perfect English (perhaps a producer?) intervened: "Why would you even try?" he said. "No one here will answer your questions honestly. They won't admit that they take bribes." It was unnerving to hear my own suspicions articulated so clearly and quickly.

My request was clearly a strange one, and no one quite knew what to do. My guide took me to one male superior, and then to another, before I finally got a chance to speak with a woman who was a supervisor. At each point, I was asked, "What do you want to know?" I answered as vaguely as I could ("I want to know what kind of work people do here") and each time, my answer was met with laughter. I had relationships with Burmese people for years before I realized that they tend to laugh when a situation is uncomfortable, as well as when it is humorous. In this case, the situation was clearly uncomfortable. No one wanted to deny my request point-blank, but it seemed dangerous to accede to it. I managed to convince them of my sincerity when I pointed out that all countries have censorship laws, and that in my own country of Canada, the government exercises strict controls over Canadian content on the airwaves. Therefore there are great debates in Canada on what constitutes "Canadian" music. I finished up with, "I want to learn about Burmese music and the laws here," and this seemed to do the trick. During the thirty-minute interview that I was finally granted, two representatives of the PSB told me the following:

Producers are responsible for submitting musical recordings to the PSB for checking. (And remember that many musicians produce their own *series*, so many performers, as well as producers, interact with the PSB.) The PSB employs forty full-time staff to censor all books, magazines, movies, and musical recordings. All of the workers have university degrees, although no special qualifications are required to work at the PSB. These staffers are paid "normal" government salaries (which is to say, they are not very well paid). The supervisor believes that workers generally like their jobs, although it can get stressful when the volume of work is very high (for example, when a worker has to check a complete novel).

The PSB representatives went on to say that their workers check all musical submissions, even those that contain only instrumental pieces. Their main concern, however, is the lyrics. They do not discriminate against particular musical styles, but they do check all the words of all songs. (When prompted, the supervisor allowed that yes, censors also evaluate performers' appearances, particularly on videos; they must "look Burmese" in order to get a pass.) Each worker is provided with the technology needed to check the submissions (cassette players, CD players, televisions, etc.). Generally, the worker listens to the song once while simultaneously reading the typed lyrics, checking to see if the words being sung match the words on the page, and determining whether those words are acceptable. (When a producer submits a *series* for censorship, he must also provide ten copies of the lyrics.)

Usually, one listening is all that is required, since "Burmese singers sing clearly." However, if the censor senses a "problem," he or she will listen to the song again. If the worker is not sure whether the recording is problematic or not, he or she can approach the manager for help. If the manager is unsure, the recording will be reviewed by the director, and so on up the chain of command. Difficult cases are sent to Naypyidaw—the new capital and the home base for virtually all government decision-makers—for censorship. But this is usually unnecessary, the PSB managers asserted, because most submissions get a "pass" right away. If a worker does perceive a problem, she or he will notify the producer, and the producer simply has to fix the problem in order to receive a pass.

Perceiving a "problem" is an art, not a science. PSB censors do not rely on any list of forbidden words or even a detailed policy. According to the supervisor I interviewed, the only document that guides their work is the Printers and Publishers Registration Act of 1962.[38] This act requires that all printing presses be registered with the government, but does not outline what can or cannot be published. Censors must therefore use their personal judgment to determine whether a recording "is acceptable to Burmese culture," in the words of my interviewee. The managers trust the workers, the supervisor said ("They grew up here, so they know Burmese culture, and they know what is acceptable"), and it seems they must do so, as a matter of logistics: there are far too many submissions for management to be able to review each case.[39]

This information accords with what I learned during interviews with musicians (with the possible exception of the assertion that "most" submissions earn a pass immediately. For example, Michael told me that "most of the time, something has to be edited.") However, some of the other information the PSB officials shared with me is not borne out by what I know to be true, based on my own observations or my interviews with musicians. Essentially, the PSB officials who spoke with me recounted the public transcript—that is, they claimed that their particular branch of the Burmese government, just like the rest of the government, works for the good of the people.

For example, the officials told me that the electricity is "always on" in their building, meaning that the PSB works efficiently. However, I could see for myself that the electricity was not working when I first arrived. In addition, they assured me that producers do not have to pay fees when they submit their work, and that the PSB does not assess fines when problematic material is discovered. Musicians, by contrast, consistently claim that they have to pay fees when they first submit their work—to shadowy "agents" who work unofficially for the PSB—and that they also have to pay a fine whenever a problem is discovered.

Some of these fees and fines seem to be standardized (10,000 *kyat* to submit a VCD, for example, and 1,000 *kyat* per spelling mistake). Since such fees and fines are not officially required, according to the PSB supervisors I interviewed, they could be described as bribes. Interestingly, none of the musicians referred to them as such. Evidently, they are so consistently required that musicians perceive them as the kinds of costs one normally pays when filing government forms. The costs that musicians most frequently complain about are those associated with rerecording songs that have been deemed problematic. In some cases, rerecording songs may be prohibitively costly or logistically impossible, and so *series* must be released without the full complement of songs originally planned.

According to the musicians I interviewed, as an application makes its way through the system, producers must grease the wheels of the PSB system by giving "presents" to officials. At each level, PSB workers expect to receive increasingly expensive gifts from musicians who have submitted their recordings. Musicians give these presents in order to ensure that the workers will process their applications in timely fashion. As producer Kaung Lin Lin explained to me, PSB officials do not actually ask for these gifts, so it is technically true to say that they do not request bribes. However, everyone involved in the "censorshit" system—as Hpone Thant called it—is well aware that these gifts are required in order to obtain a pass. In fact, producers have to factor the costs of such gifts into their budgets when they plan their projects.

The gifts, apparently, are usually not used by the recipients themselves, but are resold to supplement their salaries. Hpone Thant told me about a friend of his who wanted to prove to himself that his presents to PSB workers were not appreciated as gifts. He marked the bottom of an expensive bottle of liquor that he gave to a manager at the PSB. Sure enough, two weeks later he found that marked bottle for sale in the shop where he had originally purchased it.

Generally, though, my interview with the PSB officials produced consistent information. Interestingly, the officials confirmed for me the facets of their operation that musicians and producers find most irritating. First, they affirmed that they do not have any mechanism for notifying artists once their work has been passed. They do not phone or send out letters, and so artists must make repeated trips to the PSB to inquire in person about the progress of their submissions. Second, the PBS supervisor asserted repeatedly that workers do not have a checklist of forbidden words and phrases; workers are expected to use their own discretion in awarding passes.

This latter policy is a source of great frustration to musicians. If a list existed, composers would abide by it and thereby forestall the possibility of "problems" and the consequent expenses associated with paying fines and rerecording the music. But since no list exists, the composers are at the mercy of the censors, who can justify denying a pass, and then demand a fine, under almost any circumstances. This policy is a tool that facilitates corruption at the PSB.

It is important to note here that the Burmese government does have a written policy of sorts that lays down some ground rules for print publications (and by extension, the sheets of lyrics which accompany musical submissions to the PSB). This document was written in 1975 as an addendum to the 1962 Printers and Publishers Registration Act. It is entitled *Memorandum to All Printers and Publishers Concerning the Submission of Manuscripts for Scrutiny:*

The Central Registration Board hereby informs all printers and publishers that it has laid down the following principles to be adhered to in scrutinizing political, economic, and religious manuscripts, and novels, journals, and magazines. They must be scrutinized to see whether or not they contain:

1. anything detrimental to the Burmese Socialist Program;
2. anything detrimental to the ideology of the state;
3. anything detrimental to the socialist economy;
4. anything which might be harmful to national solidarity and unity;
5. anything which might be harmful to security, the rule of law, peace, and public order;

6. any incorrect ideas and opinions which do not accord with the times;
7. any descriptions which, though factually correct, are unsuitable because of the time or the circumstances of their writing;
8. any obscene (pornographic) writing;
9. any writing which would encourage crimes and unnatural cruelty and violence;
10. any criticism of a nonconstructive type of the work of government departments;
11. any libel or slander of any individual.[40]

Interestingly, this document was never referenced or quoted to me during my research; neither PSB officials nor musicians ever mentioned it. On the whole, I thought this made sense. Given the vagueness of these criteria, it is perhaps more accurate to say, as both PSB officials and musicians did, that "there is no list." Certainly there is no useful list. Anna J. Allott's analysis of the memorandum is a propos:

First . . . almost any written statement or piece of descriptive writing could be objected to under one or another of these headings, and second, the decision to label something "harmful" or "detrimental" would, of necessity, be arbitrary and depend on the whim of each individual censor.[41]

Censor's Experiences with Censorship

My own experience with the PSB struck me as being somewhat reflective of musicians' experiences with the board. Although the interaction produced results—I got the interview I requested—the episode was rather uncomfortable. The problem, as I saw it, was that I did not trust the PSB officials, and they did not trust me. Indeed, I was warned not to trust them, and given the fact that my request for an interview provoked debate among the staff, it seems that they were reluctant to trust me. In the end, we came to an accommodation. But I did not ask all of the questions I wanted to ask—in particular, I was itching to enquire about the Saw Wai incident (explained below), which had become public knowledge the week before—and the officials did not truthfully answer some of the questions that I did pose. Ultimately, neither I nor they were completely transparent in our dealings with each other.

And this seems to be the crux of the relationship between artists and the PSB. The artists generally assume that the workers at the PSB will deal treacherously with them, and the workers must maintain a suspicious posture toward the artists, since their work consists of being on the lookout for "problems." Because a problem is not usually self-evident (that is, it is not merely a word or phrase from a list of *verboten* vocabulary), it is difficult to detect. Indeed, as another censor explained to me at length, the essence of "checking" consists of constantly questioning an artist's motives.

This censor is U Hla Myint Swe, a retired army general and the director of City FM, Yangon's most listened-to radio station. Although he has other responsibilities, he spends two to three hours per day working on City FM tasks. He says that he devotes most of that time to censoring the station's broadcasts; he calls himself "the final decider." "I check again and again" he says, to ensure that nothing said or sung on air will be "dangerous." "My radio station is very pure," he says, adding that the programs contain "no politics" and no "wrong words." I asked him if on-air personalities or callers to the station ever make explicitly antigovernment statements, and he responded in the negative. The job is much more subtle than that. Basically, he must continually ask himself, "What is their aim in saying this?" He admits that, on occasion, on-air interviewees will make statements that have, or could have, a double meaning—that is, referring to politics. In such cases, he edits out the problematic statement. "Now with computers [i.e., digital editing], it's very easy," he says.

What is unacceptable in Burmese pop songs is not precisely defined. On the one hand, this means that censors, untrammeled by any specific policy or list of forbidden items, can deny a pass to anyone on almost any grounds. If the work is "not Burmese" enough or "dangerous" in some way, censors can edit or completely suppress it. On the other hand, they must assume that a song may contain some hidden message and then try to decipher it. After just one listening, they must determine the "meaning" of a song and decide what implications that meaning might have—no easy task, as any musicologist will attest.

Essentially, a PSB worker's job consists of trying to sustain the public transcript by ferreting out any whiff of the hidden transcript. And this is difficult to do, because the hidden transcript evolves over time. Keeping this in mind, the PSB's no-list policy makes sense: if PSB workers are going to be successful in censoring the hidden transcript, they need to exercise latitude in their work. Any list of specific words would effectively constrain them. Last year's list of problem words would not contain the vocabulary of the new and improved hidden transcript. In order to be most effective at their jobs, censors need to, as the PSB manager said, exercise their own discretion in determining whether a given song is "acceptable to Burmese culture."

Of course, they sometimes make mistakes.

One renowned example of censor error occurred in January 2008, the week before my visit to the PSB.[42] A poet named Saw Wai wrote a poem about an innocuous boy-loses-girl affair of the heart. The PSB passed this poem, and it was published in the weekly journal *Achit*. On the day of publication, delighted readers noticed that, read acrostically, the poem says *Ana-yu Bogyoke Than Shwe*—"power-crazed General Than Shwe."[43] "Power-hungry" or "power-crazed" is a deeply offensive insult in Burma. According to the value system espoused by most Buddhists, good people are always striving to lessen their attachment to the things of this world, including positions of earthly power. The junta knows this very well, and often claims in its own defense that it is not clinging to power because it is power hungry, but rather because it is obligated to ensure that the country remains stable and unified. In fact, government media even levels this accusation at its opponents, claiming that democracy activists are cynically using the vocabulary of democracy and human rights in order to gain political power.[44] So the poet's encoded insult, aimed at the head of state, was clearly an example of "wrong words."

Saw Wai was arrested immediately, and eventually sentenced to two years in prison. The journal editor (who is supposed to act as a censor in the same way that a radio station director does) also fell under suspicion.[45] For their part, PSB workers are now equipped with magnifying glasses, so they can more closely scrutinize each submission.[46] Friends who shared this story with me—and many people were happy to talk about it, seeing it as a rare victory, however short-lived, over the government—joked about the censors. They laughed when thinking about how PSB workers would now have to read each submission four times (left to right, right to left, top to bottom and bottom to top).

In fairness, I must add that there exists the possibility—however slight—that individual PSB workers do not expressly or implicitly solicit bribes and presents, and that they are uncomfortable with the current system. I deduce this from an interview I conducted with a man who is an important part of Burma's version of the *American Idol* TV show. This show, called *Melody World*, has aired on Myawaddy TV since 2007, and is by all accounts very popular. My interviewee has a history of speaking for musicians on difficult issues, and is widely perceived as a man of integrity. He says that contestants on *Melody World* frequently offer gifts to the judges, directors, and producers in the hopes that these presents will positively affect their chances for success in the contest. He claims that these presents do not, in fact, make any difference, and that the judges are committed to picking the best singer as the winner. However, he says, Burma's bribery culture is so engrained that many contestants wrongly assume that they must provide presents to those in power.

This story is distressing proof of the corruption that pervades not only the music industry but many other aspects of Burmese society. This kind of assumption may—I emphasize *may*—be at work in interactions between musicians and the PSB, and PSB workers may be unhappy with the current state of affairs; but since the present-giving culture is literally unspeakable, they cannot discuss it.

Musicians' Experiences with Censorship

The Saw Wai case is a bit of an anomaly. Usually the intended message, or meaning, of a Burmese poem or song text is not clearly spelled out. Like song texts from many other societies, Burmese lyrics depend heavily on poetic devices, especially metaphor and allusion. When censors approach such texts, they are not generally looking for an encoded phrase whose message is clear. Rather, they attempt to determine if the text's literal message could be read as an allusion to a forbidden topic (particularly if it could be read as a criticism of the government). Basically, they are looking for a disguised version of the hidden transcript.

My research revealed that Yangon-based pop musicians' predominant experience with censorship is that they are censored for lyrics that *could* be perceived as political criticism. The self-proclaimed intent of the musician usually makes no difference to the censors; when a pass is denied, generally, no appeal is possible. Musicians may argue with PSB workers, protesting that their song lyrics refer only to the topics referenced at the surface of the words (the literal meaning), but such arguments typically fall on deaf ears. An individual censor may believe a composer who says that his song was innocently meant, but this belief is somewhat beside the point. Censors are usually not interested in authorial intent. Instead, they focus on listeners: their overriding concern is to forestall any possibility that listeners could infer a forbidden meaning from the song. They worry more about audiences thinking "wrong thoughts" than about composers' intentions to provoke such wrong thoughts. To be sure, when there is no doubt that an author or composer (such as Saw Wai) has intended to make a forbidden statement, the government acts quickly and harshly. However, the more common situation among pop musicians is that composers and singers have their work edited. When their songs are judged to be potentially subversive, they are allowed to continue working, although under a cloud of suspicion.

The story of composer U Hla Kyi illustrates this point. Now aged fifty-five, U Hla Kyi has lived and worked in the Yangon-area pop scene all of his adult life, and is able to support himself and his family with this work.[47] He estimates that he has written over five hundred songs. He outlined for me four interactions he has had with the PSB—all of them negative.

First, a *series* for which he had written the songs was denied a pass. The PSB objected to the cover art, which featured a large "A.D." beside a photo of a dove. U Hla Kyi, who is a Baptist Christian, tried to explain to the PSB that the graphic was a Christian reference, with A.D. representing the *anno Domini* of the Christian calendar and the dove the Holy Spirit.[48] The censors dismissed this rationale. At the time, General Ne Win, the head of state, was living on a street in Yangon called AD Lan (or AD Road).[49] The censors believed that the cover could be interpreted as saying, "There should be peace on AD Street"— that is, the dictator should be removed from power.

On another, more recent occasion, U Hla Kyi wrote a song called "Eighteen Rains." He says he picked the number randomly, wanting to reference an extended period of time. However, the censors perceived this as a possible reference to Aung San Suu Kyi, the prodemocracy leader, who had been under house arrest for eighteen years when he submitted his song. His protests made no difference and the producer was required to remove this song from the *series*.

U Hla Kyi's third interaction with the PSB was an unofficial one. He had written a song in Sgaw Karen for a gospel *series* that was not submitted to the censors. (More about these kinds of *series* below.) The title of the song was "They Are Trying to Kill Me." Government workers heard about the song and asked acquaintances of his to enquire about the title and its meaning. U Hla Kyi told these unofficial ambassadors that indeed, the title did have a political meaning: he was alluding to the United States trying to kill Myanmar. This explanation—which he delivered to me with a wink and a nod—apparently satisfied the PSB, which was not entitled to investigate the case, anyway.

The fourth situation that U Hla Kyi told me about seems to be an outgrowth of the first three instances. He says that "the government watches me constantly now," continually questioning his work and his motives. He is never allowed to leave the country, something he dearly wishes to do. He claims that he has no fear for his physical safety, but he has genuine concerns for the viability of his career. "They will not kill me with a gun, but with a pen," he says—that is, by writing "pass denied" on his submissions to the PSB.

U Hla Kyi's story is unique to him, of course, but elements of it are common among Yangon-based pop musicians. Sporadic frustrating interactions with the PSB, which result in costly rewrites of songs or of complete *series*, the sense of being dismissed and distrusted, and the inability to travel due to government surveillance: numerous interviewees recounted these same experiences to me. Other stories are more dramatic. For example, Moe Lwin told me of being jailed for three days and then losing his sole source of income (when he was banned from performing and recording) for an entire year, after one of his recordings was deemed to be "too political" in the wake of the 1988 democracy protests. Having learned his lesson, Moe Lwin now sings only acceptable songs, and indeed is careful to cooperate with the PSB. As a result, he and his family are financially secure. His story, and the eventual outcome, mirrors the well-known story of Sai Htee Saing (now deceased).

Sai Htee Saing, a prominent composer and performer, worked as an organizer for the National League for Democracy (Aung San Suu Kyi's political party) in 1988. After being arrested, he decided to do whatever he needed to do in order to support his family. He subsequently became known as a singer of "government songs," like Moe Lwin. It is easy to criticize such musicians for giving in to government pressure (and indeed a number of my friends spoke disparagingly about both Sai Htee Saing and my interviewee), but I wonder what all the critics would do if they were faced with similar harsh treatment. In any event, while most Burmese musicians have not faced such extreme choices, they are all aware that the possibility looms in their futures, too.

Musicians can never predict how censors will react, since no document exists which clearly defines the boundaries that they must not cross. Of course, musicians can discern patterns and infer rules, and they do so constantly. Industry insiders eventually devise their own mental lists of "wrong words," and they were quick to rattle these off in interviews. Michael came up with the following list of forbidden words and topics:

> anything about sex
> any rude words
> anything to do with God
> politics
> human rights and democracy
> the country's situation (that is, the present state of Myanmar)

Michael also pointed out that, interestingly, composers are allowed to address the topics of AIDS and orphans, both of them pressing social issues in Burma, where 1.3 percent of the adult population is infected with HIV[50] and where hundreds of thousands of children live in orphanages, many of them funded by international sources.[51]

Performers also emphasize that their VCDs are censored not only for words but also for visual appearance. Other informants added the following to the list of the forbidden in musical performance:

> colored hair
> long hair (men)
> nose rings
> visible tattoos
> shorts or short skirts or split skirts
> sleeveless or wide-necked shirts (women)
> blue jeans (at least for performances aired on government TV stations)
> men and women dancing together
> vigorous dancing by either gender[52]

Soe Htun said that Myanmar TV and Myawaddy TV producers insist that performers look "neat and tidy." (Performers can deduce what "neat and tidy" is by reading the regulations posted on a billboard in front of the Myawaddy TV studio.)[53] Aye Kyi said that the justification for banning all of the above items is that they are "not Burmese," according to the PSB; and this largely accords with what I heard from censors themselves. In truth, this is an amazingly reductionist version of Burmese culture. A little more than a century ago, long hair (pinned up on the head) was the hairstyle of choice for upper-class Burmese men, and even today many get tattoos in the belief that tattoos offer protection from spiritual and physical harm. Khine Ta Tun told me that his experience convinces him that censors are not, in fact, concerned about preserving Burmese culture: "They just don't like it if you criticize *them* [i.e., the government.]"

Whatever the case—and no doubt some government officials are genuinely concerned about preserving the uniqueness of Burmese culture—it seems that the PSB standards regarding visual appearance are loosening somewhat. I have seen skirts above the knee and dyed hair on recent government TV broadcasts, for example. Of course, given the ambiguous nature of the PSB's no-list policy, standards are probably always changing. Thida Zay pointed out that standards for lyrics are even more restrictive now than they were two decades ago, and that he is quite sure he would be unable to record new versions of some songs that were popular in the 1980s—songs about marching or "showing your desire" for example. Certainly it is impossible, in the current climate, to publish songs about "standing firmly for the truth."[54]

Currently, musicians' most common generalization about the government's attitude toward musical productions is that they must meet the censor's criteria for "niceness." Musicians used various words to reference this idea. U Hla Kyi, for example, says that the PSB insists that music must always be "pretty" and "polite." Taylor says that censors seem to be continually concerned that song lyrics be "not rude." Accordingly, he was once obligated to change a line in a love song that he wrote. His original words were *ah-chit ko mohn deh*, or, "I hate her loving"; the PSB required that he rerecord the song singing *chit-ta ma chai bu*, meaning "I don't like her loving." Aung Shwe recalls that, using the same justification, the PSB once denied a pass to a song which contained a word which, in itself, was inoffensive. The word rhymes with the Burmese word for "penis" and the PSB deemed it to be potentially rude. Again, rational argument made no difference (that the word "penis" would make no sense in the context of the song and therefore listeners would be unlikely to misunderstand it). The producer had to incur the expense of rerecording the song in order to obtain a pass.

Aung Shwe summed up the situation by explaining that Burma's military government insists that TV and radio broadcasts focus on "nice things" so that the public at large will be led to reflect on those nice things—and will thereby be distracted from the grim reality of day-to-day life under a totalitarian regime. (When I told him that this sounded like the criticism of pop music lyrics leveled by a famous European scholar named Adorno, he said that he had never heard of Adorno, but that Adorno must have gotten it right.) Aung Shwe believes, though, that ultimately the government's scheme is a failure; he says that "everyone" is well aware that government-controlled TV shows and the like are "all lies," and so the public turns to foreign movies and other products for entertainment.

Clearly, the SPDC has not convinced Aung Shwe of the validity of their public transcript. (And I would say, in agreement with him, that they have failed to convince large numbers of Burmese people.) It does not directly follow from this, however, that Aung Shwe devotes his musical career to proclaiming the hidden transcript. Like virtually all of the other Burmese musicians I met, he pursues a variety of approaches in his work.

Three Strategies: Submission, Defiance, and Subversion

Yangon pop musicians use a variety of approaches, or strategies, as they negotiate their relationships with the Press Security Board. I identify the first three of these strategies as *submission, defiance,* and *subversion.* These three strategies (and a fourth that I will discuss below) largely accord with strategies identified by both James Scott, in his *Weapons of the Weak,* and Ardeth Maung Thawnghmung, who conducted a detailed study of farmers in rural Burma.[55] As we shall see, these three strategies manifest themselves quite differently in the context of pop music and censorship.

Submission

Composer and performers who submit to the PSB's rule accept the limitations imposed on their expression in order to obtain a pass from the censors. By implication, when they submit to the censors, they uphold the public transcript. As they create their music, they keep in mind all of the board's unspoken rules, and are careful to remain well within the limits of what is acceptable. In essence, they exercise self-censorship, so that they will not have to bear the expense of rerecording their work should the PSB identify a problem with their lyrics.

Taylor's attitude about his work exemplifies this strategy of submission. He quickly listed off all of the forbidden words and topics that he could think of, and then said, "But I don't worry about that when I'm composing. The government will censor it if they don't like it, so I don't think about that while writing a song." Clearly, he has internalized the PSB standards to the point that he does not bother consciously reminding himself of them while working. But more importantly, he accepts the reality that his work will be scrutinized and could possibly be rejected. (As I described above, the PSB has censored some of his lyrics in the past, so he has personal experience with the reality of censorship). He betrayed no anger or annoyance when we discussed the issue. Taylor submits himself to PSB regulations and is creating a profitable career in the music industry by selling government-approved *series* in retail outlets.

Htin Thu, a composer with twenty-five years of experience, expressed this same idea of self-censorship in response to government standards even more bluntly: "I'm immune to PSB problems," he says. "The censor lives in my hand." He, too, is accustomed to submitting to PSB standards—so accustomed, in fact, that he no longer has to consciously think about writing acceptable words. Therefore, his songs consistently earn passes from the censors. His past experiences have inoculated him against the possibility of "problems."

It is important to note here that the musicians I interviewed did not use the word "submission" (or any synonym) when describing their actions. Indeed, they were anxious to be perceived as independent actors, since they perceive themselves this way. They reject the notion that by cooperating with the censors, they are somehow aiding and abetting the promulgation of the government's public transcript. They pointed out, over and over, that their songs come from their hearts, that they are sincere expressions of real emotion and experience. That these songs are also acceptable to the PSB does not make them, perforce, mere pieces of propaganda. For example, virtually all of the pop performers in Burma regularly write and sing songs about love of family members (appropriately called "mother songs," "father songs," and "children songs.") In these kinds of songs the musician celebrates family relationships and exhorts listeners to love their closest kin. Family songs easily earn passes from the PSB, but they are not written in order to conform to some government standard of niceness. Rather, composers create these songs to reflect their own ideas and to speak to their audiences. It is simply fortuitous that these sincerely meant songs are acceptable to the censors as well.

In addition, some well-connected musicians find that even while they submit to the PSB, there is room for negotiation with the censors when a "problem" arises. Khine Ta Tun likened the whole PSB application process to a game: "It's a kind of fun challenge," he said. He pointed out that one can debate the finer points of language, and even win, if one "knows someone"—that is, if a musician has a personal relationship with a powerful personage at the PSB. Since Khine Ta Tun knows the Tatmadaw general currently in charge of the ministry, he feels free to contact this man if a lower-level employee determines that his work is problematic. This general is a former musician himself and is "a reasonable guy," according to Khine Ta Tun. Therefore, he is genuinely open to changing his mind about lyrics, provided that someone he respects offers him a good argument for doing so.

Thuza, who is currently one of the highest-paid performers in Burma, says that he, too, has found that negotiation is possible. In his case, he uses the leverage he has with PSB workers in order to help producers of *series* on which he sings. "They [the PSB clerks] are my fans," he explains, and so they respect him. They appreciate the fact that he has come to the office to discuss the problem with them. He says that his advocacy for producers and composers has paid off on a number of occasions, when he has successfully convinced PSB workers to accept and pass lyrics they had previously flagged as problematic.

Defiance

Some composers and performers defy the PSB's attempts to censor them. They write lyrics that proclaim some facet of the hidden transcript, some kind of "truth" that contradicts the public transcript. This is a very small number of artists, by all accounts, because the penalty for defiance is so severe.[56] Artists who openly promote ideas forbidden by the government risk being banned from performing for years at a time (thereby curtailing their careers) and may even be imprisoned.[57] Examples of defiance are few and far between, in part because any openly critical words which are submitted to the PSB would be censored before the public ever knows of them.[58]

The best-known instance of an artist's attempt to defy the PSB occurred in 1995, when Lay Phyu, the charismatic lead singer of the Iron Cross band, released an album titled *Power 54*. The title was widely assumed to be a reference to Aung San Suu Kyi's ongoing house arrest, because her address is 54 University Avenue, Yangon. Although Lay Phyu denied that this was his intended meaning, he was subsequently banned from performing live in Yangon. Or at least, this is the rumor; the fact is that Lay Phyu did not perform in public between 2006 and the late summer of 2008, and he has never stated why.[59]

During the course of this project, I met only one musician, Htet Aung, who spoke openly about defying the PSB. Htet Aung says that he has recently written a new arrangement of the English song "We Will Go On," and that he intends to get a group to perform it. He intends that the song be understood as a message of defiance: "We will go on" despite the regime's attempts to curtail true progress and democracy in Burma. In other words, he plans to create music that will proclaim the hidden transcript.

Subversion

When singers and composers manage to get a pass while simultaneously violating one or more of the PSB's unwritten rules, they are managing to insert the hidden transcript into the public transcript. The most immediate and obvious way for an artist to do so is to bribe a PSB official for a pass. There seems to be a perception among the Burmese public that bribery of PSB officials is a common practice.[60] Remember, for example, the anonymous young man who told me this prior to my interview at the PSB. As mentioned earlier, producers do pay bribes, or "give presents," but this is just to grease the wheels of the system. My feeling is that bribes, whether or not they are frequently offered, do not constitute an important method of subversion.

The reason is, as U Hla Kyi explained to me, that low-level officials responsible for determining whether a pass is merited are afraid of losing their jobs (or worse) if they are perceived to have passed a problematic piece of music. Interestingly, for a man who breathed fire when I first raised the topic of the censors, U Hla Kyi expressed some sympathy for the workers who review his lyrics. He believes that many of them are rational people who would, in another time and place, be willing to listen to a composer's defense should a potentially problematic lyric be identified. However, it is not politically expedient for censors to be perceived as exercising any leniency. And, he believes, a bribe offered to a superior would make no difference; once a decision is made to deny a pass, no appeal (formal or secret) is possible.

Another obvious opportunity for subversion exists due to the fact that none of the PSB staffers speak or read languages other than Burmese and English. They therefore require that all recordings made in minority languages be submitted along with translations of the lyrics in Burmese. The translator has a golden opportunity to subvert the system at this point, by submitting an innocuous "translation" of words that carry forbidden meaning in the original language. I did manage to find one person who owned up to providing such a mistranslation: he provided a softened version of lyrics which in the original Sgaw Karen spoke about a future independence for the Karen people. (His translation simply mentioned a generic "freedom.") However, this type of subversion does not seem to be common. Those few recording artists who record in minority languages and then submit their work to the PSB generally claim to provide faithful translations of their lyrics, which, of course, remain within the limits of acceptability.

It is impossible to know for certain how often artists are subverting the censorship requirements, because artists are understandably unwilling to divulge their secrets.[61] My sense of it, though, is that it is an occasional rather than a regular practice: artists who customarily submit to the PSB will, on occasion, subvert the system. What is clear is that, when they do practice subversion, the method they most commonly use is that of double entendre. They disguise the message of the hidden transcript by using ambiguous language.

Composers and performers write lyrics that have one literal and inoffensive meaning and another, usually antigovernment, message that can be plausibly denied if the censors question the intent. They usually employ metaphors to do this linguistic work. Thus we see that censors' continual concern about lyrics that *could* be dangerous is grounded in reality. As censors suspect, musicians do sometimes create lyrics with the express purpose of countering the government's version of the truth.

I present the following four examples of subversive lyrics without contextual details, in order to protect the people who shared them with me. In the first case, lyrics about a man who promised to return to his lover after ten years, and then broke his promise, were written as a criticism of the government's breaking of the Panglong Agreement.[62] In that agreement, which was signed in 1947, the newly independent government of Burma undertook to address concerns of ethnic minority groups by promising some of them the right to secede from the Union of Burma after ten years should they so choose.[63] As history shows, the agreement was not honored, and this denial of the promised right to secede fuels the ambitions of ethnic minority insurgents even today.

In another case, a song which describes a vine growing around a tree and eventually strangling it offers a criticism of the government's language policy. The BSPP (and subsequently the SPDC) frequently touted its unification of the diverse ethnic groups in Burma, and cited the Panglong Agreement as the genesis of this unity. The reality is, though, that during each iteration of its existence, the military government has enacted more and more stringent rules regarding the promulgation of minority languages, eventually banning the teaching of minority languages in public schools. Prior to 1993, no magazines in languages other than Burmese and English were permitted to be published. The result is that many members of the youngest generation of ethnic minority groups who live in urban areas can no longer speak their parents' languages. In the song being discussed here the composer, who grew up in a Sgaw Karen-speaking home in Yangon and was educated in Burmese through the public school system, condemns this government's policy using a metaphor: Burmese language instruction (the vine) is strangling the seemingly strong tree of the Sgaw Karen language.

In the third example, the composer chose to criticize the ubiquitous Tatmadaw soldiers who patrol the streets of Yangon. In the midst of a love song, he inserted the line "When I see all the stars, my eyes open wide [with astonishment]." Tatmadaw soldiers wear an olive-green uniform with a patch showing a five-pointed star on each shoulder. The lyric is therefore a veiled reference to these soldiers; the idea of eyes opening wide is rather pejorative here, conveying a sense of shock and disapproval. The lyrics articulate the hidden transcript by critiquing the totalitarian military government.

Figure 5.1. Tatmadaw soldier in uniform

The fourth example is a song which talks about always having to wait. Although the composer does not specify what the singer is waiting for (and the assumption is that it is a lover, since the song is a love song), I am assured that this song, too, is a criticism of the government. Because Burmese bureaucracy is so inefficient (and corrupt), people spend a lot of time waiting, in frustration, for government services. Yangon dwellers, for example, have to wait every afternoon for the electricity to come back on, and people across the country have to wait weeks or months for paperwork to be processed. Students have waited years to complete their degrees, because the government regularly closes universities in order to forestall student organizing. The song is an expression of anger toward a government that claims that it remains in power because an abrupt transition to democracy would disrupt the country, and yet is unable or unwilling to deliver basic services in a timely manner.

As these examples demonstrate, coded messages in Burmese pop songs are subtle, and their decoding requires detailed historical and cultural knowledge. In fact, their very subtlety is their strength. Only because each of these lyrics had a clear and logical literal meaning did they earn a pass from the censors. In each case, it is likely that some listeners did not understand the hidden message the composer was articulating. However, others certainly did—and therefore, the composers successfully subverted the PSB's censorship system.

In addition, lay people in Burma are broadly aware that such subversion is common. Some of my informants said "All songs have secret messages." Clearly, this is not true; but statements like "All songs have secret messages" are valuable because they reveal that music consumers are aware that subversion is occurring. Some listeners no doubt read unintended meanings into straightforward lyrics. As we saw above, even employees of the PSB do this. Christina Fink argues that such inferences are common among Burmese people: "People are reading meanings into everything around them," she asserts, linking this psychological tactic employed by individuals to the larger struggle for power in Burma.[64] Craig Lockard has a similar perspective; he sees this kind of assigning of meaning as a way for fans to exercise agency in the face of the government's attempt to control what they hear, and thereby, what they think.[65]

The three approaches that musicians use when they interact with the Press Security Board—submission, defiance, and subversion—mirror the strategies they use to deal with more generalized government control. Most of them submit to government requirements when planning their performances, for example. Since outdoor gatherings of more than five people are forbidden after dark, performers need to get permits to perform nighttime concerts. Although Pee Paw, the successful impresario, says that such permits are easy to get ("I just go to the local police or fire station, and I don't have to pay"), other informants said that such permits can be difficult to obtain. One performer who has spent much of her career performing at Kandawgyi Park says that permits are often denied. Her response to such denials is to submit to the limitations imposed on her. Although she is unhappy about it (describing it as the "biggest challenge" of her working life), she accepts the situation and does not attempt to change it.

Other musicians periodically defy the government. They sing antigovernment songs in private settings—inside university dormitories, for example.[66] One of the most popular antigovernment songs, "Scarecrow," speaks from the perspective of a lowly Tatmadaw soldier, one who is deeply regretful over the role he plays (note the reference to stars on the shoulder in this excerpt from the lyrics):

> Dead or alive, sacrificing my life for my country
> Gold and silver, silver stars on my shoulder
> Oh my friend, what honor and rewards I would get
> My heart is crying, while my mouth was muzzled from telling the truth
> A pierce through my eyes which have seen the truth
> Oh my friend, I am a scarecrow in human form
> Though I am alive, I am no longer living.[67]

Despite the risk involved, fans themselves sometimes also defy the Burmese government's control of music. One friend showed me some CDs that he owns, full of Karen nationalist songs (that is, songs that celebrate the Karen revolution, thereby enunciating the hidden transcript). These CDs were recorded by an artist who recently fled Yangon and is now living in one of the refugee camps on the Thai-Burma border. His CDs are smuggled back into Burma in defiance of the government's ban on any expression of support for ethnic insurgents.

Public defiance is less common, but does occur. In November of 2007, for example, a rapper named G-Tone turned his back to his audience and lifted his t-shirt, showing the crowd the tattoo on his back. The tattoo consisted of two clasped hands holding a string of beads. He and his fellow performers were immediately arrested, and G-Tone was banned from performing for one year. I heard various interpretations of his actions from my Burmese friends: he was simply being immodest; or, his tattoo was the symbol for Amnesty International; or, his tattoo was a representation of Christian or Buddhist devotional prayer. The *Irrawaddy* online magazine claimed that the Burmese government seized on the third option, and arrested him for showing support for the Buddhist monks who led the antigovernment protests that had erupted two months earlier.[68] Whatever the case, no one was surprised that a three-second public declaration of the hidden transcript was met with immediate and harsh reprisals.

From time to time, Burmese musicians successfully subvert the government's control of the music industry. For example, if they are obligated to work on a government recording project, they can prevent this from becoming known. (Composers and performers who cooperate with the junta, such as

Sai Htee Saing and Zaw Win Htut, often lose the respect of their fans, and so most musicians are reluctant to be known as composers of government songs.) Soe Htun, who played guitars on the government recording that I described in chapter 1, accepted the commission on one condition: the responsible minister had to promise that he would not put the arranger's name anywhere on the recording. The minister, needing to have the song recorded in time for the bridge opening, agreed to this condition; Soe Htun collected his money and avoided any damage to his reputation.

By submitting to the government's power over their lives, musicians endorse the public transcript. By defying it, they contest the public transcript. And by occasionally inserting the hidden transcript into the public transcript, they proclaim the hidden transcript.

A Fourth Strategy: Avoidance

Many pop musicians in Yangon supplement their repertoire of strategies for coping with government control with a fourth strategy: avoidance.

To avoid the government, musicians can either refuse to create "government songs" at the behest of the state, or they can create music intended for sale outside of mainstream retail outlets, which does not have to be vetted by the PSB. Here is an example of the first:

U Maung Zaw explained to me that when a government functionary calls the Myanmar Musicians Association to demand a composition for an upcoming ceremony, the bureaucrat may request a composer by name. In such a case, there is no avoiding it, and the composer must compose the song as required. If, however, the request does not include a specific composer, then the MMA must find someone—anyone—to do the work. Composers who are approached with the request may, and often do, turn it down. They may plead a busy schedule, for example, or even say that they are not competent to write such a song.[69] If they refuse the opportunity (and the money), they will not jeopardize their membership in the MMA and will not suffer reprisals.

The second kind of avoidance involves circumventing government control by creating recordings for distribution through private networks. Some of these recordings, which would likely not get a pass from the PSB, are made on the Thai-Burma border, and with the help of Gmail, they achieve wide distribution in Burma proper. Often, these recordings are made by members of *tain-yin-tha* communities. The lyrics of the songs are in one of the minority languages, and they usually reveal explicitly nationalistic themes. Christian *tain-yin-tha* musicians also make religious albums; my informants spoke of such recordings as "gospel *series*." The musical styles vary from hymn-singing (often by children) to soft pop to moderately-hard rock—which is to say that they sound very like mainstream Burmese pop recordings, except for the language and the lyrics. So many of these recordings are now being made that we can speak of a separate and parallel *tain-yin-tha* recording industry in Burma, one that has developed outside of the government apparatus. The people who work in this industry avoid all interaction with the censorship board and with government-approved impresarios such as Pee Paw.

Although the *tain-yin-tha* industry avoids the Burmese government, it is interwoven with the engines of the mainstream Burmese pop industry. For example, minority-language *series* are made in the same studios where mainstream *series* are recorded. Furthermore, many of the people who work in the Burmese-language industry (including performers and recording engineers) also work frequently on *tain-yin-tha* recording projects. The creators of this music are usually Christians and self-identify as ethnic *tain-yin-tha*. However, they often describe their work on *tain-yin-tha* recordings in different terms (such as "service" or "helping.") And whether they use different terminology or not, their attitude is manifest in their practice: all the Christian *tain-yin-tha* composers and performers I interviewed said that they charge different—and lower—rates for their time when they work on *tain-yin-tha* recordings or perform at *tain-yin-tha* community events.

In fact, they often perform live shows for free. Soe Htun, who was unwilling to specify exactly how much he charges for working on a *tain-yin-tha series*, simply said it was "a lot less" than his regular fee of about 200,000 *kyat*, or $200. Aung Shwe claimed that exact figures for gospel albums are hard to specify, since "it depends on the situation." He said that because ethnic minority recording artists typically have very small budgets, full-time professionals like himself will take this into consideration and adjust their fees accordingly. He claimed that the discount off the standard industry rates can be as much as seventy percent.

Ko Htwe explained this phenomenon very clearly. The *tain-yin-tha* recording industry has a different purpose, he says, and therefore those who participate in it are differently motivated. While the Burmese-language industry is intent on making money, the *tain-yin-tha* industry aims to support minority languages, cultures and religions. Therefore, when he and his colleagues work on a *tain-yin-tha* recording or play in a *tain-yin-tha* concert, they do not expect to make a profit. They participate in the mainstream and *tain-yin-tha* industries for different reasons, and have different expectations of themselves and others in each case.

These same industry insiders, who work in both camps, say that for an artist to have wide distribution in Burma—to have a chance at becoming famous—he or she must cooperate with the government's system of censorship. Retail shops do not stock *series* that have not been vetted by the PSB. However, it is my observation that some *tain-yin-tha* recording artists have a wide reach, wider in fact than that of some "famous" mainstream musicians. *Tain-yin-tha* recordings circulate primarily in ethnic minority communities in Burma. These communities constitute a small percentage of the Burmese population, but they tend to be well-organized.

Church denominations in Burma are efficient bureaucratic structures; leaders from around the country know each other, meet regularly, and work together. It is thus possible that a *series* devised by a church-based group of pop performers in northern Kachin State, for example, can be recorded in Yangon and disseminated to Kachin-speaking groups around the country, as I observed for myself during the course of my research. Furthermore, such recordings travel easily over the border and are in wide circulation in refugee camps populated by members of *tain-yin-tha* groups (Chin refugees on the India border and Shan, Karen, and Kayah refugees on the Thai border).[70]

Some *tain-yin-tha* recording artists have become refugees themselves, and others travel clandestinely to the camps to give concerts and publicize their music.[71] Since 2006 many thousands of Burmese refugees have left the camps, resettling in Western countries, bringing the music of home with them. These refugees, and other expatriate Burmese in the developed world, are now uploading clips from both Burmese and *tain-yin-tha* VCDs onto the YouTube website. As of this writing, YouTube hosts dozens of such videos. Thus we can say that Burmese pop music, both the mainstream and *tain-yin-tha* varieties, has gone global.[72]

Esther, who works exclusively as a "Karen singer" (that is, singing in Sgaw Karen on *tain-yin-tha* recordings) outlined her experiences for me, showing how it is possible to become a successful pop musician in Burma while avoiding the government at all turns. Her CDs, she says, are sold in unofficial retail outlets in Yangon, located on Christian-owned institutional property. (I encountered four such shops in my visits to churches, seminaries, and denominational headquarters in Yangon. One of them is, I believe, rather well known, since three different individuals advised me to visit it.) In addition, shops in Pa-an, Toungoo, and Dawei—all Karen population centers inside Burma—sell Karen recordings, Esther says. The owners of such shops come to Yangon and purchase hundreds of copies of her *series*, paying her either in advance or after they sell the lot.

Also, Esther visits Thailand once a year or more to perform for refugees there. While in Thailand, she mails copies of her *series* to contacts in the Karen diaspora (the Burmese postal system being vulnerable to surveillance, and more importantly, terribly inefficient). Often, she sends one master copy of the *series* and the cover art, trusting her friends abroad to reproduce it and disseminate it.[73] In this case, she accepts a flat fee of one hundred dollars from her contact in Thailand. Operating in this way, Esther has managed to sell ten thousand cassette copies and eight thousand VCD copies of her first *series*. She says that demand for this *series*, one which has become "famous among Karen people," is continual. She is still selling copies of it seven years after its release. In July 2008, when I entered her real name into the YouTube search engine, I found more than a dozen videos of this singer, in which she appears either as a featured or a guest artist. Clearly, as this singer's career illustrates, artists who avoid the Myanmar PSB can develop successful careers for themselves. Avoidance, then, is a legitimate and useful strategy for *tain-yin-tha* pop musicians in Burma.[74]

Ironically, the *tain-yin-tha* industry is able to exist and thrive because of a loophole in the system provided by the government itself. The PSB makes provision for groups who wish to record religious music with lyrics that would normally be forbidden. The board simply requires the producer of the *series* to put the following phrase on the *series* cover: *"ah-thin-daw twin kan-tha*—"For distribution within the congregation."[75] The idea is that church groups are allowed to make recordings and circulate them among the members of the church. In practice, this phrase provides cover for movement of the *series* not only within a congregation, but all over the country (and even beyond, as outlined above). Producers of *series* that are not totally devoted to gospel songs and not intended for use by one local congregation often put this phrase on the *series*. It acts as a kind of license, virtually guaranteeing that no government agent will look too closely at the contents. Again, this particular case illuminates Scott's assertions about the functioning of hidden and public transcripts. He points out that subordinate members of society often use the ideas in the public transcript to support their own agendas.[76] In Burma, producers leverage the government's stated dedication to religious tolerance for their own ends, to facilitate the movement of their hidden-transcript recordings.[77]

The creators of these "avoidance albums" express the hidden transcript in various ways. Some songs on such recordings are subtly or overtly nationalistic, affirming the long-held desire for autonomy among ethnic minority groups. Most of the songs are straightforward expressions of Christian faith, of course. But Christian faith can be a cover for an antigovernment message. For example, the Bible verse prominently displayed on the cover of one Chin-language CD says, "Our help is in the Lord, who made heaven and earth" (Psalm 124, verse 8). However, in the original context, this verse is preceded by a poem which speaks about God being "on our side," in our conflict with "our enemies." The Chin refugee who gave me this album handed it over with a snicker. Noting my confusion, he explained this verse, demonstrating his clear understanding of the hidden transcript that it references.

Much more rarely, avoidance albums convey flat-out criticism of Burma's military junta. I learned of one such example in late 2008. This album was funded by a Yangon-based parachurch organization, and the project involved some prominent pop music industry members. All the songs on the album are based on oral accounts given by child victims of Cyclone Nargis. The visuals show the tremendous devastation that the cyclone caused, including photos of corpses. The producer of the VCD explained to me that she had two equally important goals in organizing this recording.[78] First, she wanted to create a product that could be sold to raise funds for child victims of the cyclone. Second, she wanted to inform the public about what really happened in the

Figure 5.2. Censored group album showing PSB pass (lower left-hand corner)

delta area; that is, she wanted to make very clear to viewers, especially those in foreign countries, how deeply destructive the effects of the cyclone, and the government's negligible response, were to people in rural Burma. In order to achieve these goals, she decided to use photos which are banned for publication to accompany the music. The photos show weeping children, destroyed homes, and most hauntingly, dead bodies strewn in the wreckage left by the cyclone.

The VCD is a clear expression of the hidden transcript: the album shows the deep need of the victims, and by extension, the gross negligence of the SPDC, which failed to warn citizens about the coming storm, and then refused to allow international aid to enter affected areas for many weeks. As the VCD implies, the government therefore exacerbated the effects of the natural disaster and is responsible for loss of life and property. This album, then, constitutes an expression of political resistance. And this is not just my own scholarly interpretation of the work: the producer of this album, whom I interviewed, told me that she was visited by an SPDC agent and threatened with arrest shortly before she released the album. She told me that she was willing to be jailed

Figure 5.3. Album marked "For distribution within the congregation" (upper right-hand corner). The PTL studio is one of the best-known in Yangon, and the list of featured singers and lyricists includes some of the most famous artists in the mainstream Burmese pop industry.

for the cause (holding her wrists out dramatically, in a pantomime of being handcuffed) but ultimately avoided this possibility by falling back on the justification described above: "This *series* is only for circulation within my congregation," she said to the agent.

Here is another, similar example: The Christian Musicians Fellowship created a single which tells the story of the suffering that Cyclone Nargis caused. Aung Shwe, who produced the album, explained to me that, had this VCD single been submitted to the censors, the words would have earned a pass, but the visuals—which consist of a montage of banned photographs showing property damage and dead human bodies—would have disqualified it. Importantly, the CMF website has posted these visuals,[79] and this website is not blocked in

Figure 5.4. Album produced by the alternative *tain-yin-tha* recording industry

Burma, so Burmese citizens can view it in Internet cafés. It is definitely politically sensitive material, as I found out for myself when Aung Shwe gave me a hard copy of the VCD. Within minutes, he changed his mind and burned a copy on a blank CD, "because it is not approved," he said.

Government Dependence on Pop Music

Another important, but usually unacknowledged reality which impacts the power relationship between pop musicians and the Burmese government is that the government is in some ways dependent on the national pop music industry. This relationship of dependence developed very early, when the government (then in its BSPP incarnation) first leaned on pop music in order to market itself. As I explained in the introduction, *stereo* music was the creation of private citizens in Burma. In the early 1970s, when the government held a referendum, it decided to use *stereo* songs to promote its message. Ever since, bureaucrats have been paying pop musicians to write and record so-called government songs, which are used in public education campaigns, for national holidays, and on state television. This choice is a tacit acknowledgment of the public's taste. The military regime in Burma is ultranationalistic, given to jingoistic celebrations of the superiority of Burmese culture and people. (For example, for the last few years the government has been promoting the idea that the human race originated in Myanmar, proof positive that the Myanmar people are founders of all the glory of human civilization).[80] The generals therefore usually validate cultural practices that are distinctively Burmese.

Musically, they prioritize traditions such as the *hsaing waing* and the *Maha Gita*, funding state schools and music competitions which focus on exclusively promoting these musics. In late 2009, the government went as far as to ban Western instruments (including guitars and electric keyboards) from appearing with *hsaing waing* troupes.[81] The fact that the government so often pays for American-style pop music to promote their projects reads like a capitulation of sorts, a recognition that the music of the "neo-colonialist axe-handles"[82] is widely liked and that they, the leaders, have been unable to control the tastes of their citizens. In order to influence public opinion, therefore, the generals must depend on pop musicians to communicate with the public.

The government depends on pop music and musicians not only for songs but also for money. It is important to note that the Burmese junta, for all its harsh repression of basic human rights, is a rather weak government which does not effectively govern its people (nor even control all the land within its own borders).[83] For example, it does not collect taxes in a comprehensive way. To be sure, it levies taxes, but it seems to have few mechanisms for enforcing the payment of those taxes.[84] And so it is perpetually short of cash.[85]

U Hla Myint Swe, the manager of Yangon City FM, explained to me that the station is one of the branches of the Yangon City Development Committee. All the advertising revenues earned by the station go to the YCDC. "It's like a tax," he says. The national government does not provide funds to Yangon, even though it is the largest city in the country and home to some five million people, and so the radio station "raises local funds to repair roads and so on." Of course, in order for the city to raise these funds, advertisers have to be willing to purchase air time, and they will only do so if the music that the station plays is popular with a large number of potential consumers. Therefore, the largest municipal government in Burma is obliged to rely on pop music and musicians for its economic well-being.

Obviously, Burma's military junta does not hold all the cards in the game it plays with pop musicians. This became crystal clear in September 2007, when the country was convulsed by a series of antigovernment demonstrations that the government ultimately stopped with military force. In the wake of the violence, the government sought to justify itself. It therefore contacted various allies (cease-fire armed groups, state-controlled NGOs, and the like), asking them to issue statements condemning the demonstrations and the demonstrators.[86] This is a common practice: when the regime feels itself to be the subject of criticism, it demands that purportedly neutral parties defend it and its policies. To give just one example: a year earlier, when the United Nations Security Council decided to put "the situation of Myanmar" on its agenda, the Shan State Army North-Special Region 3 (a cease-fire group now allied with the SPDC) "volunteered" the following statement, which appeared in the state-run newspaper *The New Light of Myanmar*:

> We object the decision [*sic*] and declare it unacceptable as it will undermine and disturb peace and stability and the rule of law, that are prevailing in Myanmar, and the national solidarity, developments in all sectors and the ongoing democratization process.[87]

In 2007, when the junta was looking for similar statements in reference to the demonstrations, it approached the Myanmar Musicians Association. The leadership of the MMA, twenty-five persons in total, held a meeting to discuss the issue, and then voted. They decided *not* to honor the government's request. They refused to publish a statement. Importantly, neither the group nor any of the individuals in leadership suffered any reprisals because of this decision.[88] Clearly, the military regime cannot be said to control the MMA, a significant organization representing many well-respected musicians. In fact, it cannot even count on the MMA for a meaningless gesture of support at a time of great crisis.

Revisiting James Scott

As this account of the power relationship between Burmese pop musicians and their government shows, it is impossible to say that the all-powerful government renders musicians powerless by censoring their music. Clearly, as musicians and censors interact, each exercises some degree of power over the other. The government relies on pop music for financial and moral support. However, musicians sometimes refuse to lend this support. Censors attempt to prevent any songs which are not "nice"—and therefore possibly critical of the status quo—from reaching the public's ears. They often, but not always, succeed.

This detailed look at the Burmese case affirms James Scott's ideas about the exercise of power in societies where a dominant group seems to hold all the cards. Furthermore, it allows us to extend James Scott's theories in two ways. First, this study shows that the four strategies that he and others have documented among farmers and peasants can be employed at all levels of society. In this study, we see that even famous rock stars use the strategies of submission, defiance, subversion and avoidance. These strategies, therefore, are not just the weapons of the "weak." Secondly, this case study shows that the fourth strategy, avoidance, can be quite politically productive. Ethnic minority musicians (and their Burman allies) express their disagreement with the government's public transcript in recordings that successfully avoid government control. These recordings overtly celebrate ethnic and religious difference, espouse political goals that are at odds with the ruling regime, and even articulate harsh criticism of that regime. Moreover, the avoidance strategy is now embodied in an industry which reaches a worldwide Burmese audience—and therefore it is tremendously effective in disseminating the hidden transcript.

Conclusion

The Significance of the
Burmese Perspective

On April 7, 2009, the Democratic Voice of Burma (a news website maintained by Burmese journalists now living outside of Burma) published an editorial titled "The 'Victim' Treatment: A Self-Fulfilling Prophecy." It began:

> There's a tendency in the global media to portray Burma as a primitive country, held back from modernisation by the psychotic generals who would rather line their own pockets than promote the advancement of society. Thus, to the outside world its citizens are forever seen as 'victims,' given the usually negative news that filters out of the country. And there is little done to bypass this idea. Few journalists explore the effect that globalisation has had on youth culture in the country, which is now evolving rapidly. Do we wear traditional clothes on stage whilst jamming on weird, ancient instruments? Do our youths get their kicks in local moonshine places instead of hanging out at shopping malls? Yes, but not always.
>
> We like hip-hop and break dancing, and we are on Facebook and Hi5. We know Paris Hilton and have seen her sex-tapes online, and we love The Simpsons. Maybe we are not travelling at a full pace with the globalisation, but we are on the right track.[1]

The contrast between the worldview of this Burmese writer and that of liberal elites in the West could not be clearer. The author argues that the way to combat Burma's stereotypical image as a victim nation is to document its evolving youth culture. In the next paragraph, referring to Paris Hilton and The Simpsons, he claims that Burmese youths now "rush to grab hold of the Western world's finest exports." And this, he claims, is proof that Burmese society is "on the right track."

My colleagues in North American academia are likely to see this editorial as proof of the reach of Western capitalist hegemony—indeed, as a tangible example of the hard-to-define yet inexorable force of cultural imperialism. In fact, several American friends who read the excerpt above laughed aloud in disbelief. How could anyone—especially a well-educated, English-speaking journalist—assert that loving The Simpsons is proof of agency, rather than victimization? Isn't this editorial evidence of the bewitching power of Hollywood?

Of course, there is something to be said for this point of view. The advent of the Internet in Burma has brought many attractive and well-developed cultural products to a local market that has not, as yet, produced much that can compete. However, it is important to understand that Western cultural imperialism cannot entirely account for the situation in Yangon today. My analysis of pop music in Burma in the twenty-first century rests on the many interviews I conducted with members of the Yangon pop scene, and those interviews revealed that this explanation is only one part—a very small part—of the story.

Shocking as the editorial may seem to Western readers, I think it beautifully illustrates the point I have emphasized throughout this book: Burmese people have a specific perspective on American and British cultural products, including pop music. And this perspective reflects Burmese norms and values. It is these norms and values—rather than the power of the US-based industry—that largely account for the prominence of Anglo-American style pop music in Burma. While Burmese pop music sounds remarkably like Anglo-American pop music, the community that informs and produces it operates according to its own cultural logic. The musicians I describe in earlier chapters make music in a particularly Burmese way, even though the resulting sounds are putatively Western. Their music sounds like that of the best-known US pop stars precisely because of their Burmese way of thinking.

I came to understand this way of thinking as I asked Burmese pop music industry members what constituted, in their minds, a "good" song. A very few people answered by referencing sound quality (such as the guitarist who said a good song is a song in which all the parts—that is, the various instruments and voices—fit together well). But the overwhelming majority of Burmese musicians gave me a different answer: a good song is a song that is successful with audiences. For these men and women, the popularity of a song seems to be a measure of its inherent good quality. This audience-centered way of thinking about music stands in direct contrast with the philosophy so prominent in the West (especially in indie rock circles), which implies that the more popular a tune is, the more likely it is to be pandering to the lowest common denominator and, therefore, the more likely it is to be of poor quality.[2]

For most composers of Burmese pop songs, the opposite is true. According to their logic, the most commercially successful music in the world is also the best music in the world. Therefore, Anglo-American rock and pop songs are the best, highest-quality works of art being created by composers today. And so it makes sense that Burmese musicians, who place tremendous importance on copying respected models, would emulate these songs. In addition, this way of thinking explains many of Burmese pop musicians' choices when they compose their *own tune* songs.

One of Burma's most influential composers explained how this aesthetic notion influences his compositional style. U Htun Naung hosts a weekly radio show on Yangon's City FM station; the name of the show translates as

"Showing New Song Class." During this show, U Htun Naung plays an unre-leased recording and comments on its strengths and weaknesses. Up-and-com-ing artists send their recordings to the station in hopes that their song will be selected for on-air criticism. Although U Htun Naung says that he cannot iden-tify any pattern of positive and negative features in the songs he critiques ("I have to give different advice according to each song"), he does have a strong and well-articulated opinion about what makes a good song. The most impor-tant point, he says, is that a song must "coincide with the rhythm of the period [of time.]" A song must "strike at the majority of people's feelings, so the com-poser must be aware of the environment, because people's feelings coincide with [their] surrounding lives."

For U Htun Naung, as for his many colleagues, a good song will be one which is easy for the audience to relate to, to both understand and feel. A good melody, he says, is one that is "easy to get into your ear and stuck inside your heart." The melody of a good song should be "easy for you [the listener] to sing," he emphasizes. The criterion should not be whether or not it is easy for a professional vocalist: "A composer should aim to write something that is easy for the majority [of the] people. The words must be understandable to the majority. It must be up-to-date and used [i.e., useful] for all." Specifically, he adds, "If you write a melody with [the pitches] *do, so* and *ti*, it will be easy for Myanmar people, and they will like it."

Other Burmese pop music composers expressed the same idea: a good song, they say, is broadly popular and accessible to a large audience (that is, fans find it easy to sing along with the song). Composer Soe Thant summed it up most cogently. When I asked him to define a good song, he said, "I can't. The audi-ence decides that." He pointed out that every time he sits down to compose, he does his best to create a good song. However, not all of his songs become hits. Those that do not find a wide following are, evidently, not good songs.

This is not to imply that Burmese pop composers are solely concerned with writing music that will appeal to their audiences. As we saw in chapter 1, these musicians say consistently that they want to engage their fans and to entertain them (to "make them happy," as a few interviewees put it). They maintain this idea in conjunction with a seemingly competing approach: they compose in order to express their own ideas, emotions, and stories. To the musicians I met, these two notions are not mutually exclusive. In fact, they are simultaneously true. When Burmese musicians compose and perform music, they do so to express their own feelings as well as to stimulate the feelings of their listeners. Interestingly, a wide range of musicians who spoke to me in different contexts used the same expression (in Burmese and in English) to describe this phenomenon: they call it "*say pyin pya deh*," meaning "showing/revealing the heart."[3]

James Thiri first articulated this idea to me, in both languages; he explained that he performs music ultimately not for money but because he is "keen on it." "It's an outlet for me, it comes from my heart," he said. Others said similar things. Julia claimed, "My singing comes from my heart"; and Myo Myo Thant said, "When I am composing, it comes from my heart." Myo Myo Thant explained that sounds that come "from the heart" are not necessarily those that express his own emotions, or that describe events that happened to him. Indeed, his songs can tell stories based on the experiences of others, or even recount imagined events, but on some fundamental level, all of his songs are expressions of his own feelings, that is, his heart. Nu Nu Win, a recently married singer and composer, asserted the same idea: she described her about-to-be-released single as a song about a girl who is broken-hearted but proud and therefore refuses to long for the past. When I asked if this song accurately reflected her own life, she acknowledged that, well, this particular story was not her own—in fact it was a reflection of a friend's feelings. However, since she composed and performed it herself, she considered it to be the legitimate expression of her own heart.

Burmese composers especially emphasized the idea that music is a way of revealing the heart when they spoke about their compositional techniques. There was a general consensus that because music comes from the heart, composers do not have particular formulas or methods for creating songs. In vain I asked composers: Do you generally begin by writing words, or melodies, or chord progressions? Most of my interviewees puzzled over this question and then said they could not answer because the whole process is driven by emotion, and therefore does not proceed according to a series of steps. Taylor said, "When I am composing I am expressing my mood, so first I write the words, and then the melody . . . but sometimes I write the melody and chords first, and then the words."

Taylor went on to explain that the depth of his emotional involvement with the song also determines how long it takes to compose it; when his feelings are welling out of him, he can write a song in as little as ninety minutes, but at other times it can take up to three days. Ko Htwe said almost the same thing: "Sometimes I start with a story, other times with a melody, other times with a beautiful pattern of chords. Usually I start with a melody idea. If I have strong feelings about it, I can write a song in one or two hours. However if I am writing to fulfill someone else's request, it takes longer."

Michael flatly rejected the idea that composing involves some kind of planned procedure. When I asked him what he thinks about first when composing, he retorted that he never "thinks" about a song before starting, adding that his emotions, not his head, influence what he writes. U Maung Zaw acknowledged that he has a preferred method of composing (guitar in hand, he creates a chord sequence that he likes, and then adds a beat, then a melody, and finally lyrics). However, he followed this immediately by saying that "there is no formula." He smiled gently when I asked him about composing government songs; in that case, he says, he is fortunate that he has so much experience in songwriting. When writing songs for the government, he relies on that experience rather than on his heart.

Statements like these illuminate the uniquely Burmese perspective shared by the musicians that I interviewed. To understand the Burmese notion of a "good song" is to understand—and appreciate—why Burmese pop musicians are so committed to reproducing the Anglo-American pop music tradition in their own country. Cultural logic is like a hidden transcript: crystal clear to those for whom it is an everyday experience, often opaque to outsiders who study its surface phenomena. I came to understand Burmese pop musicians' way of thinking because they graciously allowed me to conduct ethnographic research in their midst.

Major scholars of ethnomusicology have issued calls for more ethnographic studies of popular music and musicians.[4] Unfortunately, as Jan Fairley points out, analyses of popular music, developing countries and cultural imperialism are not often based on culture members' first-person statements:

> Many of the arguments about world music, pessimistic and optimistic, lack the backing of ethnographic evidence, of empirical analysis of how local/global musical communication actually works. . . . I'm sometimes struck by the irony that, while not wishing to ignore macro-economic power relations, the most pessimistic readings of world music in terms of cultural imperialism tend to be the most culturally ethnocentric, showing the least understanding of the motives of either the musicians or entrepreneurs involved.[5]

I agree with Fairley. Therefore, my theories about Burmese music and musicians were developed by examining the data provided by culture members. In this book I focused on culture members' statements because I am mindful that, as Robert Walser puts it, the discourse of value is really the discourse of power.[6] Walser argues that pop music—which has received relatively little attention from "serious" musicologists—deserves the kind of analysis that classical music usually receives. Analysts should be "less interested in describing or legitimating than in understanding how music works and why people care about it," he asserts. "Ultimately, judgments of music are judgments of people."[7] To dismiss Burmese pop music as no more than the product of Western imperialism, as inauthentic, as somehow less worthy than pop music in America, would be to dismiss the people who create it and listen to it.

By observing and listening to Burmese pop musicians, I discovered (like many ethnomusicologists before me) that it is impossible to accurately understand their music making apart from their local context. It is this context—the beliefs, behaviors, and historical realities which shape their lives—that accounts for Burmese pop musicians' choices. They are heirs to a heritage which prefers to focus on imitation rather than innovation. And their local practices foster this preference: they generally do not spend much time rehearsing, so they do not have many opportunities to develop new ideas. Because their government has not enforced copyright laws, and has not educated the Burmese public about intellectual property rights, they are happy to copy foreign-made recordings, seeing this as a service they perform for local fans who have no access to the originals. Furthermore, Burmese musicians lack sustained corporate support for new projects. And they do not receive training in traditional Burmese music while attending school, so most are unlikely to combine older local music with international pop to create new fusion genres.

The similarity between Anglo-American and Burmese pop music stems from Burmese musicians' understanding of aesthetics—not from the mysterious force of cultural imperialism that issues forth from the West and homogenizes everything in its path. Burmese musicians do not create this music because they lack creativity, nor because they are trying to appropriate an American identity. Rather, they operate according to the Burmese belief that a "good song" is one that is meaningful to contemporary audiences and demonstrates its meaningfulness by selling well. Since they are not constrained by the Western scholarly belief that authenticity derives from originality, they create and perform songs that are authentically their own while also being explicit copies of English hits. Ultimately, these musicians understand Burmese pop music to be an authentic way of revealing their hearts to the world.

Notes

Introduction

1. For more on the *Maha Gita* tradition, see Judith Becker, "Anatomy of a Mode," *Ethnomusicology* 13, no. 2 (1969): 267–79; Robert Garfias, "A Musical Visit to Burma," *World of Music* 17, no. 1 (1975): 3–13; Robert Garfias, "The Development of the Modern Burmese Hsaing Ensemble," *Asian Music* 16 (1985): 1–28; Ward Keeler, "Burma," in *Garland Encyclopedia of World Music, Volume 4: Southeast Asia*, ed. Terry E. Miller and Sean Williams (New York: Garland Publishing Inc., 1998), 363–400; and Muriel C. Williamson, *The Burmese Harp: Its Classical Music, Tuning and Modes* (Northern Illinois University: Southeast Asia Publications, 2000).

2. For how this tradition is evolving today, see Gavin Douglas, "State Patronage of Burmese Traditional Music" (PhD diss., University of Washington, 2001) and Gavin Douglas, "The Sokayeti Performing Arts Competition of Burma/Myanmar," *World of Music* 45, no. 1 (2003): 35–54.

3. Gavin Douglas, "The Burmese Guitar: Local Adaptations to a World Instrument" (paper presented at the International Burma Studies Conference, DeKalb, Illinois, October 3–5, 2008).

4. Gavin Douglas, "Myanmar," in *Continuum Encyclopedia of Popular Music of the World, vol. V* (New York: Continuum, 2003), 198.

5. Note that the Myanmar Musicians Association, an important umbrella group for Burmese musicians, uses this three-part distinction to organize their members into subgroups. Musicians belong to the traditional *Maha Gita* group, the *kalabaw* group, or the *stereo* group.

6. For further explanation of popular music see Peter Manuel, *Popular Musics of the Non-Western World: An Introductory Survey* (New York: Oxford University Press, 1988), 2–3.

7. Small recording studios do exist outside of Yangon (in Mandalay, for example, and in Taunggyi), but the majority of recordings are sent to Yangon to be mixed, manufactured, and distributed from that city. As of 2010, a handful of pop-style recordings in Burmese and Sgaw Karen have been produced in Mae Sot, Thailand, and in the Mae La refugee camp. These recordings do make their way back into Burma, but are intended mostly for fans in the Burmese diaspora. Although some successful Burmese *stereo* musicians have moved to other countries, so far, none have been able to pursue their musical careers there. For all of these reasons I maintain that the Burmese *stereo* music industry is a Yangon-based industry.

8. Martin Cloonan calls for more studies of popular music at the national level, pointing out that most scholarship to date has focused on either local or global expressions of pop. This study aims to describe and discuss pop music in Burma as a national phenomenon. Of course the research was made easier by the fact that the entire national industry is located in one city. See Martin Cloonan, "Pop and the Nation-State: Towards a Theorization," *Popular Music* 18, no. 2 (1999): 193–207.

9. See Ward Keeler, "What's So Burmese about Burmese Rap? Why Some Expressive Forms Go Global," *American Ethnologist* 36, no. 1 (2009): 2–19.

10. Alison J. Ewbank and Fouli T. Papageorgiou, eds., *Whose Master's Voice? The Development of Popular Music in Thirteen Cultures* (Westport, CT: Greenwood Press, 1997), 5.

11. Krishna Sen and David T. Hill, *Media, Culture and Politics in Indonesia* (Oxford: Oxford University Press, 2000), 166.

12. Marc L. Moskowitz, *Cries of Joy, Songs of Sorrow: Chinese Pop Music and Its Cultural Connotations* (Honolulu: University of Hawai'i Press, 2010), 21.

13. John Tomlinson, *Cultural Imperialism: A Critical Introduction* (London: Continuum, 1991), 3–11. But note that later Tomlinson offers this rough-and-ready explanation: "the domination of one national culture by another" (p. 68).

14. Keith Negus, *Popular Music in Theory: An Introduction* (Hanover: Wesleyan University Press, 1996), 172 and 178.

15. Phil Zabriskie, "Hard Rock," *Time*, May 6, 2002, http://www.time.com/time/magazine/article/0,9171,235508,00.html; and Scott Carrier, "Rock the Junta," Mother Jones, July 1, 2006, http://www.motherjones.com/news/feature/2006/07/rock_the_junta.html.

16. For an English-language version of the government document that originally outlined the Burmese Way to Socialism, see http://burmalibrary.org/docs/The_Burmese_Way_to_Socialism.htm.

17. For a hilarious yet telling account of life in Burma under Ne Win, see Pico Iyer, "The Raj is Dead! Long Live the Raj!" in *Video Night in Kathmandu: And Other Reports from the Not-So-Far East* (New York: A. A. Knopf, 1988), 195–219.

18. Aung Zaw, "Burma: Music under Siege," in *Shoot the Singer: Music Censorship Today*, ed. Marie Korpe (New York: Zed Books, 2004), 41.

19. Ibid., 43.

20. Douglas, "Myanmar," 198.

21. Chris Miller, "Burmese Music on Record before 1962: A Discography in Context" (paper presented at the International Burma Studies Conference, Marseille, France, July 9, 2010).

22. Douglas, "Myanmar," 200.

23. U Htun Naung, personal interview, Yangon, February 7, 2008.

24. Moe Moe Oo, "Recording Pioneer Still Has Ear for Music," *Myanmar Times*, October 9, 2006, http://www.myanmar.com/myanmartimes/MyanmarTimes17-337/t001.htm.

25. Note that the Yangon City FM studio (located in the Yangon City Development Committee building in downtown Yangon) was constructed in 2001. The building was completed in November, but broadcasts did not begin until New Year's Day, because this date was perceived to be "lucky." U Ye Zaw Tun, personal interview, Yangon, December 17, 2008.

26. Aung Shwe, personal interview, Yangon, January 29, 2008.

27. For example, James Thiri, personal interview, Yangon, February 5, 2008; Aung Shwe, interview; and Kaung Lin Lin, personal interview, Yangon, December 27, 2008.

28. For example, Taylor, personal interview, Yangon, January 13, 2008.

29. Albin J. Zak, III, *The Poetics of Rock: Cutting Tracks, Making Records* (Berkeley, University of California Press, 2001), 192.

30. Edmund Leach, *Political Systems of Highland Burma: A Study of Kachin Social Stuctures* (London: G. Bell and Sons, 1954).

31. For examples, see Victor Lieberman, *Burmese Administrative Cycles: Anarchy and Conquest, 1580–1760* (Princeton: Princeton University Press, 1984); and Bertil Lintner,

The Rise and Fall of the Communist Party of Burma (Ithaca: Cornell University Southeast Asia Program, 1990).

32. See Mary P. Callahan, *Making Enemies: War and State Building in Burma* (Ithaca: Cornell University Press, 2003); Mary P. Callahan, *Political Authority in Burma's Ethnic Minority States: Devolution, Occupation, and Coexistence* (Washington, DC: East-West Center Institute of Southeast Asian Studies, 2007); Ingrid Jordt, *Burma's Mass Lay Meditation Movement: Buddhism and the Cultural Construction of Power* (Athens, OH: Center for International Studies, Ohio University Press, 2007); Martin Smith, *Burma: Insurgency and the Politics of Ethnicity* (London: Zed Books, 1999); David Steinberg, *Burma: The State of Myanmar* (Washington, DC: Georgetown University Press, 2001); Robert Taylor, *The State in Myanmar* (Honolulu: University of Hawaii Press, 2009); and U Thant Myint, *The Making of Modern Burma* (New York: Cambridge University Press, 2001).

33. Monique Skidmore, *Karaoke Fascism: Burma and the Politics of Fear* (Philadelphia: University of Pennsylvania Press, 2004) and Christina Fink, *Living Silence: Burma Under Military Rule* (Bangkok: White Lotus, 2001).

34. There is a burgeoning English-language literature about Burma, aimed at a general audience, written by (1) visitors to the country; and (2) exiles now living in the West. The best of each category are, in my opinion: (1) Andrew Marshall, *The Trouser People: A Story of Burma in the Shadow of the Empire* (Washington, DC: Counterpoint, 2002); Emma Larkin, *Secret Histories: Finding George Orwell in a Burmese Teashop* (London: John Murray, 2004); Emma Larkin, *Everything Is Broken: The Untold Story of Disaster Under Burma's Military Regime* (London: Granta Books, 2010); Alan Rabinowitz, *Beyond the Last Village: A Journey of Discovery in Asia's Forbidden Wilderness* (Washington, DC: Island Press/Shearwater Books, 2001; Shelby Tucker, *Among Insurgents: Walking Through Burma* (London: Radcliffe, 2000) and (2) Pascal Koo Thwe, *From the Land of Green Ghosts: A Burmese Odyssey* (New York: Harper Collins, 2002); U Thant Myint, *The River of Lost Footsteps: Histories of Burma* (New York: Farrar, Strauss and Giroux, 2006); Zoya Phan, *Little Daughter: A Memoir of Survival in Burma and the West* (London: Simon and Schuster, 2009).

35. Robert Walser, *Running With the Devil: Power, Gender, and Madness in Heavy Metal Music* (Hanover, NH: University Press of New England, 1993), 31.

36. Heather MacLachlan, "The Don Dance: An Expression of Karen Nationalism," *Voices: Journal of New York Folklore* 32, no. 3/4 (2006): 26–32.

37. Heather MacLachlan, "Innovation in the Guise of Tradition: Music among the Chin Population of Indianapolis, USA," *Asian Music* 39, no. 2 (2008): 167–85.

38. Manny Brand, *The Teaching of Music in Nine Asian Nations: Comparing Approaches to Music Education* (Lewiston, NY: The Edwin Mellen Press, 2006), 157–67.

39. Ibid., 159.

40. Ibid., 164–66.

Chapter One

1. Dr. Kaung Htun, personal interview, Yangon, January 31, 2008.

2. The Burmese currency was officially valued at six *kyat* per US dollar when I lived in Burma (2007–9). However, no one ever used the government valuation to calculate amounts in US dollars, since the black market for changing money was the only one that counted. And on the black market, $1 was worth 1,000–1,200 *kyat*. As this book went to press, the exchange rate had fallen a little, to approximately 900 *kyat* for $1. The book

reflects prices as I and my Burmese friends calculated them at the time I was conducting research.

3. Zeya Win, personal interview, Yangon, January 7, 2009.

4. Soe Htun, personal interview, Yangon, January 11, 2008.

5. Hlaing Kyi, personal interview, Yangon, December 30, 2008.

6. Ma Khin Sein, personal interview, Yangon, January 29, 2008.

7. Mavis Bayton, "Women and the Electric Guitar," in *Sexing the Groove: Popular Music and Gender*, ed. Sheila Whiteley (London: Routledge, 1997), 37.

8. Phyu Phyu Kyaw, personal interview, Yangon, February 6, 2008.

9. Theramu Blu Paw, personal interview, Yangon, February 8, 2008.

10. Gavin Douglas, e-mail message to author, May 26, 2008.

11. *Don't Fence Me In: Major Mary and the Karen Refugees From Burma*, DVD, dir. Ruth Gumnit (Watertown, MA: Documentary Educational Resources, 2004).

12. Ko Htet Aung, personal interview, Yangon, December 15, 2008.

13. The pantheon of famous singers also includes two Muslims: U Chit Kaung and Bo Phyu.

14. Aye Kyi, personal interview, Yangon, December 16, 2007.

15. Maung Maung Zin, personal interview, Yangon, December 18, 2008.

16. Moe Lwin, personal interview, Yangon, December 22, 2008.

17. Htay Cho, personal interview, Yangon, December 16, 2008.

18. Michael, personal interview, Yangon, December 28, 2007.

19. Myine Myat, personal interview, Yangon, January 24, 2008.

20. James Thiri, interview.

21. Alan P. Merriam, *The Anthropology of Music* (Evanston: Northwestern University Press, 1964), 46.

22. Ibid., 141.

23. Ibid., 137.

24. "Silver Oak's Wish for Graham," *What's Happening around Good Ol' Yangon* (blog), accessed July 28, 2011, http://www.nagani.com/news/intown/.

25. Pee Paw, personal interview, Yangon, February 8, 2008.

26. Johnson, personal interview, Yangon, January 9, 2008.

27. Terry E. Miller, "From Country Hick to Rural Hip: A New Identity Through Music for Northeast Thailand," *Asian Music* 36, no. 2 (2005): 96–106.

28. U Hla Myint Swe, personal interview, Yangon, February 1, 2008.

29. Ko Chit Min, personal interview, Yangon, January 9, 2008.

30. Shway Nyunt, personal interview, Yangon, February 7, 2008; and Ohnmar Tun, personal interview, Yangon, February 5, 2008.

31. Myo Myo Thant, personal interview, Yangon, January 10, 2008.

32. Nu Nu Win, personal interview, Yangon, January 1, 2008.

33. Ba Kaung, "Anger Over Mobile Phone Charge Hike," *Irrawaddy*, January 21, 2010, http://www.irrawaddy.org/article.php?art_id=17522Kaung 2010; and Francis Wade, "Only 4% of Burmese using cellphones," *Democratic Voice of Burma*, August 4, 2010, http://www.dvb.no/news/only-4-of-burmese-using-telephones/11082.

34. "Rock's New Rebels," in "Special Troublemaker Foldout," *Rolling Stone*, December 28, 2006–January 11, 2007, 66A.

35. "News from Yangon (Rangoon)," *Yangonow*, June 3, 2003, http://www.yangonow.com/eng/magazine/from_myanmar/200306.html.

36. Khine Ta Htun, personal interview, Yangon, December 29, 2008.

37. Thuza, personal interview, Yangon, January 1, 2009.

38. Kenneth, personal interview, Yangon, February 1, 2008.

39. Rebekah, personal interview, Yangon, December 27, 2007.

40. Ko Htwe, personal interview, Yangon, January 6, 2008.

41. Keith Negus, *Producing Pop: Culture and Conflict in the Popular Music Industry* (London: Edward Arnold, 1992), 82.

42. Theingi Zaw, personal interview, Yangon, January 7, 2009.

43. Kenneth, interview.

44. Hpone Thant, personal interview, Yangon, December 19, 2008.

45. Julia, personal interview, Yangon, January 9, 2008.

46. Jason Toynbee, *Making Popular Music: Musicians, Creativity and Institutions* (New York: Oxford University Press, 2000), 60.

47. Ibid., 64.

48. Ibid., 63.

49. Kyaw Naing Oo, personal interview, Yangon, December 31, 2008.

50. Thet Htaw Mya, personal interview, Yangon, December 30, 2008.

51. Moe Lwin, interview; and Kenneth, interview.

52. Htin Thu, personal interview, Yangon, December 24, 2008.

53. Helen James, *Security and Sustainable Development in Myanmar* (London and New York: Routledge, 2006), 167.

54. David Steinberg, *Burma: The State of Myanmar* (Washington, DC: Georgetown University Press, 2001), 120.

55. Skidmore, *Karaoke Fascism: Burma and the Politics of Fear*, 89.

56. Zunetta Liddell, "No Room To Move: Legal Constraints on Civil Society in Burma," in *Strengthening Civil Society in Burma: Possibilities and Dilemmas for International NGOs* (Chiang Mai, Thailand: Silkworm Books, 1999), 54–68.

57. Calvin Khin Zaw, "Humanitarianism in Myanmar" (paper presented at the Southeast Asia Program weekly meeting, Cornell University, Ithaca, New York, November 2, 2007).

58. Brian Heidel, *The Growth of Civil Society in Myanmar* (Bangalore: Books for Change, 2006), 60.

59. Yeni, "Support for a Stronger Civil Society," *Irrawaddy*, July 4, 2008, http://www.irrawaddy.org/opinion_story.php?art_id=13139.

60. Cho Cho Saing, personal interview, Yangon, January 17, 2008.

61. Ma Khin Sein, interview.

62. James Thiri, interview.

63. Ibid.

64. Max Horkheimer and Theodor W. Adorno, *Dialectic of Enlightenment*, trans. John Cumming (1944, repr. New York: Continuum, 1991), 17.

65. Reebee Garofalo, "Understanding Mega-Events: If We Are the World, Why Can't We Change It?" in *Rockin' the Boat: Mass Music and Mass Movements*, ed. Reebee Garofolo (Boston: South End Press, 1992), 19.

66. Ardeth Maung Thawnghmung, "Preconditions and Prospects for Democratic Transition in Burma/Myanmar," *Asian Survey* 43, no. 3 (2003): 453–54.

Chapter Two

1. "Rockin' In the Free World," *Irrawaddy*, January 2004, http://www.irrawaddy.org/article.php?art_id=3256.

2. Lay Phyu appeared again in concert with IC for the first time in August of 2008, in a concert for cyclone relief.

3. Dale Olsen observes the same behavior in Vietnam. See Dale A. Olsen, *Popular Music of Vietnam: The Politics of Remembering, the Economics of Forgetting* (New York: Routledge, 2008), 1 and 80.

4. Scott Carrier, "Rock the Junta," *Mother Jones*, July 1, 2006, http://www.motherjones .com/news/feature/2006/07/rock_the_junta.htmlCarrier 2006.

5. Don Randel, ed., "Ballad," in *The New Harvard Dictionary of Music* (London: The Belknap Press of Harvard University Press, 1986), 67.

6. See for example Aung Zaw, "Burma: Music under Siege," where the Burmese author uses this division to organize his discussion of Burmese pop music.

7. For example, Cherry, personal interview, Yangon, January 19, 2008, and Ko Htwe, interview.

8. Some musicians acknowledged the existence of political songs, but since these are so rarely heard, this seemed to be an unimportant category. Political songs—that is, songs which speak of politics, the democracy movement or the ethnic insurgency—have been performed in Yangon in the past, but their creators have been and continue to be brutally repressed (see Moe 2007). Currently, some political songs are composed and recorded on the Thai-Burma border and the recordings sometimes find their way back to Yangon. Other songs that might fit this category, such as those with coded messages (discussed in chapter 5), are still sung in Yangon, but only in private settings.

9. Esther, personal interview, Yangon, February 6, 2008.

10. U Maung Zaw, personal interview, Yangon, February 5, 2008.

11. The National Convention met in 1993 (and continued to meet sporadically for nearly two decades) in order to write a new constitution for the Union of Myanmar. (The justification for delaying elections until 2010 was that the constitution had not yet been completed.) The process was widely viewed as illegitimate, and it ultimately produced a self-serving document that guaranteed that the current junta would maintain power in perpetuity. Aung San Suu Kyi's National League for Democracy refused to participate in the convention. The government commissioned propaganda to defend the convention, and the "National Convention Song" became rather well known because it was played so often on state television.

12. Listen to "L Phyu The Last Time," YouTube video, 3:41, posted by "s2soe," March 7, 2007, http://www.youtube.com/watch?v=tbi_r38eQog.

13. "Sometimes When We Touch" was written and recorded by Canadian Dan Hill.

14. Musicologists call this kind of song, in which a new text is substituted for the original one, a *contrafactum*.

15. Paul D. Greene describes a similar phenomenon in Nepal, where he heard "Jingle Bells" while on hold during a telephone call; the song has no connection to Christmas in the minds of Nepalis. See Paul D. Greene, "Mixed Messages: Unsettled Cosmopolitanisms in Nepali Pop," in *Wired For Sound: Engineering and Technologies in Sonic Cultures*, ed. Paul D. Greene and Thomas Porcello (Middletown: Wesleyan University Press, 2005), 203.

16. Listen to May Sweet and Lay Lay War, "A pyo sin," YouTube video, 3:35, posted by "snowgirl2," January 14, 2007, http://www.youtube.com/watch?v=UEn-qoccCt8.

17. At two points, a man (presumably one of the band members) is heard singing the melody also, and he, too, sings in unison with the soloists, although one octave lower.

18. I direct the reader to YouTube for further opportunities to compare to visual and aural presentations of American hit songs and Burmese *copy thachin*. For example, (1) Bangles, "Manic Monday," 1986, YouTube video, 3:29, posted by "mattervalley," August

12, 2008, http://www.youtube.com/watch?v=s48kuKLf0mE; and (1a) Connie and Hay Mar Nay Win, "Tait Chit Lote," YouTube video, 3:07, posted by "wiseguynm," August 2, 2007, http://www.youtube.com/watch?v=m1QAITWzThU. Also (2) Air Supply, "Making Love Out of Nothing at All," 1983, YouTube video, 5:02, posted by "eos305," March 18, 2006, http://www.youtube.com/watch?v=6lE6Htee0sA; and (2a) Phyu Phyu Kyaw Thein and Gita Meit Voices, "Zat Sayar Yet A Lo :D," YouTube video, 7:39, posted by "tooto-olay," September 1, 2006, http://www.youtube.com/watch?v=6LYTt1EkOWM; and (2b) Zan Nu, "Zat Sayar A Lo Kya," YouTube video, 5:46, posted by "scGrL01," April 15, 2006, http://www.youtube.com/watch?v=EyFZ-gaLVQs. Also (3) Dan Hill, "Sometimes When We Touch," 1977, YouTube video, 3:12, posted by "a6896023," December 20, 2007, http://www.youtube.com/watch?v=-xnyHG96vY8; and (3a) Lay Phyu, "Free (But Priceless)," YouTube video, 4:07, posted by "hsathaw1970," March 19, 2008, http://www.youtube.com/watch?v=uH5eG1_5kVg.

19. To this foreigner's ears, the lyrics are therefore sometimes incomprehensible, because syllables pass by so quickly that they are, in effect, unheard.

20. Rebekah, interview.

21. As I confirmed for myself by reading the book.

22. Another glaring example—a chapter by two Burmese writers—includes long sections of text taken verbatim from BSPP publications originally issued in the 1960s, with no citations: Khin Maung Nyunt and U Gita Lu Lin Koko, "The Musical Culture of Myanmar," in *Sonic Orders in ASEAN Musics, Volume One* (Singapore: ASEAN Committee on Culture and Information, 2003), 271–72.

23. The band had no chance to rehearse with, or even warm up with, the singers who were slated to sing the songs. (See chapter 3 for more on the industry's rehearsal culture). So the show director probably played the originals so that the band could hear, once, what the song was supposed to sound like.

24. Soe Thant, personal interview, Yangon, January 12, 2009.

25. Edward Larkey, "Austropop: Popular Music and National Identity in Austria," *Popular Music* 11, no. 2 (1992): 151–85.

26. Ibid., 151.

27. Ibid., 152.

28. During my research, friends pointed me to a number of examples of what they thought of as fusion music. These usually consisted of pieces in which Western instruments and sound technology completely covered the sounds of traditional instruments, so that the Burmese instruments were, for all intents and purposes, just there for show.

29. The Burmese terminology for what Western musicologists would call simple duple time.

30. But he has to speak Sgaw Karen with them, rather than his native Bwe Karen; the two are different languages, not merely dialects.

31. Ko Sithu, personal interview, Yangon, December 25, 2007.

32. The style is the same as the singing style in the *Maha Gita* tradition.

33. "New Age" is used to describe a large number of sonically different styles. One definition of this category of music focuses not on what kinds of sounds are most common, but rather, on how listeners usually feel when listening. New Age music is supposed to be "soothing and spacious," so that it induces feelings of relaxation. See Sarah P. Long, review of *The New Age Music Guide: Profiles and Recordings of 500 Top New Age Musicians*, by Patti Jean Birosik, *Notes*, 2nd ser., 48, no. 2 (1991): 538.

34. The Oriental scale is an abstraction (like all scales) of pitches often used in Romany (so-called Gypsy) music. Beginning on C, the scale is: C D♭ E F G A♭ B C.

35. Walter Benjamin, *Illuminations*, trans. Harry Zohn (New York: Harcourt, Brace and World, 1968), 218.

36. Ibid., 221.

37. Zak, *The Poetics of Rock: Cutting Tracks, Making Records*, 19.

38. Simon Frith, "Towards an Aesthetic of Popular Music," in *Popular Music: Critical Concepts in Media and Cultural Studies, volume IV*, ed. Simon Frith (New York: Routledge, 2004), 33.

39. Richard Middleton, "Rock Singing," in *The Cambridge Companion to Singing*, ed. John Potter (New York: Cambridge University Press, 2000), 38.

40. Timothy D. Taylor, *Global Pop: World Music, World Markets* (New York: Routledge, 1997), 21–28.

41. Taylor, *Global Pop: World Music, World Markets*, 23.

42. Keeping in mind Simon Frith's comment that the word authenticity is "the most misleading term in cultural theory." See Frith, "Towards an Aesthetic of Popular Music," 36.

43. Taylor, *Global Pop: World Music, World Markets*, 21.

44. Nyunt and Koko, "The Musical Culture of Myanmar."

45. Contrary to many commentators, but see especially Thant Myint-U, *The Making of Modern Burma*, 88. Thant Myint-U contends that "Myanma" is the name of just one *lu-myo*, or descent group, that has been identified as living in the Irrawaddy delta for four centuries, in contrast to other *lu-myo* (including the the Shan, the Mon and many others we now know as "national races" in Burma). "Myanma" thus represents one particular group, and is not representative of all of the people in today's Union of Myanmar. Nyunt and Koko provide much helpful information concerning musical instruments, repertoire and the like, but when they discuss the context of the development of the music, they tend to resort to broadsides against current political foes. For example, in the midst of describing musical development in the post–World War II era: "There was thirty percent illiteracy in Myanmar as an evil result of colonialism under the British regime." See "The Musical Culture of Myanmar," 282.

46. Nyunt and Koko, "The Musical Culture of Myanmar," 264.

47. The most celebrated instance of conflict between Burma and Thailand (or Siam, as it was then) occurred in 1767. After laying siege to the Siamese capital of Ayuthia for many months, on March 28 the Burmese forces breached the walls of the city and laid it waste. They killed the Siamese king and pillaged the riches of the city. "Thousands of the population were carried away into captivity, so that many a private could boast of four slaves." (G. E. Harvey, *History of Burma: From the Earliest Times to 10 March, 1824, the Beginning of the English Conquest, 1925* [repr., London: Frank and Cass Co., 1967], 253.) It is widely believed in Burma that these great numbers of Siamese prisoners exercised an influence on Burmese culture, and in particular that their songs were the source for the Maha Gita tunes known today as "Yodiya" (or Ayuthia) songs. For more on an important composer in the Yodiya song tradition, see Muriel Williamson,"A Biographical Note on Mya-wadi U Sa, Burmese Poet and Composer," *Musica Asiatica* 2 (1979): 151–54.

48. Keeler "Burma," 398.

49. Nyunt and Koko, "The Musical Culture of Myanmar," 265.

50. Gustaaf Houtman, *Mental Culture in Burmese Crisis Politics: Aung San Suu Kyi and the National League for Democracy* (Tokyo: Institute for the Study of Languages and Cultures of Asia and Africa, Tokyo University of Foreign Studies, 1999), 91 and 103.

51. Bruno Nettl, *The Western Impact on World Music: Change, Adaptation, and Survival* (New York: Schirmer Books, 1985), 26.

52. Craig A. Lockard, *Dance of Life: Popular Music and Politics in Southeast Asia* (Honolulu: University of Hawai'i Press, 1988), 265.

53. Michael Hayes, "Capitalism and Cultural Relativity: The Thai Pop Industry, Capitalism, and Western Cultural Values," in *Refashioning Pop Music in Asia: Cosmopolitan Flows, Political Tempos and Aesthetic Industries*, ed. Allen Chun, Ned Rossiter, and Brian Shoesmith (New York: Routledge Curzon, 2004), 29.

54. Emma Baulch, *Making Scenes: Reggae, Punk, and Death Metal in 1990s Bali* (Durham: Duke University Press, 2007), 110.

55. Michael Coyle, "Hijacked Hits and Antic Authenticity: Cover Songs, Race, and Postwar Marketing," in *Rock Over the edge: Transformations in Popular Music Culture*, ed. Roger Beebe, Denise Fulbrook, and Ben Saunders (Durham: Duke University Press, 2002).

56. Don Cusic, "In Defense of Cover Songs," *Journal of Popular Music and Society* 28, no. 2 (2005): 171–77.

57. Timothy D. Taylor makes the same point, saying that consumers in the West have an overriding concern with authenticity as primality: "This is perhaps the oldest assumption made by Westerners of musics from outside the West. . . . [Music must have] some discernible connection to the timeless, the ancient, the primal, the pure, the chthonic; that is what they want to buy, since their own world is often conceived as ephemeral, new, artificial and corrupt." See Taylor, *Global Pop: World Music, World Markets*, 26.

58. From Lay Phyu, "Min Gnako Meit Leit Taw," YouTube video, 5:07, posted by "llhwilliam89," June 2, 2006, http://www.youtube.com/watch?v=5eMq7Oqw5Ls.

59. From Phyu Phyu Kyaw Thein and Gita Meit Voices, "Zat Sayar Yet A Lo :D," YouTube video, 7:39, posted by "tootoolay," September 1, 2006, http://www.youtube.com/watch?v=6LYTt1EkOWM.

60. From Lay Phyu and Chit San Maung, "Till the End of Journey," YouTube video, 4:02, posted by "myothaw," October 11, 2007, http://www.youtube.com/watch?v=8knmzscpAJw.

61. This comment also underlines an earlier point: that Burmese people often perceive high pitches as difficult and not natural to their own voices. From Lay Phyu, "Min Gnako Meit Leit Taw," YouTube video, 5:07, posted by "llhwilliam89," June 2, 2006, http://www.youtube.com/watch?v=5eMq7Oqw5Ls.

62. Callahan, *Making Enemies*, 33–36. Helen Trager is a helpful source for understanding how British colonialists came to view their Burmese subjects as dishonest and disloyal. (See Helen Trager, *Burma Through Alien Eyes: Missionary Views of the Burmese in the Nineteenth Century* [New York: Praeger, 1966].) However, the most-cited author on this issue is George Orwell, who wrote about his experiences as a police officer in colonial Burma. Although his book *Burmese Days* is a novel, it is widely hailed as an accurate description of the mistrust and misunderstanding that characterized relations between Burmese subjects and British officials. (See George Orwell, *Burmese Days* [London: V. Gollancz, 1935].)

63. Sean Turnell, "The Chettiars in Burma," Macquarie University Department of Economics Research Paper 0512 (2005), http://www.econ.mq.edu.au/research/2005/chettiar.pdf.

64. U Hla Kyi, personal interview, Yangon, February 7, 2008.

65. Cho Cho Saing said later in the interview that there are other factors which may account for her students' desire to sing English hymns: First, it is a long-standing tradition to sing in English during church services (as I experienced myself at numerous different churches). She says that this tradition developed in the early days of Christianity in Burma, when English-speaking missionaries were always present during services;

church leaders wanted to make sure that the service contained at least some English so that the missionaries could participate, if only a little. In addition, the teacher says that her students are well aware that good English skills will stand them in good stead when they graduate and so they appreciate every chance to practise their English pronunciation. Finally, she says that older congregation members appreciate the English singing because it reminds them of the British colonial era, when they were young and presumably happier. A few other informants told me that Christian Burmese people—who make up a significant number of the major players in the pop industry—like Western music because it is associated with missionaries (e.g., Ko Sithu, interview). This makes sense; Western missionaries are still venerated in Burmese Christian communities. Members name buildings after their missionaries and tend their graves with devotion. Although missionaries did not specifically introduce Christian Burmese people to the Beatles—most of them had left Burma before the Beatles became popular—they did inculcate major and minor diatonic scales and Western instruments and forms. Therefore pop music, which uses these Western features, is still redolent of Western missionaries and their musical culture.

66. Vietnamese pop musician Le Minh made a similar statement in 2001, showing that such sentiments are not limited to Burma. See Dale A. Olsen, *Popular Music of Vietnam: The Politics of Remembering, the Economics of Forgetting* (New York: Routledge, 2008),120.

67. Ewbank and Papageorgiou, *Whose Master's Voice? The Development of Popular Music in Thirteen Cultures* 7.

68. Moskowitz, *Cries of Joy, Songs of Sorrow: Chinese Pop Music and Its Cultural Connotation*, 45.

69. Keila Diehl, *Echoes From Dharamsala: Music in the Life of a Tibetan Refugee Community* (Berkeley: University of California Press, 2002), 179.

70. Alexander Dent, "Cross-Cultural 'Countries': Covers, Conjunctures, and the Whiff of Nashville in *Musica Sertaneja* (Brazilian commercial country music)," *Popular Music and Society* 28, no. 2 (2005): 207–28.

71. Ibid., 217.

72. Christine Yano, "Covering Disclosures: Practices of Intimacy, Hierarchy, and Authenticity in a Japanese Popular Music Genre," *Popular Music and Society* 28, no. 2 (2005): 193–205.

73. Jeremy Wallach, "Living the Punk Lifestyle in Jakarta," *Ethnomusicology* 52, no. 1 (2008): 103.

74. Ibid., 108.

75. Ibid., 111.

76. Other scholars draw similar conclusions. See for example Allan Moore, "Authenticity as Authentication," *Popular Music* 21, no. 2 (2002): 218. The author makes a direct comparison between British cover bands and historical performance practice. "[In both of these cases] it is the song which has an identity, which is the key to the experience."

77. The current terms are early music, or historical performance, or historical practice.

78. Richard Taruskin, "Resisting the Ninth," *19th-Century Music* 12, no. 3 (Spring, 1989): 241–56.

79. Tom Turino, "Signs of Imagination, Identity, and Experience: A Peircian Semiotic Theory for Music," *Ethnomusicology* 43, no. 2 (1999): 221–55.

Chapter Three

1. It is worth noting that Ko Htwe had never heard me play the piano or the keyboard when he wrote to me with this request. He assumed that I would be able to play competently, likely because I am an American-educated musician who was, as he well knew, completing a doctorate in music.

2. For clips of Iron Cross warming up for a live show see "Lay Phyu—Door to the Death (Rehearsal)," YouTube video, 2:51, posted by "myothaw," August 25, 2008, http://www.youtube.com/watch?v=9Xcd7GaD4lE&feature=related; and "Lay Phyu Scar (Rehearsal)," YouTube video, 4:11, posted by "myothaw," August 26, 2008, http://www.youtube.com/watch?v=7qfM1FAOxC4&feature=related.

3. U Ye Zaw Tun, interview.

4. Htay Cho, interview; Soe Htun, interview; Aung Shwe, interview; and Thuza, interview.

5. For a brief summary of this scholarship, dating back to Plato and Aristotle, see Joanne Haroutounian, *Kindling the Spark: Recognizing and Developing Musical Talent* (Oxford: Oxford University Press, 2002).

6. Henry Kingsbury, *Music, Talent and Performance: A Conservatory Cultural System* (Philadelphia: Temple University Press, 1988).

7. Ibid., 60.

8. Thida Zay, personal interview, Yangon, January 4, 2009.

9. Kaung Lin Lin, interview.

10. Interviewees used these English terms in response to my questions.

11. Compare this with Kingsbury's articulation of the Western notion of talent: "Talent . . . is understood as located 'in' the person's mind, psyche, or perceptual apparatus, and is widely felt to be transmitted genetically, like hair and eye color." See Kingsbury, *Music, Talent and Performance*, 63.

12. For example, Ma Khin Sein, interview.

13. Kingsbury, *Music, Talent and Performance*, 76.

14. This seems to be a hypothetical proposition, however. No one mentioned any examples of untalented musicians who had succeeded because they worked hard.

15. Khine Ta Tun, personal interview, Yangon, December 29, 2008.

16. Khin Nyein Aye Than, "More People Tune In to Myanmar's Music Schools," *Myanmar Times*, August 22, 2005, http://www.myanmar.gov.mm/myanmartimes/no280/MyanmarTimes14-280/t003.htm.

17. R Zani, personal interview, Yangon, January 1, 2009.

18. The idea that artistic talent boils down to the ability to learn by following along was made clear to me by a teacher at the State School of Music and Drama in Yangon during my visit on February 13, 2008. Students at this school learn the venerable arts of traditional Burmese music and dance by following teachers' examples, rather than by reading notation or dance choreography. The dance teacher explained to me that she knows right away if students in her classes are talented or not, because she observes how quickly they can follow her (reproduce her example). She showed me the basic dance posture (feet together, knees bent outward, chest forward, and hands at sides) and told me that students who can perform this posture as soon as it is shown to them, and then hold it for five minutes without shaking, will be able to succeed in the school's dance program. I tried out the posture myself, trembling after only thirty seconds or so. She looked at me sadly; clearly, I am not talented.

19. Haroutounian, *Kindling the Spark: Recognizing and Developing Musical Talent*, xvi.

20. Susan O'Neill, "The Self-Identity of Young Musicians," in *Musical Identities*, ed. Raymond A. R. MacDonald, David Hargreaves and Dorothy Miell (Oxford: Oxford University Press, 2002), 82.

21. Kingsbury, *Music, Talent and Performance*, 68.

22. Saw Leh Dah, personal interview, Yangon, December 29, 2007.

23. Michael A. Aung-Thwin, *Myth and History in the Historiography of Early Burma: Paradigms, Primary Sources and Prejudices* (Athens, OH: Ohio University Center for International Studies, 1998), 150.

24. Note that the capital *c*'s in figure 3.2 are written with curlicues, making them appear somewhat like lowercase *e*'s.

25. For example, Nu Nu Win, interview; and Shway Nyunt, interview.

26. Keeler, "Burma," 379.

27. That is, the colotomic structure.

28. In traditional Burmese music, phrases always end on the *wah* beat, so the analogy with the third beat of a four-beat measure is problematic. Nevertheless, this is what is now taught in Burma.

29. The Burmese scale contains seven pitches, as does the European major scale. However, in the Burmese scale, the fourth scale degree is slightly higher in pitch and the seventh degree is slightly lower in pitch than the corresponding notes in the European major scale.

30. Ko Sithu, interview.

31. Nyunt and Ko Ko, "The Musical Culture of Myanmar," 244.

32. Tulip, personal interview, Yangon, Janury 5, 2008.

33. Kyaw Naing Oo, interview.

34. I was able to document only one exception to this trend. Cherry—the same woman who told me that her foreign-trained church choir conductor had given her an outstanding education in singing—said that good singing involves pronouncing words correctly and performing in the range that is most comfortable for one's voice.

35. Thuza, interview; Chit Nyein, personal interview, Yangon, December 27, 2008; and Thida Zay, interview.

36. Htin Thu, interview.

37. Ma Khin Sein, interview; Ko Sithu, interview; and Myine Myat, interview. This is an impressive feat, considering that these musicians perform almost all of these songs in English, which is not their first language.

38. Hotel performers often learn repertoire at the behest of the hotel managers with whom they work. The managers anticipate that certain new songs will begin to be popular with patrons. In at least one case, a hotel manager requires the house band to learn music representing certain ethnic traditions for theme weeks such as "Arabia." Johnson, interview.

39. Meaning, there is no school where Western theoretical concepts are taught. The musicians are of course aware of government-run Fine Arts High Schools and the University of Culture, where students receive formal instruction in the *Maha Gita* tradition.

40. Kit Young, the founder of Gita Meit, is actively working to get the school accredited to offer ABRSM (Associated Board of the Royal Schools of Music) theory exams, for two reasons: She says that her students really want to have an international evaluation and affirmation of their learning, and that earning such certificates is the usual route to success in international classical music.

41. Kit Young, personal interview, Yangon, January 4, 2008.

42. For a look at the Gita Meit Voices performing with Phyu Phyu Kyaw Thein, Burma's most prominent female pop singer, see Phyu Phyu Kyaw Thein and Gita Meit Voices, "Zat Sayar Yet A Lo :D," YouTube video, 7:39, posted by "tootoolay," September 1, 2006, http://www.youtube.com/watch?v=6LYTt1EkOWM.

43. For more information on Dr. Zipper's life and career, see Paul F. Cummins, *Dachau Song: The Twentieth Century Odyssey of Herbert Zipper* (New York: Peter Lang, 1992). Kit Young says that this book was important in helping her to plan Gita Meit.

44. See Gita Meit's website for more information on their social service projects: http://www.gitameit.com/wp/.

45. Than, "More People Tune In to Myanmar's Music Schools," *Myanmar Times*, August 22, 2005, http://www.myanmar.gov.mm/myanmartimes/no280/MyanmarTimes14-280/t003.htm.

46. Ko Doo, personal interview, Yangon, December 18, 2008.

47. To watch Nge Nge Lay (the young daughter of Chit San Maung, the lead guitarist in Iron Cross) performing, see "Chit San Maung's Daughter," YouTube video, 4:49, posted by "dennispuia," October 7, 2006, http://www.youtube.com/watch?v=uUrznS1lzx0; and Nge Nge Lay, "Meme Thachin," YouTube video, 4:42, posted by "maythe84," January 22, 2009, http://www.youtube.com/watch?v=0Jgt3YcczWQ.

48. This is the famous gospel song copied from "Sometimes When We Touch."

49. In Burma, being a choir leader and being a choral conductor are two different things. The conductor leads rehearsals and the choir leader functions more like a secretary, taking care of the paperwork and logistics involved.

50. The committee discussed the possibility of having this certificate recognized by the Myanmar Institute of Theology, the flagship institution of Christian higher education in Burma.

51. Rebekah, interview.

52. For example, Kit Young, interview; Cho Cho Saing, interview; and Wunna Khin Win, personal interview, Yangon, January 23, 2008.

53. This movie is based on the life story of the Australian classical pianist David Helfgott.

54. Three musicians who are currently at the top of the Burmese pop music scene did mention a Burmese *kya-saya-myin-saya*. Interestingly, they all identified the same man, Htoo Ein Thin, an *own-tune* composer and performer who is now deceased (Ko Htet Aung, interview; Chit Nyein, interview; Thuza, interview).

55. For example, see Melford E. Spiro, *Anthropological Other or Burmese Brother? Studies in Cultural Analysis* (London: Transaction Publications, 1992), 148, and Fink, *Living Silence: Burma Under Military Rule*, 253.

56. Lucy Green, *How Popular Musicians Learn: A Way Ahead for Music Education* (Aldershot: Ashgate, 2001), 60–61.

57. Ibid. 76–77.

58. Ibid., 38.

59. Ibid., 184.

60. Htay Cho, interview; Myint Oo, personal interview, Yangon, January 10, 2009; Aung Shwe, interview; U Ye Zaw Tun, interview; and Thet Htaw Mya, interview.

61. Daw Khin Soe, personal interview, Yangon, January 6, 2009.

62. And she believes that this is because the government censors are "concerned."

63. However, "sensitive" facts that come to light in the interview are usually suppressed, either by the Press Security Board or by the writer herself. She recalled one specific example: an actor overdosed on drugs, but "we would never write this." My own

limited experience bears this out. During an interview, a composer showed me three recent articles that had been written about him in Burmese journals (Soe Thant, interview). Each of them focused to some extent on his life with his wife and daughter. None of them mentioned the fact that he had been married once before. Here again, the concern seems to be that journalists do not want to be perceived as criticizing famous artists—either for their personal choices or for their artistic ones.

64. Virginia Danielson argues that celebrity is created by an entire society, which includes the celebrity herself, her fans, critics, and others. Society may include critics in many countries, but in Burma, there are few critics to "contribute to the public understanding" of the celebrity. See Virginia Danielson, "Theorizing Musical Celebrity Across Disciplines: Singing Celebrities and Their Publics" (paper presented at the annual international meeting of the Society for Ethnomusicology, Middletown, CT, October 27, 2008).

65. Than, "More People Tune In to Myanmar's Music Schools," *Myanmar Times*, August 22, 2005, http://www.myanmar.gov.mm/myanmartimes/no280/MyanmarTimes14-280/t003.htm.

Chapter Four

1. "Bomb Explosions Occur in Yangon Due to Inhumane Acts Committed by Terrorists," *The New Light of Myanmar*, May 8, 2005, http://www.myanmar.gov.mm/NLM-2005/may/enlm/May08_h2.html.

2. Shway Nyunt, interview.

3. Kit Young, interview.

4. Heather MacLachlan, "Bombings in Burma" (paper presented at the SEASSI Student Forum, University of Wisconsin-Madison, Madison, WI, August 2006).

5. Which is not to say that Burmese people conflate all English speakers with citizens of the United States. Caucasian speakers of English in Burma are almost always referred to as "foreigners" rather than "Americans."

6. For example, staff at my guest house, which caters to foreigners, make between 24,000 and 30,000 *kyat* per month, working twelve hours per day, six days a week. In the current economy, these are relatively desirable jobs.

7. A Pensioner, "Living in Myanmar Is Worth It," *New Light of Myanmar*, December 31, 2007, 11, http://myanmargeneva.org/NLM2007/eng/12Dec/n071231.pdf 2007.

8. Note that I do not include in this analysis people and products that are part of the alternate recording industry, that is, the growing industry which creates *series* recorded in minority languages, aimed at *tain-yin-tha* customers. For more on this, see chapter 5.

9. Richard A. Peterson, "The Production of Culture: A Prolegomenon," in *The Production of Culture*, ed. R. A. Peterson (Beverly Hills, CA: Sage, 1976), 10.

10. Lewis A. Coser, Charles Kadushin, and Walter W. Powell, *Books: The Culture and Commerce of Publishing* (Chicago: University of Chicago Press, 1982).

11. Diana Crane, *The Production of Culture: Media and the Urban Arts* (Newbury Park, CA: Sage Publications, 1992), 4.

12. Richard A. Peterson and N. Anand, "The Production of Culture Perspective," *Annual Review of Sociology* 30 (2004): 313.

13. Ibid., 318.

14. See, for example, Robert Burnett, *The Global Jukebox: The International Music Industry* (New York: Routledge, 1996).

15. Ohnmar Tun, interview; and Kaung Lin Lin, interview.

16. The personal nature of these relationships became very clear to me when, during the last week of my research, I attended the wedding of a musician who is quoted in this book. At the wedding I encountered two other music industry members whom I had previously interviewed. Although there was no formal business relationship between the groom and these other two people, so far as I am aware, the friendship was strong enough to merit a wedding invitation and wedding gifts in return.

17. See the MMRDS website at: http://www.mmrdrs.com/Default.aspx.

18. Peter Thein, personal interview, Yangon, February 4, 2008.

19. Kenneth, interview.

20. I assume that prizes are awarded this way in part because the management of the station wants to avoid the appearance of bias and corruption. Burma's annual prizes for movies (The Academy Awards) are given to the Best Director, Best Sound Editor, and so on. The judges are widely believed to be either accepting bribes or working at the behest of the junta, since the prizes frequently go to movies that the majority of the Burmese people do not like. One of my Burmese friends sarcastically calls these prizes "The Government Awards." And Aung Shwe, who told me that he was asked to serve as a judge for the movie awards, admitted that he had not seen any of the movies on which he was expected to render judgment.

21. Lwin Moe, personal interview, Yangon, December 22, 2008; and Kenneth, interview.

22. N. Anand and Richard A. Peterson, "When Market Information Constitutes Fields: Sensemaking of Markets in the Commercial Music Industry," *Organization Science* 11 (2000): 270–84.

23. Kyaw Kyaw Tun, "New Blood Injected to Bring Myanmar Music Association Back to Life," *Myanmar Times*, October 17, 2005, http://www.myanmar.gov.mm/myanmartimes /no288/MyanmarTimes15-288/t005.htm.

24. James Thiri, interview; Ohnmar Tun, interview; U Maung Zaw, interview; Kyaw Naing Oo, interview; and Ko Chit Min, interview.

25. Kenneth, interview.

26. Khine Ta Tun's insider perspective on music production companies allows him to see a side of the industry many others, including most Burmese music professionals, are not aware of: these companies, by and large, operate on shoestring budgets and do not turn large profits. He says that the money made by Burmese companies pales in comparison to that earned by their counterparts in Thailand.

27. For example, Aung Shwe, interview; Kenneth, interview; and Peter Thein, interview.

28. James Thiri, interview.

29. Kaung Lin Lin, interview.

30. To cite just one statistic: according to the World Health Organization, in 2003 the government of Burma devoted only ten dollars (international dollar rate) per capita to health expenditures (see the WHO 2006 report archived at http://www.who.int /whr/2006/annex/06_annex3_en.pdf).

31. And I have every sympathy with their confusion. Despite asking many people for information about these laws, I am still uncertain that I understand what Burmese law says, because I heard so many different answers from so many people who claimed to know. Here is one example: the *Myanmar Times* reports that the country became a member of the World Intellectual Property Organization in 2001. (See Khin Hninn Phyu, "Laws Drafted on Intellectual Property," *Myanmar Times*, April 11, 2005, http://www .myanmar.gov.mm/myanmartimes/no262/MyanmarTimes14-262/n009.htm). However,

the country is not listed as one of WIPO's member states on the WIPO website (see http://www.wipo.int/members/en/).

32. Saw Hser Ler, personal interview, Yangon, December 20, 2008.

33. Although there is some indication that some middle-class and high-income people are starting to view copied recordings as somehow inferior to originals: Kaung Lin Lin shared with me that "a few people" are ashamed of owning pirated CDs and never give them as presents, especially to family and friends living abroad.

34. Smuggling goods into and out of Burma is such a big business now that international sanctions against the country have hardly any noticeable effect, at least on the availability of recorded music. Foreign recordings come into the country in the luggage of citizens who travel abroad to acquire them. This has apparently been true since at least the 1970s, according to my interviewees. Recently, though, smuggling has become a desirable profession. One friend (Rebekah, interview) shared with me the story of two acquaintances, a married couple who are both medical doctors. They have given up their medical careers to work full-time as porters. They charge fees to Burmese folks who want to send local goods (often food and medicines) to relatives living in the diaspora, and to those same relatives who send Western-made goods and currency back home. They fly in and out of the country, toting their bulging suitcases, twice a month. This couple, and people like them, effectively make a mockery of sanctions. Porters can and do bring the best-selling albums from the West into Burma shortly after their official release in Australia or Japan (of course, they need to bring only one copy of each album, since the duplicates can quickly be made in Yangon).

35. This movie features Rambo fighting on the Thai-Burma border against SPDC soldiers. Rambo is victorious, of course, and so the movie is banned in Burma.

36. "What Is WIPO?," World Intellectual Property Organization, accessed January 18, 2011, http://www.wipo.int/about-wipo/en/what/.

37. Roger Wallis and Krister Malm, *Big Sounds from Small Peoples: The Music Industry in Small Countries* (New York: Pendragon Press, 1984), 164.

38 "General Information on Copyright," World Intellectual Property Organization, accessed January 18, 2011, http://www.wipo.int/copyright/en/general/about _copyright.html.

39. Ibid.

40. Ibid.

41. Wallis and Malm, *Big Sounds from Small Peoples*, 168.

42. Ibid., 171.

43. Ibid., 173.

44. One might even say many Burmese musicians seem ill-informed. For example, musicians—MMA members—told me a variety of different target dates for the country to join WIPO. I am quoting 2014 in this book, since that date was told to me by two MMA board members who seemed to be particularly knowledgeable about the process.

45. Theramu Blu Paw, interview.

46. Crane, *The Production of Culture*, 152.

47. Ahunt Phone Myat, "Censor Board to Switch to Digital Submissions," *Democratic Voice of Burma*, February 26, 2009, http://www.dvb.no/english/news.php?id=2261.

48. Electronic equipment, most of which has to be imported into the country, is more costly in Burma than in the G8 countries where it is made. Burmese people pay the equivalent of hundreds of American dollars for used cell phones, for examples. Cars, computers, videocameras and the like are all more expensive in real terms. I once

paid sixty dollars for a disposable camera, an item that would cost me less than 5 dollars in New York.

49. See Richard A. Peterson and N. Anand, "The Production of Culture Perspective" and Richard A. Peterson and D. G. Berger, "Cycles in Symbol Production: The Case of Popular Music," *American Sociological Review* 40 (1975): 158–73.

50. Note that Burnett modifies this assertion. See Robert Burnett, *The Global Jukebox*, 115.

51. Paul DiMaggio and Paul Hirsch, "Production Organizations in the Arts," *American Behavioral Scientist* 19, no. 6 (1976): 745.

52. Anand and Peterson, "When Market Information Constitutes Fields."

53. Keith Negus, *Producing Pop: Culture and Conflict in the Popular Music Industry*, 16.

54. The "Big Four" record companies (EMI, Sony BMG, Warner Music Group, and Universal Group) control approximately 85 percent of the music recorded and sold worldwide.

Chapter Five

1. Fink, *Living Silence: Burma under Military Rule* and Skidmore, *Karaoke Fascism*.

2. Reporters Without Borders, "Worldwide Press Freedom Index 2007," press release, October 16, 2007, http://www.rsf.org/IMG/pdf/index_2007_en.pdf.

3. Ibid.

4. I am depending on Martin Cloonan's definition of censorship here: "Censorship is: the attempt to interfere, either pre- or post-publication, with artistic expressions of popular musicians, with a view to stifling, or significantly altering, that expression. This includes procedures of marginalization, as well as the overt banning, of such expressions." See Martin Cloonan, *Banned! Censorship of Popular Music in Britain: 1967–92* (Aldershot, UK: Ashgate Publishing Ltd., 1996), 23.

5. For a concise overview of the development of laws governing written expression in Burma, see "Chronology of Burma's Laws Restricting Freedom of Opinion, Expression and the Press," *Irrawaddy*, May 1, 2004, http://www.irrawaddy.org/research_show .php?art_id=3534.

6. See Fink, *Living Silence*, 197–212.

7. Anna J. Allott, *Inked Over, Ripped Out: Burmese Storytellers and the Censors* (New York: PEN American Center, 1993).

8. Zaw, "Burma: Music under Siege," 39–61.

9. Cloonan, *Banned! Censorship of Popular Music in Britain: 1967–92*.

10. For some particularly well-written examples, see Burnett, *The Global Jukebox*, 29–32 and Richard Middleton, *Studying Popular Music*, 34–63.

11. Max Horkheimer and Theodor W. Adorno, *Dialectic of Enlightenment*, trans. John Cumming (New York: Continuum, 1991).

12. Ibid., 137.

13. Ibid., 133.

14. Jerry Rodnitzky, "A Rocky Road to Respect: Trends in Academic Writing on Popular Music and Popular Music and Society," *Popular Music and Society* 21, no. 1 (1997): 99.

15. Craig A. Lockard, *Dance of Life: Popular Music and Politics in Southeast Asia*, 263. But Lockard is sensitive to the implications of his conclusion. He notes that it is not clear that overtly resistant music has been able to foster significant change (p. 206). He says that the political impact of this kind of popular music is indirect, at best (p. 267).

16. Timothy Ryback, *Rock Around the Bloc: A History of Rock Music in Eastern Europe and the Soviet Union* (New York: Oxford University Press, 1990), 233.

17. Jeff Chang, *Can't Stop Won't Stop: A History of the Hip-Hop Generation* (New York: St. Martin's Press, 2005), 111.

18. Ibid., 419.

19. Michael Bodden, "Rap in Indonesian Youth Music of the 1990s: 'Globalization,' 'Outlaw Genres,' and Social Protest," *Asian Music* 36, no. 2 (2005): 1–26.

20. Walser, *Running with the Devil: Power, Gender and Madness in Heavy Metal Music*, xiv. For similar wording see Richard Middleton, *Studying Popular Music*, 249.

21. Toynbee, *Making Popular Music*, 45.

22. Wallis and Malm, *Big Sounds from Small Peoples*, 302. (See also Negus, *Popular Music in Theory*, 174.) Note that Wallis and Malm do not consequently argue for cultural imperialism; in fact they explicitly state that the flow of cultural influence is not a one-way movement from the West to the Rest.

23. Andreas Gebesmair, "Measurements of Globalization: Some Remarks on Sources and Indicators," in *Global Repertoires: Popular Music Within and Beyond the Transnational Music Industry*, ed. Andreas Gebesmair and Alfred Smudits (Aldershot, UK: Ashgate, 2001), 131.

24. Marcus Breen, "The End of the World As We Know It," in *Popular Music: Style and Identity*, ed. Will Straw et al. (International Association for the Study of Popular Music: Seventh International Conference on Popular Music Studies. Montreal: Centre for Research on Canadian Cultural Industries and Institutions, 1995), 45–53.

25. Negus, *Popular Music in Theory*, 178.

26. Hayes, "Capitalism and Cultural Relativity" 30 (see chap. 2, n. 51).

27. Indeed, cultural theorist Slavoj Zizek claims that the hegemony-resistance discourse has become the new dominant discourse in academia more generally. See Slavoj Zizek, *Welcome to the Desert of the Real* (London: Verso, 2002), 66.

28. James C. Scott, *Domination and the Arts of Resistance: Hidden Transcripts* (New Haven: Yale University Press, 1990), 2.

29. Ibid., 4.

30. Ibid., 114.

31. Ibid., 136.

32. Ibid., 166.

33. Callahan, *Making Enemies*, 191 (see introduction, n. 31).

34. This is the usual English translation of the regime's constant proclamation. It appears frequently in English-language propaganda.

35. "Perspectives: Unity is Dignity of the Union," *The New Light of Myanmar*, January 8, 2009.

36. See especially Skidmore, *Karaoke Fascism*.

37. Allot, *Inked Over, Ripped Out*, 16.

38. For a translation of this document see http://burmalibrary.org/docs3/Printers _and_Publishers_Registation_Act.htm. I suspect the supervisor intended to reference this document along with the 1975 Memorandum to Printers and Publishers Concerning the Submission of Manuscripts for Scrutiny—an addendum that amplifies the 1962 regulation by describing unacceptable content.

39. One producer says that the PSB sometimes farms their work out to other government ministries, such as the Ministry of Health, to ensure that the recording meets the government standard of "Burmese culture" (Kaung Lin Lin, interview).

40. Translation quoted in Allott, *Inked Over, Ripped Out*, 6.

41. Allott, *Inked Over, Ripped Out*, 7.

42. For a more complete accounting, see Yeni, "Burma: The Censored Land," *Irrawaddy*, March 2008, http://www.irrawaddy.org/article.php?art_id=10648.

43. Written Burmese uses a syllabic script. Sounds are written in syllable combinations (rather than as separate letters). Therefore, the first grapheme of each line of a poem is not a letter, but a syllable. In addition, there are many monosyllabic words in Burmese, so many single syllables carry meaning. Thus it is possible to write the message "Power-Hungry General Than Shwe" using only the first grapheme in each line of an eight-line poem.

44. For an example, see Kyaw Min Lu, "Rights and Wrongs of Today's Political Arena of Myanmar," *New Light of Myanmar*, September 28, 2007, 8, http://myanmargeneva .org/NLM2007/eng/9Sep/n070928.pdf. Scholar Michael Aung-Thwin makes the same argument, albeit in a more graceful manner. See Aung-Thwin, *Myth and History in the Historiography of Early Burma: Paradigms, Primary Sources and Prejudices*, 145–60, and especially p. 159.

45. For more information on the Saw Wai case and other similar cases, see Naw Say Phaw, "Censor and Editor Give Evidence at Poet's Trial," *Democratic Voice of Burma*, July 9, 2008, http://english.dvb.no/news.php?id=1518; and Saw Yan Naing, "Suppressed," *Irrawaddy*, February 2009, http://www.irrawaddy.org/article.php?art_id=1,5004.

46. Saw Yan Naing, "Burma's Censors Are Now Also Code-Breakers," *Irrawaddy*, February 4, 2008, http://www.irrawaddy.org/article.php?art_id=10151.

47. Interestingly, he described himself as a "famous songwriter," not as a composer, insisting on the difference between the two. He believes that the word "composer" should be used to describe people who write music using "international notes" (discussed in chapter 2). He was the only musician I met who made this distinction.

48. Note that the Buddhist calendar differs from the Gregorian calendar; the Buddhist calendar dates from the birth of Buddha, 543 years earlier than the birth of Christ. The Buddhist calendar was used across Lower Burma for centuries, and when Burma became a part of the British empire, the BC-AD system did not entirely dislodge it. Most Burmese are equally comfortable with both. The Buddhist calendar is a lunar calendar, and in my experience most Burmese people are much more aware of the waxing and waning phases of the moon than are Westerners, even if they commonly refer to dates using the Gregorian terms.

49. This street is now called Parami Lan, although many Yangonites still know it as AD Lan.

50. See the USAID 2008 report on HIV prevalence in Burma, archived at http:// www.usaid.gov/our_work/global_health/aids/Countries/ane/burma_profile.pdf.

51. For other lists of forbidden words derived from Burmese musicians' experiences, see Zaw, "Burma: Music under Siege," 45 and 56.

52. Nu Nu Win, interview; Aye Kyi, interview; and Soe Htun, interview.

53. When I announced my intention to head over to the studio to photograph this billboard, the respondent and two friends reacted with alarm. "You can't do that!" they said. I offered that I would simply stand in front of the billboard and write down the rules in a notebook, but they said that this was not permitted, either. I asked whether Burmese people could do this and they said, "No, no one is allowed to make a copy of the rules. People are only allowed to read the rules and memorize them."

54. Ko Chit Min, interview.

55. Ardeth Maung Thawnghmung, *Behind the Teak Curtain: Authoritarianism, Agricultural Policies, and Political Legitimacy in Rural Burma/Myanmar* (New York: Kegan Paul, 2004).

56. Saw Yan Naing, "Suppressed," *Irrawaddy*, February 2009, http://www.irrawaddy.org/article.php?art_id=1,5004.

57. Zaw, "Burma: Music under Siege."

58. And there are persistent reports of politically defiant hip-hop recordings being made, although these are not circulating openly. For one such report see Naw Seng, "Political Hip Hop Released," *Irrawaddy*, September 15, 2003, http://www.irrawaddy.org/article.php?art_id=1765.

59. "A Rocker's Return," *Irrawaddy*, September 2008, http://www.irrawaddy.org/article.php?art_id=14153.

60. See Zaw, "Burma: Music under Siege," 46.

61. For example, one singer-composer who was active in the early 1980s and who now lives in Switzerland acknowledged to me that some of his songs contained coded messages, but was unwilling to discuss the issue further (and was specifically unwilling to "decode" the secret messages for me). He pointed out that he still has family living in Burma, and fears that they could be the subject of reprisals if he were to reveal this information (e-mail message to author, March 4, 2007).

62. See also Amporn Jirattikorn, "Shan Noises, Burmese Sound: Crafting Selves Through Music" (paper presented the Conference on Shan Buddhism and Culture, School of Oriental and African Studies, London, UK, December 8, 2007), 9, http://eprints.soas.ac.uk/5339/. The author claims that anonymous Burmese fans made the exact same interpretation of "A Song for Silver Mountain Ranges," composed by Sai Khamlek.

63. See the English translation of the text of the Panglong Agreement at http://www.burmalibrary.org/docs/panglong_agreement.htm.

64. Fink, *Living Silence*, 229.

65. Lockard, *Dance of Life*, 265.

66. Zaw, "Burma: Music under Siege," 47.

67. Quoted in Aung Zaw, "And the Band Played On," *Irrawaddy*, September 2002, http://www.irrawaddy.org/article.php?art_id=2707&page=1.

68. "Burma's Hip-Hop Under Attack," *Irrawaddy*, May 2008, http://www.irrawaddy.org/article.php?art_id=11646.

69. For example, Htay Cho, interview; and Ko Chit Min, interview.

70. See Jane Ferguson, "Rocking in Shanland: Histories and Popular Culture Jams at the Thai-Burma Border" (PhD diss., Cornell University, 2008).

71. Three of the Karen musicians I met during my second trip to Yangon left the city for the camps on the Thai-Burma border in mid-2008. Therefore I was unable to reinterview them during my third trip.

72. I asked a number of musicians in Yangon about YouTube. They were mostly unaware of it, but a handful said that they had been able to view it via Internet connections in Burma. Based on this, I assume that *tain-yin-tha* videos on YouTube reach viewers inside the country, but only rarely.

73. In December 2008, I became part of the dissemination of *tain-yin-tha* music when I was asked to take a master copy of a new Karen *series* in my suitcase back to the United States, for sale to people in the Karen diaspora there.

74. A foreigner friend of mine who has lived and worked in Burma for six years asserts that avoidance is *the* dominant strategy employed by Burmese people in the face of a repressive government. She argues that people generally survive by avoiding conflict, or even contact, with government bureaucracy as much as possible (Kit Young, interview). I do not care to make such a broad statement about a large and diverse

group of people, but intriguing traces of this idea seemed to pop up every so often. For example, I once met a retired diplomat who regaled me with stories about working as a representative of the Burmese government in various First World countries over thirty years. When I responded, "You should write a book!" he said very seriously, "I would like to, but I never will. My goal for my retirement is to simply not be noticed by the government." Two of my respondents for this project claimed that "the Karen way" is to want to stay away from government bureaucracy, and that this stems from the traditional Karen way of life: villagers live in isolated communities where they are not dominated by a central political authority. This "simple" and "honest" life is directly tied to the idea that Karen people like to be left to themselves, according to these two Yangon-dwelling Karen leaders (Bo Bo Mya, personal interview, January 14, 2008; and Aung Shwe, interview). The same themes (preference for simplicity, isolation, and independence from the Burmese central government) are evoked in a recent article about the Wa people of the Shan State (see Tor Norling, "Haven or Hell," *Irrawaddy*, July 11, 2008, http://www.irrawaddy.org/highlight.php?art_id=13275). In addition, author Anna Allott implies that avoidance is a common life strategy for Burmese people in general. She offers this analysis of a Burmese expression, which translates as, "If you don't do anything, and don't get involved, you won't get fired": "[This expression] suggests that the best way to keep out of (political) trouble and avoid personal loss and suffering is to keep one's head down and avoid taking initiative" (see Allott, *Inked Over, Ripped Out*, 39).

75. Censored recordings are labeled also. The official label is a multicolored, one-inch-square sticker which shows the date when the *series* was approved.

76. Scott, *Domination and the Arts of Resistance*, 96–102.

77. Interestingly, some producers of religious and nationalistic recordings do not make even this minimal attempt to disguise their normally forbidden product. I have in my own collection a handful of CDs and cassette tapes containing explicitly Christian content that are not so labeled. Evidently, the likelihood of such recordings being discovered by government agents is very slight, so slight that it is not worth the trouble of asserting in print that they will only be circulated "within the congregation."

78. Naw Hsa Paw, personal interview, December 24, 2008.

79. See http://cmfmyanmar.multiply.com/.

80. "Fossils Found Reveal the Origin of Human Beings in Myanmar," *New Light of Myanmar*, December 20, 2007, 2, http://myanmargeneva.org/NLM2007/eng/12Dec/n071220.pdf.

81. Arkar Moe, "Western Instruments Outlawed from Traditional Orchestras," *Irrawaddy*, December 29, 2009, http://www.irrawaddy.org/article.php?art_id=17491.

82. This is another oft-used phrase in the state media. For whatever reason, "axe-handle" seems to be extremely insulting, although it doesn't sound so when translated.

83. Callahan, *Political Authority in Burma's Ethnic Minority States*, 10.

84. Brian Heidel reveals a fascinating fact: Most of the NGO workers who were surveyed in his large-scale survey of 64 NGOs in Yangon were confused about their organizations' tax-exempt status. (Although nonprofit organizations in Burma are tax exempt, workers did not know this.) These workers represent some of the best-educated people in the country. Clearly, the government is not even effectively educating the population about tax requirements. See Heidel, *The Growth of Civil Society in Myanmar*, 18.

85. A significant portion of the Burmese economy consists of remittances. In fact, the government requires that Burmese citizens employed abroad deposit remittances in the Myanmar Foreign Trade Bank. This rule especially impacts sailors and seamen. In addition, millions of Burmese are being supported by relatives who are unofficially abroad,

especially migrant workers in Thailand and other Southeast Asian countries. See Sean Turnell, Alison Vicary and Bradford Wylie, "Migrant Worker Remittances and Burma: An Economic Analysis of Survey Results," *ANU E Press* (2007), http://epress.anu.edu.au/myanmar02/mobile_devices/ch05.html.

86. The term "NGO" is popular in Burma now, and people use it to describe any kind of group that is supposedly devoted to the public good. For instance, the government creates so-called NGOs that conduct public health campaigns.

87. Archived at http://mission.itu.ch/MISSIONS/Myanmar/06nlm/n060929.htm.

88. James Thiri, interview.

Conclusion

1. Ye Thu, "The 'Victim' Treatment: A Self-Fulfilling Prophecy," *Democratic Voice of Burma*, April 7, 2009, http://www.dvb.no/features/the-victim-treatment-a-self-fulfilling-prophecy/2127.

2. Holly Kruse, *Site and Sound: Understanding Independent Music Scenes* (New York: P. Lang, 2003), 14.

3. The syllable *say* is usually translated as "mind" in English. It is used in many Burmese expressions that convey emotion (such as confusion or calm). The Burmese word for the organ that pumps blood is *nilohn*.

4. See Sara Cohen, "Ethnography and Popular Music Studies," *Popular Music* 12, no. 2 (1993): 123–38; Martin Stokes, "Talk and Text: Popular Music and Ethnomusicology," in *Analyzing Popular Music*, ed. Allan Moore (Cambridge: Cambridge University Press, 2003), 218–39; Robert Walser, "Popular Music Analysis: Ten Apothegms and Four Instances," in *Analyzing Popular Music*, ed. Allan F. Moore (Cambridge: Cambridge University Press, 2003), 16–38.

5. Jan Fairley, "The 'Local' and 'Global' in Popular Music," in *The Cambridge Companion to Pop and Rock*, ed. Simon Frith, Will Straw, and John Street (Cambridge: Cambridge University Press, 2001), 275.

6. Walser, "Popular Music Analysis," 19.

7. Ibid.," 38.

Bibliography

Ahunt Phone Myat. "Censor Board to Switch to Digital Submissions." *Democratic Voice of Burma*, February 26, 2009. http://www.dvb.no/english/news.php?id=2261.

Allott, Anna J. *Inked Over, Ripped Out: Burmese Storytellers and the Censors.* New York: PEN American Center, 1993.

Anand, N. and Richard A. Peterson. "When Market Information Constitutes Fields: The Sensemaking of Markets in the Commercial Music Industry." *Organization Science* 11 (2000): 270–84.

"A Rocker's Return." *Irrawaddy*, September 2008. http://www.irrawaddy.org/article.php?art_id=14153.

Arkar Moe. "Western Instruments Outlawed from Traditional Orchestras." *Irrawaddy*, December 29, 2009. http://www.irrawaddy.org/article.php?art_id=17491.

Aung Zaw. "And the Band Played On." *Irrawaddy*, September 2002. http://www.irrawaddy.org/article.php?art_id=2707&page=1.

———. "Burma: Music under Siege." In *Shoot the Singer: Music Censorship Today*, edited by Marie Korpe, 39–61. New York: Zed Books, 2004.

Aung-Thwin, Michael A. *Myth and History in the Historiography of Early Burma: Paradigms, Primary Sources, and Prejudices.* Athens, OH: Ohio University Center for International Studies, 1998.

Aye, Moe. "Interview: Burma's Declining Basic Education." *Democratic Voice of Burma*, July 10, 2008. http://english.dvb.no/news.php?id=1519.

Ba Kaung. "Anger over Mobile Phone Charge Hike." *Irrawaddy*, January 21, 2010. http://www.irrawaddy.org/article.php?art_id=17522.

Baulch, Emma. *Making Scenes: Reggae, Punk, and Death Metal in 1990s Bali.* Durham: Duke University Press, 2007.

Bayton, Mavis. "Women and the Electric Guitar." In *Sexing the Groove: Popular Music and Gender*, edited by Sheila Whiteley, 37–49. London: Routledge, 1997.

Becker, Judith. "The Anatomy of a Mode." *Ethnomusicology* 13, no. 2 (1969): 267–79.

Benjamin, Walter. *Illuminations.* Translated by Harry Zohn. New York: Harcourt, Brace and World, 1968.

Bodden, Michael. "Rap in Indonesian Youth Music of the 1990s: 'Globalization,' 'Outlaw Genres,' and Social Protest." *Asian Music* 36, no. 2 (2005): 1–26.

"Bomb Explosions Occur in Yangon Due to Inhumane Acts Committed by Terrorists." *New Light of Myanmar*, May 8, 2005. http://www.myanmar-information.net/infosheet/2005/050508.htm.

Brand, Manny. *The Teaching of Music in Nine Asian Nations: Comparing Approaches to Music Education.* Lewiston, NY: Edwin Mellen, 2006.

Breen, Marcus. "The End of the World as We Know It." In *Popular Music: Style and Identity*, edited by Will Straw, Stacey Johnson, Rebecca Sullivan, and Paul Friedlander, 45–53. IASPM: Seventh International Conference on Popular Music Studies. Montreal: Centre for Research on Canadian Cultural Industries and Institutions, 1995.

"Burma's Hip-Hop Under Attack." *Irrawaddy*, May 2008. http://www.irrawaddy.org/article.php?art_id=11646.

Burnett, Robert. *The Global Jukebox: The International Music Industry*. New York: Routledge, 1996.

Callahan, Mary P. *Making Enemies: War and State Building in Burma*. Ithaca: Cornell University Press, 2003.

———. *Political Authority in Burma's Ethnic Minority States: Devolution, Occupation, and Coexistence*. Washington, DC: East-West Center Institute of Southeast Asian Studies, 2007.

Carrier, Scott. "Rock the Junta." *Mother Jones*, July 1, 2006. http://www.motherjones.com/news/feature/2006/07/rock_the_junta.html.

Chang, Jeff. *Can't Stop Won't Stop: A History of the Hip-Hop Generation*. New York: St. Martin's Press, 2005.

"Chronology of Burma's Laws Restricting Freedom of Opinion, Expression and the Press." *Irrawaddy*, May 1, 2004. http://www.irrawaddy.org/research_show.php?art_id=3534.

Cloonan, Martin. *Banned! Censorship of Popular Music in Britain: 196792*. Aldershot, UK: Ashgate Publishing Ltd., 1996.

———. "Pop and the Nation-State: Towards a Theorization." *Popular Music* 18, no. 2 (1999): 193–207.

Cohen, Sara. "Ethnography and Popular Music Studies." *Popular Music* 12, no. 2 (1993): 123–38.

Coser, Lewis A., Charles Kadushin, and Walter W. Powell. *Books: The Culture and Commerce of Publishing*. Chicago: University of Chicago Press, 1982.

Coyle, Michael. "Hijacked Hits and Antic Authenticity: Cover Songs, Race, and Postwar Marketing." In *Rock Over the Edge: Transformations in Popular Music Culture*, edited by Roger Beebe, Denise Fulbrook, and Ben Saunders, 133–57. Durham: Duke University Press, 2002.

Crane, Diana. *The Production of Culture: Media and the Urban Arts*. Newbury Park, CA: Sage Publications, 1992.

Cummins, Paul F. *Dachau Song: The Twentieth-Century Odyssey of Herbert Zipper*. New York: Peter Lang Publishing, 1992.

Curtis, Jessicah. "Shipping Markets Inconsistent." *Myanmar Times*, December 8, 2003. http://www.myanmar.gov.mm/myanmartimes/no195/MyanmarTimes10-195/021.htm.

Cusic, Don. "In Defense of Cover Songs." *Journal of Popular Music and Society* 28, no. 2 (2005): 171–77.

Danielson, Virginia. "Theorizing Musical Celebrity Across Disciplines: Singing Celebrities and Their Publics." Paper presented at the annual international meeting of the Society for Ethnomusicology, Middletown, CT, October 27, 2008.

Dent, Alexander. "Cross-Cultural 'Countries': Covers, Conjectures, and the Whiff of Nashville in *Musica Sertaneja* (Brazilian Commercial Country Music)." *Popular Music and Society* 28, no. 2 (2005): 207–28.

Diehl, Keila. *Echoes From Dharamsala: Music in the Life of a Tibetan Refugee Community.* Berkeley: University of California Press, 2002.

DiMaggio, Paul, and Paul Hirsch. "Production Organizations in the Arts." *American Behavioral Scientist* 19, no. 6 (1976): 735–52.

Douglas, Gavin. "The Burmese Guitar: Local Adaptations to a World Instrument." Paper presented at the International Burma Studies Conference, DeKalb, Illinois, October 3–5, 2008.

———. "Myanmar." *Continuum Encyclopedia of Popular Music of the World* Vol. V, 196–202. New York: Continuum, 2003.

———. "The Sokayeti Performing Arts Competition of Burma/Myanmar." *World of Music* 45, no. 1 (2003): 35–54.

———. "State Patronage of Burmese Traditional Music." PhD diss., University of Washington, 2001.

Ellingson, Ter. "Notation." In *Ethnomusicology: An Introduction*, edited by Helen Myers, 153–64. New York: W. W. Norton, 1992.

Ewbank, Alison J., and Fouli T. Papageorgiou, eds. *Whose Master's Voice? The Development of Popular Music in Thirteen Cultures.* Westport, CT: Greenwood Press, 1997.

Fairley, Jan. "The 'Local' and 'Global' in Popular Music. In *The Cambridge Companion to Pop and Rock*, edited by Simon Frith, Will Straw, and John Street, 272–89. Cambridge: Cambridge University Press, 2001.

Ferguson, Jane. "Rocking in Shanland: Histories and Popular Culture Jams at the Thai-Burma Border." PhD Diss., Cornell University, 2008.

Fink, Christina. *Living Silence: Burma Under Military Rule.* Bangkok: White Lotus, 2001.

"Fossils Found Reveal the Origin of Human Beings in Myanmar." *New Light of Myanmar*, December 20, 2007, 2. http://myanmargeneva.org/NLM2007/eng/12Dec/n071220.pdf.

Frith, Simon. "Towards an Aesthetic of Popular Music." In *Popular Music: Critical Concepts in Media and Cultural Studies, Volume 4*, edited by Simon Frith, 32–47. New York: Routledge, 2004.

Garfias, Robert. "The Development of the Modern Burmese *Hsaing* Ensemble." *Asian Music* 16 (1985): 1–28.

———. "A Musical Visit to Burma." *World of Music* 17, no. 1 (1975): 3–13.

Garofalo, Reebee. "Understanding Mega-Events: If We Are the World, Why How Do We Change It?" In *Rockin' the Boat: Mass Music and Mass Movements*, edited by Reebee Garofalo, 15–35. Boston: South End Press, 1992.

Gebesmair, Andreas. "Measurements of Globalization: Some Remarks on Sources and Indicators." In *Global Repertoires: Popular Music Within and Beyond the Transnational Music Industry*, edited by Andreas Gebesmair and Alfred Smudits, 137–52. Aldershot: Ashgate, 2001.

Green, Lucy. *How Popular Musicians Learn: A Way Ahead for Music Education.* Aldershot: Ashgate, 2001.

Greene, Paul D. "Mixed Messages: Unsettled Cosmopolitanisms in Nepali Pop." In *Wired For Sound: Engineering and Technologies in Sonic Cultures*, edited by Paul D. Greene and Thomas Porcello, 198–221. Middletown: Wesleyan University Press, 2005.

Don't Fence Me In: Major Mary and the Karen Refugees From Burma. DVD. Directed by Ruth Gumnit. Watertown, MA: Documentary Educational Resources, 2004.

Habermas, Jurgen. *Toward a Rational Society: Student Protest, Science, and Politics*. Translated by Jeremy J. Shapiro. Boston: Beacon Press, 1970.

Haroutounian, Joanne. *Kindling the Spark: Recognizing and Developing Musical Talent.* Oxford: Oxford University Press, 2002.

Harvey, G. E. *History of Burma: From the Earliest Ttimes to 10 March, 1824, the Beginning of the English Conquest.* 1925. Reprint London: Frank and Cass Co., 1967.

Hayes, Michael. "Capitalism and Cultural Relativity: The Thai Pop Industry, Capitalism, and Western Cultural Values." In *Refashioning Pop Music in Asia: Cosmopolitan Flows, Political Tempos and Aesthetic Industries*, edited by Allen Chun, Ned Rossiter, and Brian Shoesmith, 10–30. New York: Routledge Curzon, 2004.

Heidel, Brian. *The Growth of Civil Society in Myanmar*. Bangalore: Books for Change, 2006.

Horkheimer, Max, and Theodor W. Adorno, *Dialectic of Enlightenment*. 1944. Translated by John Cumming. New York: Continuum, 1991.

Houtman, Gustaaf. *Mental Culture in Burmese Crisis Politics: Aung San Suu Kyi and the National League for Democracy*. Tokyo: Institute for the Study of Languages and Cultures of Asia and Africa, Tokyo University of Foreign Studies, 1999.

Howley, Kerry. "Students Help Music 'Dream School' Make Comeback." *Myanmar Times*, March 8, 2004. http://www.myanmar.gov.mm/myanmartimes /no207/MyanmarTimes11-207/026.htm.

Iyer, Pico. "The Raj is Dead! Long Live the Raj!" In *Video Night in Kathmandu: And Other Reports from the Not-So-Far East*, 195–219. New York: A. A. Knopf, 1988.

James, Helen. *Security and Sustainable Development in Myanmar*. London and New York: Routledge, 2006.

Jirattikorn, Amporn. "Shan Noises, Burmese Sound: Crafting Selves Through Music." Paper presented the Conference on Shan Buddhism and Culture, School of Oriental and African Studies, London, UK, December 8, 2007. http://eprints.soas.ac.uk/5339/

Jordt, Ingrid. *Burma's Mass Lay Meditation Movement: Buddhism and the Cultural Construction of Power*. Athens, OH: Center for International Studies, Ohio University Press, 2007.

Kayasha Mon. "A Famous Mon Singer and Actor." *Independent Mon News Agency*, November 9, 2005. http://www.monnews-imna.com/featureupdate.php?ID=1.

Keeler, Ward. "Burma." In *Garland Encyclopedia of World Music, Volume 4: Southeast Asia*, edited by Terry E. Miller and Sean Williams, 363–400. New York: Garland Publishing Inc., 1998.

———. "What's So Burmese About Burmese Rap? Why Some Expressive Forms Go Global." *American Ethnologist* 36, no. 1 (2009): 2–19.

Khin Hninn Phyu. "Laws Drafted on Intellectual Property." *Myanmar Times*, April 11, 2005. http://www.myanmar.gov.mm/myanmartimes/no262/Myanmar-Times14-262/n009.htm.

Khin Nyein Aye Than, "More People Tune In to Myanmar's Music Schools," *Myanmar Times*, August 22, 2005. http://www.myanmar.gov.mm/myanmartimes/no280/MyanmarTimes14-280/t003.htm.

Khin Nyein Aye Than and Kyaw Kyaw Tun. "Blasts from the Past Are Back on Stage and Rocking." *Myanmar Times*, May 9, 2005. http://www.myanmar.gov.mm/myanmartimes/no265/MyanmarTimes14-265/t001.htm.

Kingsbury, Henry. *Music, Talent and Performance: A Conservatory Cultural System*. Philadelphia: Temple University Press, 1988.

Khoo Thwe, Pascal. *From the Land of Green Ghosts: A Burmese Odyssey*. New York: Harper Collins, 2002.

Kruse, Holly. *Site and Sound: Understanding Independent Music Scenes*. New York: P. Lang, 2003.

Kyaw Kyaw Tun. "First Complete DVD Made." *Myanmar Times*, April 12, 2004. http://www.myanmar.gov.mm/myanmartimes/no212/MyanmarTimes11-212/28.htm.

———. "New Blood Injected to Bring Myanmar Music Association Back to Life." *Myanmar Times*, October 17, 2005. http://www.myanmar.gov.mm/myanmartimes/no288/MyanmarTimes15-288/t005.htm.

Kyaw Min Lu. "Rights and Wrongs of Today's Political Arena of Myanmar." *New Light Of Myanmar*, September 28, 2007, 8. http://myanmargeneva.org/NLM2007/eng/9Sep/n070928.pdf.

Larkey, Edward. "Austropop: Popular Music and National Identity in Austria." *Popular Music* 11, no. 2(1992): 151–85.

Larkin, Emma. *Everything Is Broken: The Untold Story of Disaster Under Burma's Military Regime*. London: Granta Books, 2010.

———. *Secret Histories: Finding George Orwell in a Burmese Teashop*. London: John Murray, 2004.

Leach, Edmund. *Political Systems of Highland Burma: A Study of Kachin Social Stuctures*. London: G. Bell and Sons, 1954.

Liddell, Zunetta. "No Room To Move: Legal Constraints on Civil Society in Burma." In *Strengthening Civil Society in Burma: Possibilities and Dilemmas for International NGOs*. Chiang Mai, Thailand: Silkworm Books, 1999.

Lieberman, Victor. *Burmese Administrative Cycles: Anarchy and Conquest, 1580–1760*. Princeton: Princeton University Press, 1984.

Lintner, Bertil. *The Rise and Fall of the Communist Party of Burma*. Ithaca: Cornell University Southeast Asia Program, 1990.

Lockard, Craig A. *Dance of Life: Popular Music and Politics in Southeast Asia*. Honolulu: University of Hawai'i Press, 1988.

Long, Sarah P. Review of *The New Age Music Guide: Profiles and Recordings of 500 Top New Age Musicians*, by Patti Jean Birosik. *Notes*, 2nd ser., 48, no. 2 (1991): 538–39.

MacLachlan, Heather. "The Don Dance: An Expression of Karen Nationalism." *Voices: Journal of New York Folklore* 32 no. 3/4 (2006): 26–32.

———. "Bombings in Burma." Paper presented at the SEASSI Student Forum, University of Wisconsin-Madison, Madison, WI, August 2006.

———. "Innovation in the Guise of Tradition: Music among the Chin Population of Indianapolis, USA." *Asian Music* 39, no. 2 (2008): 167–85.

"Maj-Gen Tha Aye Honours Outstanding Students, Teachers of Kayin State." *New Light of Myanmar,* December 27, 2007, 1. http://myanmargeneva.org/NLM2007/eng/12Dec/n071227.pdf.

Manuel, Peter. *Popular Musics of the Non-Western World: An Introductory Survey.* New York: Oxford University Press, 1988.

Marshall, Andrew. *The Trouser People: A Story of Burma in the Shadow of the Empire.* Washington, DC: Counterpoint, 2002.

Merriam, Alan. *The Anthropology of Music.* Evanston: Northwestern University Press, 1964.

Middleton, Richard. *Studying Popular Music.* Philadelphia: Open University Press, 1990.

———. "Rock Singing." In *The Cambridge Companion to Singing,* edited by John Potter, 28–41. New York: Cambridge University Press, 2000.

Miller, Chris. "Burmese Music on Record before 1962: A Discography in Context." Paper presented at the International Burma Studies Conference, Marseille, France, July 9, 2010.

Miller, Terry. "From Country Hick to Rural Hip: A New Identity through Music for Northeast Thailand." *Asian Music* 36, no. 2 (2005): 96–106.

Min Zin. "Burmese Pop Music: Identity in Transition." *Irrawaddy,* September 2002. http://www.irrawaddy.org/article.php?art_id=2710&page=3.

Moe Moe Oo. "Recording Pioneer Still Has Ear for Music." *Myanmar Times.* October 9, 2006. http://www.myanmar.com/myanmartimes/MyanmarTimes17-337/t001.htm.

Moore, Allan. 2002. "Authenticity as Authentication." *Popular Music* 21, no. 2 (2002): 209–23.

Moskowitz, Marc L. *Cries of Joy, Songs of Sorrow: Chinese Pop Music and Its Cultural Connotation.* Honolulu: University of Hawai'i Press, 2010.

Naw Seng. "Political Hip Hop Released." *Irrawaddy,* September 15, 2003. http://www.irrawaddy.org/article.php?art_id=1765.

Naw Say Phaw. "Censor and Editor Give Evidence at Poet's Trial." *Democratic Voice of Burma,* July 9, 2008. http://english.dvb.no/news.php?id=1518.

Negus, Keith. *Popular Music in Theory: An Introduction.* Hanover: Wesleyan University Press, 1996.

———. *Producing Pop: Culture and Conflict in the Popular Music Industry.* London: Edward Arnold, 1992.

Nettl, Bruno. *The Western Impact on World Music: Change, Adaptation, and Survival.* New York: Schirmer Books, 1985.

Norling, Tor. "Haven or Hell." *Irrawaddy,* July 11, 2008. http://www.irrawaddy.org/highlight.php?art_id=13275.

Nyunt, Khin Maung, and U Koko Gita Lu Lin. "The Musical Culture of Myanmar." In *Sonic Orders in ASEAN Musics, Volume One,* 236–89. Singapore: ASEAN Committee on Culture and Information, 2003.

Olsen, Dale A. *Popular Music of Vietnam: The Politics of Remembering, the Economics of Forgetting.* New York: Routledge, 2008.

O'Neill, Susan A. "The Self-Identity of Young Musicians." In *Musical Identities,* edited by Raymond MacDonald, David Hargreaves, and Dorothy Miell, 70–96. Oxford: Oxford University Press, 2002.

Orwell, George. *Burmese Days.* London: V. Gollancz, 1935.

Pensioner, A. "Living in Myanmar is Worth It." *New Light of Myanmar,* December 31, 2007, 11. http://myanmargeneva.org/NLM2007/eng/12Dec/n071231.pdf.

"Perspectives: Unity Is Dignity of the Union." *New Light of Myanmar,* January 8, 2009.

Peterson, Richard A. "The Production of Culture: A Prolegomenon." In *The Production of Culture,* edited by R. A. Peterson, 7–22. Beverly Hills, CA: Sage, 1976.

Peterson, Richard A., and N. Anand. "The Production of Culture Perspective." *Annual Review of Sociology* 30 (2004): 311–34.

Peterson, Richard A., and D. G. Berger, "Cycles in Symbol Production: The Case of Popular Music." *American Sociological Review* 40 (1975): 158–73.

Phan, Zoya. *Little Daughter: A Memoir of Survival in Burma and the West.* London: Simon and Schuster, 2009.

Pleasants, Henry. "Elvis Presley." In *Popular Music: Critical Concepts in Media and Cultural Studies, Volume 3,* edited by Simon Frith, 251–63. New York: Routledge, 2004.

Rabinowitz, Alan. *Beyond the Last Village: A Journey of Discovery in Asia's Forbidden Wilderness.* Washington, DC: Island Press/Shearwater Books, 2001.

Randel, Don, ed. "Ballad." In *The New Harvard Dictionary of Music,* 67–68. London: The Belknap Press of Harvard University Press, 1986.

"Rockin' in the Free World." *Irrawaddy,* January 2004. http://www.irrawaddy.org/article.php?art_id=3256.

Rodnitzky, Jerry. "A Rocky Road to Respect: Trends in Academic Writing on Popular Music and Popular Music and Society." *Popular Music and Society* 21, no. 1 (1997): 99–103.

Ryback, Timothy. *Rock Around the Bloc: A History of Rock Music in Eastern Europe and the Soviet Union.* New York: Oxford University Press, 1990.

Saw Yan Naing. "Burma's Censors Are Now Also Code-Breakers." *Irrawaddy,* February 4, 2008. http://www.irrawaddy.org/article.php?art_id=10151.

———. "Suppressed." *Irrawaddy,* February 2009. http://www.irrawaddy.org/article.php?art_id=1,5004.

Scahill, Jeremy. *Blackwater: The Rise of the World's Most Powerful Mercenary Army.* New York: Nation Books, 2007.

Scott, James C. *Domination and the Arts of Resistance: Hidden Transcripts.* New Haven: Yale University Press, 1990.

———. *Weapons of the Weak: Everyday Forms of Peasant Resistance.* New Haven: Yale University Press, 1985.

Sen, Krishna, and David T. Hill. *Media Culture and Politics in Indonesia.* Oxford: Oxford University Press, 2000.

Skidmore, Monique. *Karaoke Fascism: Burma and the Politics of Fear.* Philadelphia: University of Pennsylvania Press, 2004.

Smith, Martin. *Burma: Insurgency and the Politics of Ethnicity.* London: Zed Books, 1999.

Spiro, Melford E. *Anthropological Other or Burmese Brother? Studies in Cultural Analysis.* London: Transaction Publications, 1992.

Steinberg, David. *Burma: The State of Myanmar.* Washington, DC: Georgetown University Press, 2001.

Stokes, Martin. "Talk and Text: Popular Music and Ethnomusicology." In *Analyzing Popular Music,* edited by Allan Moore, 218–39. Cambridge: Cambridge University Press, 2003.

Taruskin, Richard. "Resisting the Ninth." *19th-Century Music* 12, no. 3 (Spring, 1989): 241–56.

Taylor, Robert. *The State in Myanmar.* Honolulu: University of Hawaii Press, 2009.

Taylor, Timothy D. *Global Pop: World Music, World Markets.* New York: Routledge, 1997.

Thant Myint-U. *The River of Lost Footsteps: A Personal History of Burma.* New York: Farrar, Strauss and Giroux, 2006.

———. *The Making of Modern Burma.* New York: Cambridge University Press, 2001.

Thawnghmung, Ardeth Maung. *Behind the Teak Curtain: Authoritarianism, Agricultural Policies, and Political Legitimacy in Rural Burma/Myanmar.* New York: Kegan Paul, 2004.

———. "Preconditions and Prospects for Democratic Transition in Burma/Myanmar." *Asian Survey* 43, no. 3 (2003): 443–60.

Tomlinson, John. *Cultural Imperialism: A Critical Introduction.* London: Continuum, 2002.

Toynbee, Jason. *Making Popular Music: Musicians, Creativity and Institutions.* New York: Oxford University Press, 2000.

Trager, Helen. *Burma Through Alien Eyes: Missionary Views of the Burmese in the Nineteenth Century.* New York: Praeger, 1966.

Tucker, Shelby. *Among Insurgents: Walking through Burma.* London: Radcliffe, 2000.

Turino, Tom. "Signs of Imagination, Identity, and Experience: A Peircean Semiotic Theory for Music." *Ethnomusicology* 43, no. 2 (1999): 221–55.

Turnell, Sean. "Burma's Economy: Current Situation and Prospects for Reform." Paper presented at the Association for Asian Studies Conference, Atlanta, GA, April 2008.

———. "The Chettiars in Burma." Macquarie University Department of Economics Research Paper 0512 (2005), http://www.econ.mq.edu.au/research/2005/chettiar.pdf.

Turnell, Sean, Alison Vicary, and Bradford Wylie. "Migrant Worker Remittances and Burma: An Economic Analysis of Survey Results." *ANU E Press* (2007). http://epress.anu.edu.au/myanmar02/mobile_devices/ch05.html.

Wade, Francis. "Only 4% of Burmese Using Cellphones." *Democratic Voice of Burma,* August 4, 2010. http://www.dvb.no/news/only-4-of-burmese-using-telephones/11082.

Wai Moe. "Popular Musician and Friends Arrested in Rangoon." *Irrawaddy,* November 28, 2007. http://www.irrawaddy.org/article.php?art_id=9445.

Wallach, Jeremy. "Living the Punk Lifestyle in Jakarta." *Ethnomusicology* 52, no. 1 (2008): 97–115.

Wallis, Roger, and Krister Malm. *Big Sounds from Small Peoples: The Music Industry in Small Countries.* New York: Pendragon Press, 1984.

———. *Media Policy and Music Activity*. London: Routledge, 1992.

Walser, Robert. "Popular Music Analysis: Ten Apothegms and Four Instances." In *Analyzing Popular Music*, edited by Allan F. Moore, 16–38. Cambridge: Cambridge University Press, 2003.

———. *Running With the Devil: Power, Gender, and Madness in Heavy Metal Music*. Hanover, NH: University Press of New England, 1993.

Williamson, Muriel C. "A Biographical Note on Mya-wadi U Sa, Burmese Poet and Composer." *Musica Asiatica* 2 (1979): 151–54.

———. *The Burmese Harp: Its Classical Music, Tunings, and Modes*. Northern Illinois University: Southeast Asia Publications, 2000.

Yano, Christine. "Covering Disclosures: Practices of Intimacy, Hierarchy, and Authenticity in a Japanese Popular Music Genre." *Popular Music and Society* 28, no. 2 (2005): 193–205.

Ye Thu. "The 'Victim' Treatment: A Self-Fulfilling Prophecy." *Democratic Voice of Burma*, April 7, 2009. http://www.dvb.no/features/the-victim-treatment-a-self-fulfilling-prophecy/2127.

Yeni. "Burma: The Censored Land." *Irrawaddy*, March 2008. http://www.irrawaddy.org/article.php?art_id=10648.

———. "Support for a Stronger Civil Society." *Irrawaddy*, July 4, 2008. http://www.irrawaddy.org/opinion_story.php?art_id=13139.

Zabriskie, Phil. "Hard Rock." *Time*, May 6, 2002. http://www.time.com/time/magazine/article/0,9171,235508,00.html.

Zak, Albin J. *The Poetics of Rock: Cutting Tracks, Making Records*. Berkeley, University of California Press, 2001.

Zaw, Calvin Khin. "Humanitarianism in Myanmar." Paper presented at the Southeast Asia Program weekly meeting, Cornell University, Ithaca, New York, November 2, 2007.

Zizek, Slavoj. *Welcome to the Desert of the Real*. London: Verso, 2002.

Index

Note: Page numbers in *italics* indicate illustrations.

CPSIA information can be obtained at www.ICGtesting.com
Printed in the USA
BVOW03s1909081013

333231BV00009B/91/P

9 781580 464710